MODERN FASHION TRADITIONS

Dress and Fashion Research

The bold *Dress and Fashion Research* series is an outlet for high-quality, in-depth scholarly research on previously overlooked topics and new approaches. Showcasing challenging and courageous work on fashion and dress, each book in this interdisciplinary series focuses on a specific theme or area of the world that has been hitherto under-researched, instigating new debates and bringing new information and analysis to the fore. Dedicated to publishing the best research from leading scholars and innovative rising stars, the works will be grounded in fashion studies, history, anthropology, sociology, and gender studies.

ISSN: 2053-3926

Previously published in the Series

MODERN FASHION TRADITIONS

Negotiating Tradition and Modernity through Fashion

EDITED BY
M. ANGELA JANSEN AND JENNIFER CRAIK

Bloomsbury Academic
An imprint of Bloomsbury Publishing Plc

BLOOMSBURY
LONDON · OXFORD · NEW YORK · NEW DELHI · SYDNEY

Bloomsbury Academic

An imprint of Bloomsbury Publishing Plc

50 Bedford Square	1385 Broadway
London	New York
WC1B 3DP	NY 10018
UK	USA

www.bloomsbury.com

First published 2016
Paperback edition first published 2018

British Library Cataloguing-in-Publication Data
A catalogue record for this book is available from the British Library.

ISBN: HB: 978-1-4742-2949-4
PB: 978-1-3500-5849-1
ePDF: 978-1-4742-2951-7
ePub: 978-1-4742-2950-0

Library of Congress Cataloging-in-Publication Data
Names: Jansen, M. Angela, editor. | Craik, Jennifer, editor.
Title: Modern fashion traditions : negotiating tradition and modernity through fashion / edited by M. Angela Jansen, London College of Fashion, University of the Arts London, UK and Jennifer Craik, Queensland University of Technology, Australia.
Description: London ; New York, NY : Bloomsbury Academic, an imprint of Bloomsbury Publishing, Plc., [2016] | Includes index.
Identifiers: LCCN 2016003922| ISBN 9781474229494 (hardback) | ISBN 9781474229500 (epub) | ISBN 9781474229517 (ePDF)
Subjects: LCSH: Clothing and dress--Asia. | Fashion--Asia. | Fashion design--Asia. | Fashion--Social aspects--Asia.
Classification: LCC GT1370 .M64 2016 | DDC 391.0095--dc23 LC record available at https://lccn.loc.gov/2016003922

Series: Dress and Fashion Research, 20533926

Cover image: © Hassan Hajjaj
Wamuhu, photograph by Hassan Hajjaj
Metallic Lambda on Dibond
2014/1435
Edition of 5
Courtesy of Taymour Grahne Gallery, New York, U.S.A.

Typeset by Fakenham Prepress Solutions, Fakenham, Norfolk, NR21 8NN

CONTENTS

PART III: SELF-ORIENTALISM OR NATION BRANDING?

PART IV: LOCAL CONSTRUCTS OF THE GLOBAL

PART V: CONCLUSION

LIST OF ILLUSTRATIONS

Napoleon Oui; photography by Michael Greves. Courtesy of QUT Creative Enterprise Australia. 107

Figure 5.2 AKIN Collection 2012 collaborative fashion project: Top and pants designed by Shea Cameron, and textiles by Tommy Pau; coat and visor designed by Monique White, and textiles by Arone Meeks; photography by Michael Greves. Courtesy of QUT Creative Enterprise Australia. 109

Figure 5.3 AKIN Collection 2012 collaborative fashion project: Shirt, shorts, and scarf designed by Hayley Elsaesser; textiles designed by Sharon Phineasa; photography by Michael Greves. Courtesy of QUT Creative Enterprise Australia. 110

Chapter 6

Figure 6.1 A piece from Atıl Kutoğlu's more recent fashion show, held on March 24, 2014, in İstanbul, Turkey. In this collection, he used printed abstract Ottoman floral motifs on long dresses combined with boleros and jackets. Photograph: Vittorio Zunino Celotto/Getty Images. 132

Figure 6.2 A piece from Dilek Hanif's Haute Couture Show held on January 23, 2012, in Paris, as a part of the Paris Haute Couture Week. In this piece, tinsel floral motifs were applied to a dress that seems to be an intensively stylized caftan. Photograph: Victor Virgile/Getty Images. 133

Chapter 7

Figure 7.1 A so-called "traditional" tailor in the old Arab city center of Fes, Morocco. Photograph by the author. 145

Figure 7.2 Cover of the Moroccan fashion magazine *Ousra*. Photograph by the author. 148

Figure 7.3 The first Zara store on Massira El Khedra in the center of Casablanca, Morocco. Photograph by the author. 150

Figure 7.4 A boutique selling Moroccan fashion in the shopping mall Twin Centre in Casablanca, Morocco. Photograph by the author. 151

Figure 7.5 Modern Moroccan fashion used in a billboard advertisement of a telephone provider. Photograph by the author. 158

Chapter 8

Chapter 9

LIST OF CONTRIBUTORS

M. Angela Jansen obtained her PhD in 2010 from Leiden University, the Netherlands, for a dissertation on the Moroccan fashion industry. Her monograph, *Moroccan Fashion: Design, Tradition and Modernity*, was published in 2014 by Bloomsbury. She is currently an independent scholar based in Brussels, as well as a Visiting Scholar at the Research Department at the Victoria and Albert Museum in London, and an Associate Researcher at the Centre Jacques Berque in Rabat, Morocco. Her research interests are fashion anthropology, Eurocentricity in academic practice, globalization, and modernity. In 2012, she initiated the NWFashionConference (NWFC), which is in its fourth edition (Rabat 2012, London 2013, Hong Kong 2014). In addition to publishing and lecturing on the Moroccan fashion industry, she is involved in fashion events and museum exhibitions.

Jennifer Craik is Professor and Head of Fashion at Queensland University of Technology in Brisbane, Australia. Her research interests include interdisciplinary approaches to the study of fashion and dress. She has also researched aspects of cultural studies, cultural policy, and arts funding. Her publications include: *The Face of Fashion* (Routledge, 1993), *Uniforms Exposed: From Conformity to Transgression* (Berg Publishers, 2005), and *Fashion: The Key Concepts* (Berg Publishers, 2009).

Toby Slade is Associate Professor at the University of Tokyo, researching Asian modernity and the history and theory of fashion. His previous research focused on Asian responses to modernity, seen through art objects of the everyday like fashion, the suit, and its role in modernity, the ideas of style and the classic, and the governing dynamics of systems of fashion. His doctoral research at the University of Sydney, Australia, examined the Modernity of Japanese clothing and the implications of that unique sartorial history for contemporary theories of fashion. His book *Japanese Fashion: A Cultural History*, published by Berg, covers the entire sweep of fashion and clothing in Japan from the earliest times to today.

Christine Tsui was a 2013–14 Fulbright Scholar at Parsons the New School for Design. At Parsons she taught "China Fashion/Nation" along with Professor Hazel Clark. She obtained her Master's degree in Fashion Marketing and Management from the London College of Fashion in 2003. She was Visiting Associate Professor of the Shanghai Design Institute of China Academy of Arts from 2004 to 2010. Her publications include: *China Fashion: Conversation with Designers* (Chinese edition, 2013); *Workbook for Fashion Buyers* (Chinese edition, 2009).

Janaki Turaga is an independent researcher based in New Delhi. She finished her doctoral research at Jawaharlal Nehru University, New Delhi. Her PhD dissertation, "Ecological Movements as People's Response to Alternative Development: A Study in Westerns Ghats in Karnataka", deals with ecological movements and the emerging development paradigm. She is engaged in areas of environment and development, textiles, handicrafts, microfinance, sustainable livelihoods, and sustainable appropriate development paradigms. She has presented her research work in both the academic and development world, at conferences and seminars, and has published independent research work, as articles in scholarly journals, such as *Security and Society*, and development sector magazines.

Şakir Özüdoğru is Research Assistant at the Department of Fashion Design Anadolu University, Eskişehir, Turkey, from which he graduated in 2008. He did his Master's degree in the field of industrial arts at Anadolu University on the "Interaction between Fashion and Art from 19th Century until Today." His publications in various journals include poems, criticisms, and short stories. His book of poems, *Garipsemeler*, was published in 2005. His current research interests include: experimental, visual, phonetic poetry and design, postmodernisms, queer theory, sociology of perception and drug culture, subcultures, contemporary art theory, and cultural studies on fashion and art.

Victoria L. Rovine is Associate Professor of Art History at the University of North Carolina at Chapel Hill, USA. Her research focuses on clothing and textiles in Africa, with particular attention to innovations in forms and meanings across cultures. Her first book, *Bogolan: Shaping Culture through Cloth in Contemporary Mali* (Smithsonian Press, 2001 and Indiana University Press, 2008), examined the recent transformations of a richly symbolic textile. Her second book, *African Fashion, Global Style: Histories, Innovations, and Ideas You Can Wear* (Indiana University Press, 2015), explores the innovations of designers from Africa, past and present, as well as Africa's presence in the Westerns fashion imaginary. Rovine is also Research Associate with the Visual Identities in Art and Design Research Centre (VIAD) at the University of Johannesburg, South Africa.

Emma Dick is Lecturer in Visual Culture Fashion at Middlesex University London and Director of Projects & Training for SPINNA Circle (www.spinna.org) a non-profit organisation working to empower women in fashion and textiles globally. She read Turkish with Islamic Art & Archaeology at the University of Oxford and holds a Masters degree in Design Practice (Textiles as Fashion) from Glasgow School of Art. Emma has lived and worked in Turkey and Singapore, where she was Head of Fashion at LASALLE College of the Arts (2007–2010) and collaborated on the vocational curriculum in Tailoring project for the Royal Government of Bhutan with UNDP Bhutan and Singapore International Foundation, about which her chapter in this volume is based. Emma travels frequently throughout Central Asia and is currently working on development projects in the region, linking textile artisans to global markets. During 2014 SPINNA Circle managed and implemented a USAID-funded grant in Kazakhstan and Uzbekistan, 'Empowering women in Central Asia by building capacity and linking markets through setting up SPINNA Circle hubs' working with over 100 women from the region. This work is continuing in 2016 with further research and project implementation in the Central Asian region.

Sandra Niessen is an independent scholar based in The Netherlands. In 1979, she began to study, lecture, and write about the Batak cultures of North Sumatra, Indonesia. In 1985, she obtained her PhD in anthropology from Leiden University in The Netherlands, and subsequently taught until 2001 at the University of Alberta in Canada. Her book publication, *Legacy in Cloth: Batak Textiles of Indonesia* (2009) documents the full repertory of textile types of the Toba, Karo, and Simalungun Batak of North Sumatra, including design history and techniques of production. In 2013, she produced a film about Batak weaving techniques entitled *Rangsa ni Tonun*. Sandra is co-editor of *Re-Orienting Fashion: The Globalization of Asian Dress* (2003), and *Consuming Fashion: Adorning the Transnational Body* (1998).

1
INTRODUCTION

M. ANGELA JANSEN AND
JENNIFER CRAIK

The aim of this volume, *Modern Fashion Traditions*, is to disrupt a persistent euro- and ethnocentricity in fashion discourse by bringing together research by authors who are engaged in creative and critical thinking concerning fashion, in a wide scope of geographical areas, from a wide variety of disciplines, and from a cross-cultural perspective. The key premise is that fashion in a non-Western context is not a mere adoption of a European phenomenon or a recent outcome of globalization. Non-Western fashion has its own historical and socio-cultural relevance. To this end, the objectives of this volume are:

- to disrupt persistent euro- and ethnocentric academic practice in fashion studies by challenging simple, linear, oppositional, and essentialist thinking, resulting in false dichotomies like tradition versus modernity, dress versus fashion, West versus Non-West, local versus global, etc.

- to contest the idea that fashion outside of Europe and North America is a recent phenomenon and/or a result of globalization.

- to acknowledge that different fashion systems have been, and are, located all around the world, and that these have been developing in conjunction, competition, collaboration, and independently from the European fashion system.

- to not only dispute misassumptions concerning non-European fashion as being static, authentic and symbolic, but also concerning European fashion as being arbitrary, innovative, and, most importantly, detached from its cultural context.

- to provide a platform for developing alternative, inclusive theoretical frameworks to analyze fashion from a global perspective, and to establish new terminology that surpasses current Eurocentric discourse in relation to fashion.

This is an ambitious remit as it seeks to challenge deeply held assumptions about Western culture and its distinctiveness from, and superiority over "Other" cultures and traditions. The authors in this volume are thinking outside the box and testing new ideas and propositions in an effort to develop new conceptual and analytic frameworks. As such, the intellectual understanding of non-Western fashion is still a neophyte field that is developing, and this volume, therefore, represents a work in progress.

First, there is an urgent need to problematize persisting dichotomies like traditional versus fashionable, tradition versus modernity, local versus global, and the West versus the Rest in fashions studies. For, as Sandra Niessen (2003: 264) argues, the weaknesses and limitations in the dichotomous model are evident from the complex way in which these oppositions are manipulated and combined, such that binary distinctions are blurred and proliferate in new forms. Ironically, however, by trying to transgress these dichotomies, there is a real danger of reinforcing them and reproducing the very stereotypes we set out to critique.

Second, it is imperative to redefine existing concepts and/or introduce new ones, starting by searching for a synonym for the concept "non-Western fashion" that escapes the implicit polarization of that term. Alternatives in use are "ethnic fashion," "world fashion," "global fashion," "postmodern fashion," and "fusion fashion," but all are problematic in their own way. Ethnic fashion, for example, as defined by Joanne Eicher and Barbara Sumberg (1995: 300), refers to garments that are "worn by members of one group to distinguish themselves from another by focusing on differentiation," but many so-called "ethnic" people, and especially fashion designers, feel stigmatized by the term, emphasizing a distinction between "them" and "mainstream fashion" (e.g. Western fashion) (Akou 2007: 403). World fashion, in its turn, generally refers to European fashion (trends) like blue jeans, the business suit, T-shirts, etc. that have been adopted by the rest of the world due to processes of globalization (Eicher and Sumberg 1995; Maynard 2004; Eicher et al. 2000; Lillethun et al. 2012), whereas we are looking to acknowledge a large diversity of fashion systems within their own right. World fashion research also usually insinuates that something is only fashion if it has a global scale (Eicher and Sumber 1995; Hansen 2004; Akou 2007; Lillethun, Welters and Eicher 2012), whereas we believe fashions can also be local. José Teunissen (2005: 11) defines "fusion fashion" as a mixture of traditional dress with contemporary fashion trends that, to a certain extent, is embedded in one's own culture, and to a certain extent grounded in international fashion, neglecting the force of fashion trends instigated by local developments.

Unfortunately, all these terms are, in one way or another, always in relation to Western fashion. Until there is a consensus about a satisfying substitute term, this volume reverts to the (equally problematic) use of "non-Western fashion" as shorthand for a large diversity of fashion systems outside and beyond dominant fashion from Europe and North America. Simultaneously, just as problematic as "non-Western fashion," are terms like "Western fashion," "European fashion," and "North American fashion," which, too, are far from homogenous categories. Although rarely produced in Europe and/or North America and strongly influenced by fashion systems from other regions, these terms are used in this volume to refer to fashion that is culturally associated with these geographical areas.

Moreover, the chapters in this volume were not necessarily selected on their specific geographical focus, but rather because of their significant contribution to the discussion as well as their uniqueness as case studies to represent non-Western fashion. Simultaneously, one of the ambitions of the volume is to reach out to scholars who have remained invisible in the academic landscape due to all sorts of barriers, be it financial, linguistic, or Eurocentric. Therefore, we have favored to include a number of researchers who are unpublished (in English and/or mainstream publications), as well as researchers who represent their own culture as opposed to Western researchers representing non-Western cultures.

Although fashion globalization has become a well-established topic of research since the 1990s (Skov 1996; Maynard 2004; Teunissen 2005; Eicher et al. 2000; Rabine 2002; Niessen 2003; Monden 2008; Riello and McNeil 2010), case studies from different geographical areas have rarely been assembled in a single volume with the purpose of cross-cultural comparison. Too often non-Western fashion systems are studied in comparison, or in relation to the Western fashion system, and/or in the context of globalization, whereby new economies, especially, have earned their right to join the fashion discourse, based on their recent socio-economic achievements, their convergence with the West, and/or their successful engagement with fashion as both consumers and producers (Riello and McNeil 2010: 5). As Giorgio Riello and Peter McNeil (2010: 4) argue, if we wish to understand fashion beyond Europe, we must refrain from thinking that this has suddenly emerged in the past few decades as the result of globalization and the growth of new middle classes. The fact that these historical traditions of fashion are not as well-known, they say, or advertised as the European one, should not diminish their value. This volume aims to take a clear stand by explicitly contesting that European fashion is at the origin of all other fashion systems, or that non-Western fashions are a (recent) result of globalization. Its contributors argue that fashion has been historically located all around the world, but that it is the Eurocentric representations of hegemonic fashion that have generally emphasized European bourgeois and upper-class women's attire as the site of newness and now-ness, while other nations/cultures/spaces have been depicted as static and exotic; as fixed in earlier times (Kaiser 2012: 173).

The case studies gathered in this volume set out to illustrate that non-Western fashions are far from static, but rather powerful tools in an ongoing negotiation of continuity and change, of tradition and modernity, of local developments and global influences. Both Western and non-Western fashions are continuously invented and reinvented following social, cultural, political, religious, and economic developments, and are equally used to formulate and express unique local cultural identities. Contemporary fashion designers are increasingly tapping into their local cultural heritage (tradition) for inspiration to create distinctive design identities, while simultaneously reinventing/modernizing it. On the one hand, in a globalized world, this allows designers to differentiate themselves in a highly competitive international fashion market, while on the other hand, on a national level, it makes them successful as a result of a general revaluation of local cultural heritage as a counter reaction to cultural globalization. Consequently, the research cases in this volume contest the idea that globalization would lead to cultural homogenization; on the contrary, they show how it feeds into cultural heterogenization through the (re)invention of local cultural heritage and vestimentary traditions as a powerful means of distinction.

Nevertheless, we argue that when non-Western designers are using their cultural heritage as a source of inspiration, it is considered "traditional," whereas when Western fashion designers incorporate their cultural heritage, it is categorized as "fashionable." In the same way, when non-Western fashion designers incorporate Western fashion aesthetics, it is often perceived as westernization and a loss of local culture, whereas when Western fashion designers turn to non-Western cultures for inspiration, it is seen as innovative and fashionable. Think of designers like Yves Saint Laurent and John Galliano, who owe their success, to a large extent, to their collections inspired by Eastern Europe, North Africa, and Asia, while the actual designers from these regions have rarely succeeded in truly penetrating the global fashion industry, apart from the Japanese.

This volume aims to illustrate that despite so-called fashion globalization, the epicenter of fashion is still very much concentrated in Europe. Despite trends are coming from London, New Delhi, Milan, Shanghai, New York, São Paolo, Casablanca, and Dakar, Western designers predominantly still have the opportunity to put them on the global fashion map, while Indian, Chinese, Hispanic, Latin American, Moroccan, and Sub-Sahara African fashion designers continue to be categorically excluded from Western catwalks, and are categorized as "ethnic fashion." As Sandra Niessen argues in the concluding chapter to this volume, despite so-called "fashion globalization," the reins of fashion economics have never been more tightly held in the West. Despite the fact that fashion weeks are happening all over the world, she says, a handful of holding companies are disproportionately huge players. She asserts that it is no longer the styles that reveal the social ladder of fashion, but that the game is about manipulating style to suck money upward. Niessen emphasizes that it is important to demystify how style interacts with the global politics of fashion. As fashion is about economics, she argues that holding companies are dangling the strings, whereby fashion designers are hired and fired and that fashion producers no longer vie for the top independently. Fashion globalization is hegemonic and no holds barred, with the fashion weeks outside of the West still at the dispensable bottom rungs, while immense power is held in the hands of a Western few. As such, this volume addresses an emerging agenda about the role of new fashion cities and spaces of fashion consumption, as a counterbalance to the global dominance of the "conventional" world fashion cities.

A legacy of Eurocentric fashion discourse

Abby Lillethun, Linda Welters, and Joanne Eicher (2012: 76) argue in their article *(Re)Defining Fashion* that Social Darwinism, in the nineteenth and early twentieth centuries, is at the origin of the embedding of perceived ownership of fashion in Western culture. Social Darwinism's paradigm, they argue, included a hierarchical construct of human typologies shaped by Westerners, which, therefore, positioned their own cultures at the top of the hierarchy. The definition of fashion that came into use was shaped to fit the perspective of the people defining it. They state:

> For them fashion occurred in a capitalist production system of innovation, distribution, and consumption wherein the social structure enabled, even fostered, emulation of adjacent status groups. (Lillethun, Welters, and Eicher 2012: 76)

Fashionable behaviors, they continue, particularly the adoption of rapidly changing styles, were assigned to European urban culture, while dress-practices that appeared to them to be unchanging—that is, those dress practices in cultures registering below European urban culture in the Social Darwinist hierarchy—were not fashion. Qualifying them initially as primitive, savage and exotic and later as traditional, folkloric and ethnic, mainly allowed Western researchers to initially dehumanize and later depower these fashions as well as differentiate themselves from them (Baizerman, Eicher and Cerny (2008: 126). According to Suzanne Baizerman, Joanne Eicher and Catherine Cerny (2008: 126) in their article "Eurocentrism in the Study of Ethnic Dress," terminology has been used to establish boundaries between Euroamerican society and the rest of the world, and to validate a hierarchical relationship between a powerful Euroamerican elite and a less powerful Other. It aims to deny a complexity and elegance, they say, that otherwise exemplifies dress among, for example, the nobility of the Han Dynasty, or of the ancient Maya, both of which developed independent of European influence.

Baizerman, Eicher, and Cerny (2008: 127) argue that the non-historical reputation of "primitive" societies is a construction of Western cultural biases and the limitations of traditional Western modes of scholarship. As Eicher (2005: 17) formulates it, in her introduction to *National Geographic Fashion*, from a Eurocentric point of view, people whose past does not include written history, paintings, or drawings, are easily categorized as coming from static worlds. Even though documenting change represents a challenge, she says, it is mandatory to find out how change occurred and accept evidence of it, for example through the oral histories of elders that relate to dressing the body. She explains that these fashions may seem not to change over the years to untrained outsiders, but the insiders who wear these garments know very well what is in fashion and what is not (2005: 21).

Gertrud Lehnert and Gabriele Mentges (2013: 10) in their book *Fusion Fashion: Culture beyond Orientalism and Occidentalism*, argue that Orientalism as an important part of Eurocentric perspectives on culture and history implicitly suggests that global history is organized around Western history. Simultaneously, they say, it presupposes the Western modernization process to be a generalized or generalizable schema. They argue there is an urge to rewrite the history of material culture in another perspective than the "orientalized and Euro-centered" ones in order to discover the different voices of a multiple Other. Western fashion, they say, has long claimed an aesthetic, technical, as well as moral/ethical superiority over the non-Western sartorial otherness, even though it has always adopted "oriental" practices, yet in different ways and with different goals (2013: 11). The development of European fashion, they point out, is due substantially to the cultural transfer of techniques, materials, tastes, and aesthetics.

The first critiques of the conceptualization of fashion as the product and domain of Western capitalism began appearing in the 1980s, reflecting global social changes of the twentieth century, whereby the movements for native independence from colonialism were nearly complete, and the era of multiculturalism thrust ethnic identity to the forefront (Lillethun, Welters, and Eicher 2012: 76). According to Lillethun, Welters, and Eicher (2012: 76–7), the current era of globalization is also one of contestation and challenges for inclusion, whereby the increased pace of globalism and the inclusion of voices of the marginalized in postmodern and globalization theory furthered awareness of the so-called "others" in the world. As a result, the concept of fashion as purely Western has been challenging, and many scholars have been advocating reframing the concepts of fashion within broader and more diverse parameters by detailing other possible fashion systems (Niessen 2003; Eicher 2005; Akou 2007; Baizerman, Eicher, and Cerny 2008; Craik 2009; Lillethun, Welters, and Eicher 2012; Lehnert and Mentges 2013). While the fundamental urge to decorate the self was considered "primitive," rather than a key concept of fashion, Jennifer Craik (2009) emphatically places this trait in the foreground in conceptualizing fashion.

Heather Akou (2007: 408), in her article "Building a New World Fashion," proposes a framework to conceptualize fashion consisting of three levels of cultural systems: microcultures, cultures, and macrocultures. Each level, she argues, is accompanied by a different kind of aesthetic system, respectively street styles and local dress practices, ethnic dress and national dress, and world fashions. This framework, she says, allows us to recognize multiple "world fashion" systems associated with different macrocultures—Western, Islamic, African, Asian, Latino, etc.

Emma Dick in her chapter on Bhutanese fashion in this volume, critiques Joanne Entwistle's (2000) definition of fashion formulated as "a system of dress found in societies where social mobility is possible," and argues that this concept does not correlate with Bhutanese ideas of state sovereignty, which are fundamentally different to those espoused by European history. Fashion from a Eurocentric point of view, she argues, is overwhelmingly construed as a materialistic and superficial field of practice, which seems difficult to reconcile with the non-materialistic philosophy of Buddhist culture:

> Changes in style may happen more subtly and at a slower rate in Bhutan than in a highly developed economy, but an alternative system of social identification through dress and appearance, governed by its own logic of temporality and location is visible in the traditional dress practices of people throughout Bhutan.

Therefore, Dick asserts that there are multiple fashion systems in the world, operating under different logics and notions of temporality. Key to the problem, however, is that there is no consensus on what fashion is exactly. Different disciplines use different definitions of fashion which add considerably to the amalgam of misunderstandings (Welters and Lillethun 2011: xxvii). In general, fashion is characterized by both its ephemerality and also its rapid and incessant stylistic changes (Wilson 1985; Davis 1992; Purdy 2004; Barnard 2007). However, as Niessen argues in this volume, in today's fast-changing world, (rapid) change has become empty of definitional value.

In a search for an all-inclusive, non-Eurocentric definition and analytical framework for fashion, the emerging sub-discipline of fashion anthropology offers some important tools. Particularities of the anthropological perspective are cross-cultural, inclusive, holistic and relativistic, whereby a cross-cultural perspective implies that human behavior is studied in a wide and inclusive sense, embracing many or potentially all human ways of being (Eller 2015: 12). Only through cross-cultural perspectives can both the commonalities/ universals across cultures be discovered, as well as the full range of variations between cultures. Holism, in its turn, means that each particular culture is, and must be, approached as a whole, not just as a single trait (e.g. fashion) or as a disconnected list of traits. A culture is a system containing multiple parts that are in some kind of integrated relationship with each other. Every part of a culture relates in some way to every other part and each part has its unique function and each contributes to the function of the whole (Eller 2015: 12). Therefore, each specific fashion system can only be analyzed in relation to the historical, cultural, social, political, religious, and economic context within which it exists. Different fashion forms have different origins, are set in different geographies, and have different ways of evolving. For example, when a curator tried to identify fashionable garments in an ethnographic museum collection, those deemed "fashionable" all showed traces of Western fashion influences. Due to prevalent Eurocentric perceptions of fashion, even in an ethnographic museum, people fail to comprehend that fashion is not inherent to an object, but rather that its socio-cultural-historical context renders it fashionable. It is only through intensive field research that fashion as a specific part of culture can be studied as well as its interconnectedness to the whole. Most importantly, cultural relativism asserts that an observer cannot apply the standards of its own culture to another culture. Rather, a phenomenon in a culture must be understood and evaluated in relation to, relative to, that culture. Ethnocentrism, therefore, is the attitude or practice of assuming that one's own cultural point of view is the best, the right, or even the only point of view. Each judgment about another culture is made from one's own cultural point of view in relation to some standard of "right/normal," and a culture is precizely a set of standards for such judgment (Eller 2015: 12).

As such, fashion can be conceptualized as a universal phenomenon with a full range of local variations, in the same way that political or economic systems are universal systems with local variations. Central to fashion is dress, defined as everything that one does to or puts on one's body as a material embodiment of one's culture (Barnes and Eicher 1992: 15). The most important difference between dress and fashion, as formulated by Yuniya Kawamura (2005: 2–4), is that while dress refers to tangible objects, fashion is intangible and provides added value to dress that only exists in people's imaginations and beliefs. An all-inclusive definition of fashion then, is desirable dress at a given moment and place (Entwistle 2000: 1), whereby its desirability can be based on a wide-range of values, be it social, political, nostalgic, exclusivity, modernity, innovation, nationalism, etc. As soon as a person (consciously or unconsciously) prefers one body adornment over another, one can speak of fashion. Only in very rare and extreme circumstances, such as poverty, refugee status, or being party to religious doctrines, might people not have a choice and fashion be absent. The simplicity or complexity of a fashion system should not be based on the simplicity or complexity of the bodily adornment, but rather on the simplicity or complexity of the wearer's motivations behind his or her choices.

Due to a hegemonic Eurocentric fashion discourse, non-Western countries have come to believe that fashion is a Western phenomenon (just like modernity) and that it has only recently been introduced through globalization. On the one hand there is a lack of elaborate research on non-European fashion histories while on the other hand, as Giorgio Riello and Peter McNeil (2010: 4–5) formulate it, European fashion history already comes packaged with strong "stories" or "narratives," and even its set areas of debate—these might be the consumer revolution of the "long" eighteenth century; the birth of couture in the last third of the nineteenth century; or the importance of subcultural style in the mid- to late twentieth century. Such narratives, they say, form the basic ways in which histories of fashion are written and taught and are underpinned by chronologies, facts and a cast of characters straight from European history. This then becomes the framework with which non-Western fashion histories are studied.

Consequently, European fashion has been the ultimate reference for many contemporary non-Western fashions, often resulting in bad copies of European fashion. Juanjuan Wu (2009: xi), for example, explains how the "chinoizerie" collections by European designers were at first a more important source of inspiration for Chinese designers than their own rich indigenous fashion history. While European fashion was considered fashionable, she says, their own fashion was considered "traditional." Therefore, Chinese designers initially started by distorting French haute couture in an attempt to create "Chinese" haute couture and it was only at a much later stage that they started turning to their own clothing traditions as a source of inspiration (Tsui 2009). From a Eurocentric perspective, it is often asserted that only through a formal training in (European fashion) design, people are taught to isolate elements from (either their own or other) culture and to turn them into elements of a visual language to create a certain aesthetic that is no longer bound by its cultural restrictions. But not only have (non-Western) craftsmen for a long time been isolating and appropriating elements from a wide variety of cultural influences, the other way around, Western fashion is not completely free from its cultural restrictions.

At this point, It is important to note that contesting Eurocentricity in fashion discourse does not mean denying altogether the significant influence that European fashion has had, and continues to have, on a wide range of fashions around the world. French fashion, in particular, has been, and still is, an important influence on many fashions, including various European ones, and stands predominantly at the origin of what is referred to as European/Western fashion today. In the course of the nineteenth century, for example, French fashion, which had come to represent cosmopolitanism and (Euro)modernity, overshadowed many other European fashions, which had come to be considered provincial, coarse, and old-fashioned. This resulted in a stagnation and reduction to what is now referred to as Dutch, Belgian, German, etc. traditional dress. This nomination, in the same way as many non-Western fashions, ignores the once vivid and transnational dynamics of these fashions (Feitsma 2014).

Interestingly, the introduction of European fashion in many non-Western countries has not threatened the continuity of local fashions, but rather increased processes of selection, appropriation, hybridization, reinvention, and redefinition. As Jansen illustrates in her contribution to this volume, for example, the introduction of foreign fashion brands on a large scale at the turn of the twenty-first century, did not threaten Moroccan fashion, but on the contrary, boosted its development through the introduction of new consumption patterns and marketing strategies. Simultaneously, adopting European fashion aesthetics in many case studies is an important way to engage with a global (cultural) discourse, but without the willingness to give up one's cultural distinctiveness. As Niessen (2003: 259) explains it, appropriately modern styles are cued by Western trends, but the Western look is not adopted wholesale. To be fit to represent the non-Western-but-developing state, she says, they must be modified by elements of traditional heritage:

> The resulting blend of modernity and tradition is colored by both, but not too much by either one. Their modern-dress performance is as much in process as their performance of traditional dress. (Niessen 2003: 260)

Tradition and modernity in fashion

Just as there are many misconceptions about fashion as a result of Eurocentric analyzes, there are persistent misapprehensions about the concepts of tradition and modernity. As Leslie Rabine (2002: 10) puts it, tradition is probably the most problematic of terms inherited from colonial discourse. In her research on the globalization of African fashion, she criticizes the static tradition/modernity binary, as it was used by missionaries, colonialists and anthropologists to "oppose an Africa deemed traditional in the sense of primitive and static to a modern Europe as transmitter of enlightened values" (Rabine 2002: 10). Although local fashions mostly are encoded as traditional by their consumers, they are far from embodying the timeless, closed societies evoked by the colonial notions of tradition (Rabine 2002: 11). On the contrary, they result from centuries-old histories of the weaving together of local development and foreign influence. Today, local fashions have become the focal point for anxieties, attachments, and criticisms that attend the ever-changing status of tradition in societies that are subject to increasing influences of industrialization, modernization, and globalization. Rather than tradition being an unchanging trope of the past, it is a dynamic encapsulation of the fusion of global trends and successive innovations. The more foreign influence there is, the more need is felt to create, define, and categorize indigenous fashions.

The concept of tradition is a construct rather than a given that is constantly redefined and reinvented and that has more to do with ideological thinking than with a faithful representation of historical facts. As Eric Hobsbawm and Terence Ranger (1983) argue in *The Invention of Tradition*, although traditions can be ancient, they are often quite new and sometimes even literally invented in a single event or over a short period of time. The authors define tradition as:

> a set of practices, normally governed by overtly or tacitly accepted rules and of a ritual or symbolic nature, which seeks to inculcate certain values and norms of behaviour by repetition and to imply a continuity with a suitable historic past. (Hobsbawm and Ranger 1983: 1)

This continuity with a historic past, however, they emphasize, is often largely fictitious, whereby invented traditions are most often a response to new situations (Hobsbawm and Ranger 1983: 4). Foreign influences are continuously appropriated through what Joanne Eicher and Tonye Erekosima (1995: 145) describe as a process called "cultural authentication," whereby foreign elements become authentic by being assimilated into an already existing system, and foreign influences come to symbolize what they call ethnic identity:

> The construct of cultural authentication applies to specific articles and ensembles of dress identified as ethnic and considered indigenous when the users are not the makers or when the material used is not indigenous in origin. (Eicher and Erekosima 1995: 140)

In general, authenticity does not apply well to fashion because it is always a product of cultural encounters as well as processes of hybridization (Kaiser 2012: 59) and authenticity is a slippery concept (Jansen 2014: 118). Most of all, as Charles Lindholm (2008: 1) argues, authenticity gathers people together in collectives that are felt to be real, essential and vital, providing participants with meaning, unity and a surpassing sense of belonging. Marilyn Halter (2000: 17), in her book *Shopping for Identity: The Marketing of Ethnicity*, argues that the increasing popularity of authenticity in the past few decades is related to nostalgia for an idealized and fixed point in time when folk culture was supposedly untouched by the corruption that is automatically associated with commercial development. Hence, she says, the more artificiality, anonymity, and uncertainty apparent in a postmodern world, the more driven is the quest for authentic experiences and the more people long to feel connected to localized traditions seeking out timeless and pure culture (Halter 2000: 17). As such, modernity is a catalyzer for tradition.

Simultaneously, notions of modernity are just as much misinterpreted and mainly narrowed down to euromodernity. As Jonathan Inda and Renato Rosaldo (2002: 3) formulate it, ideologies related to modernity are mainly made up of elements of the (European) Enlightenment worldview such as freedom, welfare, human rights, democracy, and sovereignty, initiated in the West. According to them:

> many developing nations adhere to policies which at least ostensibly aim to modernize their politics, infrastructures and economies, but often their own prevailing ideologies do not correspond with those proposed by the West. (Inda and Rosaldo 2002: 3)

Dick argues in this volume that it is not meaningful to impose such values of European enlightenment on Bhutanese culture that independently developed its own entirely different logic of enlightenment. In Buddhist terms, she says, to be enlightened means to have woken up and to understand the world, so that the mind and the body are not separated but are in perfect harmony with one another. Binary systems inherent to Western thinking, she concludes, which exist to impose "rational" order on the world, are deeply unenlightened from this perspective.

Over time, concepts like "alternative" or "multiple" modernities have been introduced in the context of non-Western societies, but as Rovine demonstrates in her chapter on the South-African case study, the alternative-modernity formulation misses what may be most important about the current mutation in the meaning of "modernity" for Africans. Theoretically, she explains, modernity replaces tradition and it is marked by cultural practices that share more with other "modern" societies than with long-standing local practices. But this is not the lived expectation of modernity in much of Africa, she says. Instead, modernity means economic and personal security, access to funds, goods and services that ensure a good life. For people whose standard of living is declining, she argues, who are denied access to the trappings of modernity, aware of yet experiencing only vicariously its comforts and privileges, the modern may be a remembered past rather than a promised future.

The Japanese anthropologist Chie Nakane (1967 in Iwabuchi 1994: 23) argues that other societies should not be measured with a Western yardstick, but rather with an indigenous one. Her call for cultural specificity is a challenge to Eurocentric definitions of modernity and suggests an alternative way of theorizing modernization without regarding the Western experience as the model path to the modern stage. Modernity has been monopolized by the West and, as Longxi Zhang (1988) proposes:

> it is time to recognize the Other as truly Other, that is, the Other in its own Otherness [...] The Other that does not just serve the purpose of being a foil or contrast to the Western self. (Zhang 1988 in Iwabuchi 1994: 18)

Toby Slade (2009: 4), in his book on Japanese fashion, also calls for alternative analyzes of modernity based on the fact that Eurocentric models of modernity do not fit the Japanese experience. The use of theoretical constructs from Western philosophy, he explains, when related to the Japanese context, bring up many potential difficulties in applying what should be considered culturally specific tools to a different cultural context. According to him, essential to modernity is the idea of reflexivity—the continual re-examination and re-evaluation of knowledge in every sphere—and, therefore, its central precept of progress is the end of certainty. Unchallenged sources of authority, whether political, religious or scholastic, he explains, are all overthrown by modernity, whereby scientific and technological advances and social and economic reforms create anxiety since the reassurance of traditional sources of knowledge are continuously questioned (Slade 2009: 4). The result, he continues, is continually changing practices and fads—fashions—in ideas and things that become repositories for those ideas, like clothing, which is, before almost everything else, *the* repository for conceptions of individual and collective identity. In modernity, he adds, progress is constantly sought, yet constantly questioned, undermined and remodelled (Slade 2009: 4). Simultaneously, he adds, the perceived unstoppable trajectory of modem progress results in nostalgia and, if not an overt longing for the past, then at least a formless melancholy and regret that some essence or intangible element has been lost. Modernity everywhere, he says, repeatedly clothes itself in reconstructions of the past, recreating national fashions and inventing traditions to authenticate this past and to authenticate the very idea of a nation itself (Slade 2009: 5).

Tradition is most often emphasized when discussing non-Western fashion, while hardly referred to in the context of Western fashion which is argued to be synonymous for modernity (Wilson 1985; Purdy 2004; Barnard 2007). According to José Teunissen (2005: 9), contrary to traditional dress, fashion is never based on fixed principles (traditions) that are transmitted. Fashion, she says, is attached to nothing, but creates every season a complete new atmosphere with new meanings that are loosely inspired by and taken from fashion history, art, or exotic cultures that are used in its own favor. After only one season, she continues, a certain element, representing a certain desirability in society, can be discarded and replaced by another symbol. As Craik (2009: 234) formulates it, however, fashion is a relentless cycle of anticipating the future, yet drawing on resonances of the past and this involves balancing the now with the future and the past. Consumers, she says, may be frightened by trends that are too different from what they wear now, but reject anything that looks old fashioned or out of fashion, so a careful balancing act is needed to predict a newness that is exciting, but that still has some familiarity.

Formulated by Sarah Cheang who references Georg Simmel and Roland Barthes, fashion is predicated on a "liberation from tradition," on a "refusal to inherit," while simultaneously being obsessed with the past as a measure of how far it has traveled in a theological project of modernity. The past, she says, is a source of inspiration for the recycling of styles that make fashion's newness paradoxical in its content. Trends, she continues, are nourished by repetition and deconstruction and in a constant drive to leave the present behind, fashion is blind to a constantly changing modernity.[1] As Rovine asserts in this volume, because fashion is defined by change from what has come before, it is inextricably connected to chronology. Referring to Walter Benjamin (1999: 252), she argues that even when clothing trends reach into the past for sources of inspiration, their focus on innovation gives the past "the scent of the modern." Teunissen (2005: 19) arguably contradicts herself by explaining modernity in fashion as a reinterpretation of existing things with current influences and as a translation into contemporary fabrics and technologies.

According to Teunissen, (2005: 17) what differentiates European from non-European fashion is that the first always aimed to move away from local distinctiveness based on tradition in a search for modern cosmopolitanism while the second would be characterized by local distinctiveness based on local cultural heritage, but this again is a very Eurocentric interpretation. Susan Kaiser (2012: 54) argues that European nations view and represent themselves as "being too complex" to have national fashions. To be modern, after all, she says, means continual change and progress. This urge for local distinctiveness, however, is only a relatively recent development as a counter reaction to cultural globalization and is not limited to the non-West. Since the success of Japanese fashion designers in the 1980s, and that of the Belgian Six right after, national identity has become a powerful marketing tool for European fashion designers, and one's own local cultural heritage has become a growing source of inspiration on which to build distinct characteristic national design identities. As Teunissen (2005: 17–19) explains, this revaluation of one's own cultural heritage represents a general melancholy based on a general fear for the loss of local traditions and craftsmanship due to industrialization and globalization. She argues that the link with the past becomes more and more direct and the urge for "authenticity" is remarkably strong.

The contribution by Angela Jansen to this volume clearly illustrates how the unprecedented success of contemporary Moroccan fashion is due to a revaluation of local cultural heritage following increasing external cultural influences through processes of globalization. Moroccan culture materialized through Moroccan fashion has become a brand under the name *beldi*—meaning "traditional/local/authentic" in Moroccan Arabic—and has come to represent everything that is "good" about Morocco. Moroccan fashion plays on people's nostalgic longing for nationalism, tradition and authenticity, while simultaneously representing promises of change, progress and participation in global (cultural) discourse. Where *beldi* only a few years ago was still associated with the countryside, backwardness and old-fashionedness, today, in a rapidly developing urban society, it allows people to escape for a moment and dream about Morocco's glorious past.

Şakir Özüdoğru, however, accuses contemporary Turkish fashion designers of self-Orientalism because, he argues, they look at their Ottoman cultural heritage through Westerners' eyes, presenting it as an exotic fantasy, detached from its historical and socio-cultural context. Instead of reinterpreting and modernizing their vestimentary heritage in order to adapt it to contemporary Turkish society, they rather mystify it with the sole aim of appealing to the international fashion market. Contrary to many other non-Western fashions, these designers are primarily aiming at a foreign clientele rather then a local one; this might have to do with the fact that the "natural" development of Ottoman fashion was disrupted by the establishment of the Turkish Republic and the subsequent prohibition of Ottoman fashion in public life.

Furthermore, the use of cultural heritage by contemporary non-Western fashion designers is not always without protest and controversy, as is well illustrated by Turaga Janaki's contribution on Indian fashion. Consumers of "holy writing" fashion, she says, cross traditional rules of engagement with the sacred and take elements of it to the non-sacred domain, which ironically, proclaims the fashionableness of the wearer, while at the same time proclaiming and underscoring his or her underlying religious and spiritual beliefs. This concurrent rediscovery of its rich and diverse heritage, on the one hand, and the ever increasing exposure to global developments and worldviews, on the other, she explains, has given rise to multiple frames of reconstruction of the self by objectifying some elements of culture, reframing and appropriating them.

The book

This volume consists of five sections. **Part 1** shows that fashion outside of Europe should not be solemnly seen as a simple result of encounters with Europe or as a consequence of recent processes of globalization. As Toby Slade's contribution demonstrates, in the beginning of the Meiji period (1868–1912) in Japan and the opening up of the country after centuries of seclusion, the primary shift in tastes that accompanied early economic and social embourgeoisement, following the abolition of feudal sumptuary laws, was the adoption of samurai tastes, previously inaccessible, financially and legally, to other classes. The ascendancy of finer materials, such as cotton and silk, among the greater populace and the very fact that choice for the lower classes now existed (they had the opportunity to formulate new identities and express previously dormant aesthetic impulses) created the wellspring of modernity in fashion in

Japan. The installation of change as an acceptable and preferable value was, in the context of Japan, the central formulation of modernity. European fashion consisting of tailcoats and bustle dresses, at this time only interested a tiny elite which was keen to demonstrate its nation's equality with foreign powers. While Japanese men rapidly adopted the suit—considered exemplary of modernism because it balanced being true to the body and the clothing without emphasizing either one—Japanese women, in contrast, took much longer to adopt European dress. According to Slade, this was mainly because "the imported women's fashions of the 1870s were a profound reaction against modernity and were consequently immoderately ornamental, anatomically perfidious and formally arbitrary."

Christine Tsui uses textual analysis to explore Chinese characters and vocabularies that are related to fashion to demonstrate that fashion dynamics in China preceded any significant exchange with Europe. She argues that while in Europe a "sense of style, fashion, manner of dress" was firstly recorded in 1300, the word "fashion" only came to signify "a popular style of clothes or way of behaving" in the sixteenth-century. In Chinese, however, there are several ancient terms that signify something similar, whereby the term *Shishizhuang* was first introduced by a Chinese poet who lived between 772 and 846. Initially, it referred to a particular makeup style for women that was in vogue at the time, but eventually it evolved into meaning "the prevalent style fit for the time." The Chinese term *Shiyang,* she explains, first appeared in a poem between 1053 and 1102, and implied a similar meaning. This shows that China distinguished between "prevalent" clothing styles from ordinary ones at a much earlier time than Europe did and therefore is not a mere nor recent imported European phenomenon. Unlike Japanese and Korean, which both directly adopted the pronunciation and transliteration form of the English word "fashion," Chinese has its own term for it, *shizhuang*. The two Chinese characters used signify "clothing (*zhuang*) that fits the time (*shi*)."

Next, the volume builds on Sandra Niessen's (2003) idea that the classification of dress as fashionable and traditional is retained by both sides of the divide in the construction of a conceptual Other for self-definitional purposes. **Part 2** focuses on the use of local cultural heritage in the construction of unique fashion identities. The case studies in this section contribute in a refreshing way to the discussion about cultural appropriation in fashion, whereby instead of focusing on how foreign fashion designers tap into non-Western cultures for inspiration without respecting historical or socio-cultural contexts, these two case studies illustrate how local designers make use of their own cultural heritage without necessarily retaining spiritual and/or religious connotations. Janaki Turaga, for example, analyzes a recent trend of holy writing on fashion. Although sacred garments and textiles were initially the esoteric preserve of the initiated and worn only in culturally prescribed sacred contexts, "secularized sacred" fashion items are now worn in non-sacred contexts to primarily make fashion and lifestyle statements. Highly popular among the growing middle classes, she argues that these garments are used to show a presumably perfect combination of materialism and spiritualism with an aesthetic fashion sense. The simultaneous rediscovery of a rich and diverse heritage on the one hand, and the ever increasing exposure to global developments and worldviews on the other, she explains, has given rise to multiple frames of reconstruction of the self by objectifying elements of culture.

Jennifer Craik, in her chapter, analyzes exotic narratives in Australian fashion, in particular, and examines why Western cultures draw both on the exotica of non-Western cultures as well as past (Western) cultures (e.g. folk cultures, traditions, historical cultures) to add an element of frisson to everyday culture; to imbue the everyday with a special—almost magical—quality. Alongside diverse forms of exotica, she reflects on the ongoing fascination with Aboriginal motifs in Australian fashion and textiles in a cyclical process of acclamation followed by renunciation coinciding with periods of nationalistic fervour (Craik in press). Through *avant-garde* fashion, she argues, Australian designers have popularized the sophisticated blending of indigenous and Australiana inspirations in colorful textiles, fashion and artwork. The underpinning of this trend according to Craik, has been the desire to create a new sense of national culture in order to reconcile the traditional myth of Australian identity as the bush and the outback with the recognition of a modern urban culture fanned by the energy of youth and popular culture. Simultaneously, there has been the politicization of indigenous culture and the recognition of the sovereignty of Aboriginal people. As a result, the use of Australiana motifs—especially indigenous ones—has become increasingly tinged by the overt and implicit politics of inspiration and appropriation.

In **Part 3**, the essays focus on discussions concerning self-Orientalism as a means of establishing a characteristic and distinctive design identity, which in its turn is used as a powerful marketing tool for nation branding. Self-Orientalism is defined as a practice of adopting and absorbing a Western gaze to deliberately turn oneself into the Other (Iwabuchi 1994). It can function in two ways: on the one hand, the characteristics of the East are mythicized and transformed into national symbols by elevating them to become agents for an international audience while on the other hand, cultural heritages are transformed through Western references whereby traces of the past are ignored/progressively erased. A frequent critique of self-Orientalism is that non-Western designers are looking at their own past and culture through Westerners' eyes by mythicizing it and as such, that they are reproducing the idea that the only way to modernize is according to Western ideologies (Shih 2001 in Sakir Özüdoğru chapter). This way, the East contributes just as much to an East–West binary. Sakir Özüdoğru, for example, argues that Turkish designers are only incorporating Ottoman clothing elements in their collections as a commercial strategy to get recognition from the international fashion scene, without really investing in their socio-cultural values. He argues that Ottoman clothing is merely used as a visual source of inspiration by contemporary Turkish fashion designers and that their collections are an embodiment of Western Orientalism. In the same way that Western designers are picking from a wide range of cultural sources without referencing, he accuses contemporary Turkish designers of making anachronistic selections based on visual characteristics solely rather than conceptualizing their heritage as insiders. The way he formulates it, "Ottoman clothing is transformed into either pastiche of the past or ultra modern forms where the past is only an ornamentation."

Angela Jansen's chapter, in its turn, focuses on the commodification of cultural heritage and the growing success of consumption driven by national identity. In the last decade, Moroccan culture, as materialized through Moroccan fashion, has become a successful brand under the name *beldi*, which meets people's longing for authenticity, craftsmanship, and national glory. Its unprecedented success is related to a general nostalgia for an idealized and fixed point in time when culture was supposedly untouched by the corruption that is automatically associated with commercial development. Referencing Marilyn Halter (2000), the more artificiality, anonymity and uncertainty apparent in a postmodern world, the more driven is the quest for authentic experiences and the more people long to feel connected to localized traditions seeking out the timeless and truth. The fact that these localized traditions are constructed and invented by contemporary fashion designers does not devaluate the experience. On the contrary, the fact that these fashion designer continuously modernize Moroccan fashion by adapting it to continuously changing circumstances, adds to their success.

Part 4 sets out to contest simple, oppositional and essentialist thinking by problematizing persisting dichotomies like tradition versus fashion, and local versus global. Both case studies presented testify in refreshing ways as to how the global is constructed locally while the local is constructed globally (Appadurai 1996). Victoria Rovine's chapter focuses on the local interpretation of a global commodity. Through the work of two South African fashion designers, she explores the lives of the plastic containers often called "China bags." The life stories of these bags, she argues, illustrate how fashion can be used to investigate local constructions of modernity that emerge out of global markets and media, as these humble containers defy their rootlessness to become deeply local. The work with China bags of the fashion collaborative Strangelove, she explains, evokes the paradoxical experience of modernity in contemporary Africa, where the modern is for many an absence and an aspiration. The China bag is a distinctively modern product, yet it emerges out of a modernity that might also be past, or just out of reach. Therefore she speaks of a failed modernity.

Emma Dick, in her chapter, analyzes how the development of a curriculum for "Western-style" tailoring at a training institute in Bhutan in the early 2000s has influenced the construction of Bhutanese fashion and identity. She analyzes the relationship between international fashions and national dress in the construction of a street-style identity in Bhutan. She shows how both traditional media and new social network technology are playing an important role in mediating and creating a fashionable Bhutanese identity. On the one hand, the national press regulates and mediates local concerns about how to interpret the ruling Buddhist monastic dress code correctly alongside an emergent discourse of nostalgia for the loss of authentic national dress practices as older styles of garments become superseded by modern hybrid garments with stitched elements to emulate the appearance of wrapped and folded cloth and modern closures and fastenings adopted for reasons of practical wearability. On the other hand, the same newspapers are encouraging their readers to wear stiletto gladiator sandals with their *kira*, to adopt Korean-style spectacles and tweed jackets that emulate characters in the *Twilight* movie franchize, and advising how to style cardigans imported from Bangladesh. She argues that the seeming contradictions of change and continuity, tradition and modernity, are encapsulated by the dual consciousness of dress in Bhutan.

Finally, the volume concludes with an afterword by Sandra Niessen in which she focuses on some of the major fallacies of the "global fashion system." She argues that the fashion/non-fashion dichotomy is a mystification and a buy-in. Fashion, she explains, is only a particular case of a universal phenomenon, a clothing adaptation to a particular economic situation. The Western fascination with its own clothing system, she says, is reified in the word "fashion" itself and simply defining it as "change over time" conveys nothing. She demonstrates that fashion studies have remained narcissistic and that the fashion history trope is not adapted to accommodate a broader definition of fashion; rather, she critiques, the Other is admitted in a cursory way without any clear criteria of selection and no cross-cultural analysis. A serious history of fashion, she adds, would need to include a self-reflexive and critical evaluation of the development of the concept of fashion. It would need to explore why definitions and descriptions of fashion have the stubbornness of a mantra and what is at stake such that fashion's conventional definition is retained. The symptoms of the fashion syndrome, she says, increase as the terminology and biases rooted in the West/rest dichotomy build upon one another. This powerful conclusion encapsulates the themes and agendas of this volume as well as being a clarion cry to shape new directions in the future scholarship on challenges to the hegemony of Western fashion as modernity and tradition as the past.

Note

1 See also Sarah Cheang, 2013.

References

Akou, Heather Marie. "Building a New 'World Fashion': Islamic Dress in the Twenty-First Century." *Fashion Theory,* vol. 11(4), (2007): 403–22.

Appadurai, Arjan. *Modernity at Large*. Minneapolis, MI: University of Minnesota Press, 1996.

Baizerman, Suzanne, Joanne B. Eicher, and Catherine Cerny. "Eurocentrism in the Study of Ethnic Dress." In *The Visible Self: Global Perspectives on Dress, Culture and Society*, eds J. Eicher, S. Evenson, and H. Lutz, 97–106, 4th ed. New York: Fairchild Books, 1996.

Barnard, Malcolm, ed. *Fashion Theory: A Reader*. London, New York: Routledge, 2007.

Barnes, R., and J. B. Eicher. *Dress and Gender: Making and Meaning in Cultural Context*. New York: Berg, 1992.

Benjamin, Walter. "Theses on the Philosophy of History." In H. Arendt (ed.), *Illuminations*, ed. H. Arendt trans. Harry Zohn, 245–56. London: Pimlico, 1999 [1968].

Cheang, Sarah. "Fashion and Ethnicity." Paper presented for the 1st Non-Western Fashion Conference, Rabat, 2012.

Cheang, Sarah. "To the Ends of the Earth: Fashion and Ethnicity in the Vogue Fashion Schoot." In *Fashion Media: Past and Present*, eds Djurdja Bartlett and Agnes Rocamora. London: Bloomsbury, 2013. pp. 35–49.

Craik, Jennifer. *Fashion: The Key Concepts*. New York: Berg, 2009.

Craik, Jennifer. "From Iconography to Inspiration in Australian Indigenous Fashion." *Journal of Fashion, Style and Popular Culture*, 1(3) (2016).

Davis, Fred. *Fashion, Culture and Identity*. Chicago: The University of Chicago Press, 1992.

Eicher, Joanne, and Tonye Erekosima. "Why Do They Call it Kalahari? Cultural, Authentication and the Demarcation of Ethnic Identity." In *Dress and Ethnicity: Change across Space and Time*, ed. J. B. Eicher, 139–64.Oxford, New York: Berg, 1995.

Eicher, Joanne, and Barbara Sumberg. "World Fashion, Ethnic and National Dress." In *Dress and Ethnicity: Change across Space and Time* 295–306. Oxford, New York: Berg, 1995.

Eicher, Joanne, Sandra Lee Evenson, and Hazel A. Lutz. *The Visible Self: Global Perspectives on Dress, Culture, and Society,* 2nd ed. New York: Fairchild, 2000.

Eicher, Joanne B."Introduction: The Fashion of Dress." In Cathy Newman, *National Geographic Fashion*. Washington, D.C.: National Geographic, 2005.

Eller, Jack David. *Cultural Anthropology: Global Forces, Local Lives*. New York: Routledge, 2015.

Entwistle, Joanne. *The Fashioned Body: Fashion, Dress and Modern Social Theory*, Cambridge. Oxford: Polity Press, 2000.

Feitsma, Maaike. *Dutch Fashion? An Exploration of Myths and Meanings*. PhD Thesis. Nijmegen: Radboud University, 2014.

Halter, Marilyn. *Shopping for Identity: The Marketing of Ethnicity*, New York: Schocken Books, 2000.

Hansen, Karen Transberg. "The World in Dress: Anthropological Perspectives on Clothing, Fashion and Culture." *Annual Review of Anthropology* (2004) 33: 369–92.

Hobsbawm, Eric, and Terence Ranger. *The Invention of Tradition*. Cambridge: Cambridge University Press, 1983.

Inda, Jonathan, and Renato Rosaldo. *The Anthropology of Globalization: A Reader*, Oxford:Blackwell Publishers, 2002.

Iwabuchi, Koichi. "Complicit Exoticism: Japan and its Other." *Continuum: The Australian Journal of Media and Culture* 8(2), (1994): 49–82.

Jansen, M. Angela. *Moroccan Fashion: Design, Tradition and Modernity*. London: Bloomsbury, 2014.

Kaiser, Susan. *Fashion and Cultural Studies*. New York: Berg, 2012.

Kawamura, Yuniya. *Fashion-ology: An Introduction to Fashion Studies*. New York: Berg, 2005.

Lehnert, Gertrud, and Gabriele Mentges. *Fusion Fashion: Culture Beyond Orientalism and Occidentalism*. Frankfurt: Peter Lang, 2013.

Lillethun, Abby, Linda Welters, and Joanne B. Eicher. "(Re)Defining Fashion," *DRESS*, (2012), vol. 38: 75–97.

Lindholm, Charles. *Culture and Authenticity*, Malden. Oxford: Blackwell Publishing, 2008.

Maynard, Margaret. *Dress and Globalization*. Manchester: Manchester University Press, 2004.

Monden, Masafumi. "Transcultural Flow of Demure Aesthetics: Examining Cultural Globalization through Gothic & Lolita Fashion." *New Voices* vol. 2, (2008): 21-40.

Niessen, Sandra. 2003. "Afterword: Re-Orienting Fashion Theory." In *Re-Orienting Fashion: The Globalization of Asian Dress*, eds. S. Niessen, A. M. Leshkowich, and C. Jones, 243–67. Oxford: Berg, 2003.

Purdy, Daniel Leonhard. *The Rise of Fashion: A Reader*. Minneapolis: University of Minnesota Press, 2004.

Rabine, Leslie. *The Global Circulation of African Fashion*. Oxford: Berg, 2002.

Riello, G., and Peter McNeil, eds *The Fashion Reader: Global Perspectives*. London: Routledge, 2010.

Skov, Lize. "Fashion Trends, Japonisme and Postmodernism, or 'What is so Japanese about *Comme des Garçons*?'" *Theory, Culture and Society* 13(3), (1996): 129–51.

Slade, Toby. *Japanese Fashion: A Cultural History*. Oxford: Berg, 2009.

Teunissen, José. "Global Fashion, Local Tradition: Over de Globalizering van Mode." In *Global Fashion, Local Tradition: Over de Globalizering van Mode*, eds José Teunissen and Jan Brand, 8–23. Utrecht: Terra, 2005.

Tsui, Christine. *Chinese Fashion: Conversations with Designers*, Oxford: Berg, 2009.

Welters, Linda, and Abby Lillethun, eds *The Fashion Reader*. Oxford: Berg, 2011.

Wilson, Elizabeth. *Adorned in Dreams: Fashion and Modernity*. London: Virago, 1985.

Wu, Juanjuan. *Chinese Fashion: From Mao to Now*. Oxford, New York: Berg, 2009.

FASHION HISTORY REVISED

2

NEITHER EAST NOR WEST: JAPANESE FASHION IN MODERNITY

TOBY SLADE

Japan occupies a unique position in the study of non-Western fashion as it was the first non-Western nation to fully engage with euromodernity, and the first to develop ways to integrate the Western fashion system into its own fashion system based on its indigenous clothing. The unique history of Japanese clothing fashions has led to some particular lingering characteristics in present fashions that do not exist in the same form elsewhere. This chapter will examine the history of Japanese clothing styles from the end of isolation of the Edo period, and the sudden influx of foreign clothing from 1868 and the Meiji period, to the present, with particular attention to the ongoing negotiation between the Western idea of fashion and the constantly changing native fashion. While often clearly delineated into indigenous kimono, and foreign or "Western" clothing, the full story is a much more complex process of negotiating sartorial modernity via both modernizing Japanese traditional clothing while, at the same time, localizing foreign influences and building a unique dual structure or "double life," with two fashion systems operating concurrently at different levels.

In many ways, Japan is a somewhat artificial example of non-Western fashion because of the extreme nature of its self-imposed isolation and then the suddenness of its reopening. However, this artificiality gives a unique vantage point from which to critique many of the assumptions within contemporary fashion theory, and also shows that fashion was not a European invention, and that despite the conceptualization of a monolithic Other threatening a traditional, static cultural core, it was actually the indigenous kimono fashions that underwent the largest changes and were the subject of the biggest trends. Japan engaged with modernity on its own terms and found sartorial forms to suit its particular needs, and did not simply replay a European fashion history. The Japanese example shows clearly the existence of fashion systems in the complete absence of foreign contact, and also the exponential growth in the intensity of fashion that comes with modernity. Yet, modernity was an accelerant, not a cause of fashion.

Globalization too, always increases the variety of fashion, whether by globalization is meant the trade on the Silk Road or the ubiquity of the Internet, but it in itself does not create fashion. And, most crucially, the paths of modernity and globalization are not one-way, from West to East, but rather a complex network expanding in many directions. The Japanese example also demonstrates that the distinction between a *fashion* which emanates from Western Europe and a traditional, indigenous *costume* is a false one, as the trends in Japanese kimono most often outpace the minority foreign fashions. Finally, the Japanese encounter with foreign fashion helps to demonstrate the previous gap between the academic discipline of fashion and the actual phenomenon as lived by the peoples of the world. Academic conveniences, such as the assumption of a clear hierarchical fashion relationship between an essentialized West and an essentialized East is shown to be far more complex and difficult to generalize in a modernizing Japan that defies this, and many other too simplistic dichotomies.

The reopening of Japan

In the beginning of Meiji period and the sudden opening of Japan to the world after centuries of seclusion, sartorial modernity was not initially the coveted dress modality of the modernizing Japanese. In 1868, sartorial modernity meant tail coats and bustle dresses, and, while this interested a tiny elite, keen to demonstrate their nation's equality to foreign powers, the vast majority were more interested in demonstrating the changing class dynamic. With the abolishing of feudal sumptuary laws, the primary shift in tastes that accompanied early economic and social embourgeoisement was a more conservative adoption of samurai tastes, previously inaccessible, both financially and legally, to other classes. The ascendancy of finer materials, such as cotton and silk, among the greater populace was the background tendency of much of the Meiji period, and experimentation with tailoring, divided garments, shifting erogenous display, and other facets of modernity in dress, were left to an exclusive few. The very fact that choice for the lower classes now existed—that they had the opportunity to formulate new identities, and express previously dormant aesthetic impulses—was the wellspring of modernity in fashion. The installation of change as an acceptable and preferable value was, in the context of Japan (where in many ways modernity preceded modernization), the central formulation of its modernity. The paradox that conservative vestimentary behavior was actually progressive and an act of modernism, as it denoted a social mobility in which people were self-actualizing, is a central formulation of modernity in Japanese clothing. At the level of form, however, the modernist project was a limited phenomenon. The application of Kantian aesthetic values to sartorial forms, although instituted in formal, male, occupational dress very early, took a long while to be manifested more widely. This was not the case in the related comportment modifications of hairstyling and cosmetics, where their relative accessibility allowed the early manifestation of naturalism, reductionism, and streamlining—all ventures in achieving a Kantian truth in form.

While male Japanese dress adopted the suit briskly—and this, it will be argued, is an exemplary example of modernism, as it balances being true to the body and the clothing without emphasizing either one—women's dress waited a long time before it could assert the same proposition. This is mainly because the imported women's fashions of the 1870s were a profound reaction against modernity, and were consequently immoderately ornamental, anatomically perfidious, and formally arbitrary. Indigenous women's styles in Japan already fulfilled many of these requirements for the reactionary performance of femininity in early modernity, which was characterized by the full weight of display being transferred to women, and male dress demonstrating seriousness and utility in contrast. It was not until the 1920s that the need for political emancipation, appropriate mobility, and aesthetic modernity were finally reflected in female dress. The male adoption of sartorial modernity, by way of the suit, was only half the story, as the phenomenon of the "double life" meant that sartorial modernity was adopted only for public life, while private life, in the home and the leisure quarters, remained partial to traditional dress forms. The "double life" was partly to do with the practical consideration of clothing appropriate to furniture and living arrangements. Domestic interior design remained predominantly traditional until the advent in the 1920s of the *bunka seikatsu* (cultured life) and *bunka jūtaku* (cultured houses)—which meant Western-style houses with Western-style furniture (Sand 2003). Desks with chairs were introduced to the civil service around 1872, making it practical to wear suits at work, though leisure and home life remained floor-based, and, thus, at variance with fitted garments, difficult-to-remove shoes, and the other attributes of Western garb.

Figure 2.1 *Concert of European Music*, 1889, Toyohara Chikanobu (1838–1912). The Metropolitan Museum of Art, New York.

The invention of tradition

The invention of tradition in the Meiji period, which accompanied the general inclination of all classes toward samurai tastes and sartorial practices, meant that indigenous styles were far from stationary, and they adapted dialectically to the provocation of imported styles. The refinement and adaptation of "traditional" clothing forms facilitated the construction of Japanese identity as something both adaptable and modern, and, at the same time, unique and uncontaminated. The monarchy was often constructed as the pioneer in this, demonstrating sartorially the military and economic sophistication of Japan, while at other times stressing the importance of continuity, and racial and cultural integrity. The invention of dress practice and its authentication as "traditional" was the primary engine of early Meiji reinvention, once the sumptuary laws were lifted and the newly permitted importation of cheaper fabrics, mainly from China, allowed the bulk of the population to reinvent itself as much closer to samurai styles than before (Minnich 1963; Rathbun 1993). This realignment of class tastes was not limited to dress, but also permeated custom, morality, and ritual, with the result that while the economic currents moved toward embourgeoisement, the cultural currents moved, at least initially, toward "samuraization." The cultural confines of "samuraization," as they were codified in the Meiji period, allowed participation in it with limited means; stoicism, abstemiousness, and Zen-restraint being key features in the abstract that easily translated into consumption patterns, interior design, and conventions of sartorial array.

In Japanese fashion, in general, sartorially *avant-garde* practice was at odds with early social trends. The move toward modernity in dress, which can be generally defined as a Kantian veracity in forms of dress, did not become the predominant trend until the Taishō period, even, perhaps for the vast majority, until after the Second World War (Hirano and Chen 1993). Modernity was not the dominant tendency and it was not performed by traditionally *avant-garde* sections of the populace: the adoption of suits was a state-instituted fashion among the political and bureaucratic elite, normally a very sartorially conservative group. Later styles were promulgated by the *mobo* (modern boys) and *moga* (modern girls) urban youth, another demographic not considered economically endowed, or socially liberated enough to act as a generator of sartorial trends, until after the youth-quakes of the 1960s. Top-down formulations of fashion were inapplicable in both cases, with only the Imperial Household as an example of elite provision of vestimentary models, and even that was highly unusual use of a monarchy, as an engine of progressive reform rather than conservative continuity.

Figure 2.2 *A Garden Refreshed by the Passing Rain*, 1888, Toyohara Chikanobu (1838–1912). The Metropolitan Museum of Art, New York.

The Rokumeikan Period

In 1883, Japan built an entertaining hall in the style of a Western casino, where the most elite levels of government would host foreign guests, dress in perfect Japanese versions of Western fashions, and dance perfect Japanese versions of Western dances, with the idea of impressing foreign dignitaries and making them feel among equals. The construction of the Rokumeikan, and its employment as a means of demonstrating cultural sophistication and adaptability through carefully replicated dress and the more formal leisure customs of international diplomacy in the 1870s, was an example of deliberate and politically motivated sartorial modernity. Perhaps because early sartorial modernity was merely a political maneuver, born of anxiety about the unequal treaty arrangements and put into place as a calculated demonstration of cosmopolitanism, it lacked the validity to be considered a real tendency toward modernity in Japanese culture. Yet, though the Rokumeikan was a failure in its political objective of restoring equality to the treaty arrangements of Japan through charm alone, it was a defining product of the particular experience of early modernity of the Meiji political elite, whose members were fascinated by American and European culture and technology, and particularly enthusiastic about a cultural program which equated modernization with westernization. As a sartorial event that went against the general tendency of samuraization in early modern Japan, early sartorial modernity can be considered an *avant-garde* dress experiment, conducted by the educated and newly empowered political elite. Besides early sartorial modernity's limitation to a very small class, and, especially in the case of women's dress, its later repudiation, there are also reservations that can be made regarding the concept of the "double life," in which sartorial modernity was limited to public and formal life, but was also deliberately prevented from infiltration into other areas like leisure activities or the home. This was perhaps part of a cultural strategy which the Japanese adopted, consciously or unconsciously, to limit the potency of foreign cultural influence, in reaction to the rapidity of the arrival of external cultural ideas. The designation of certain foreign cultural practices as "play" enables a divide to be maintained between what is Japanese and what is foreign. It permanently positions some customs as non-serious, and perhaps even not real, which prevents them from ever being fully assimilated into authentic Japanese culture. This strategy for maintaining a kind of cultural purity, or a veneer thereof, is something that continues to exist in various forms.

The events that ran counter to the general trends, or were decades ahead of where those general trends would eventually lead (and thus *avant-garde*), were in general performed by groups that can be seen to have been non-typical when compared to sartorial *avant-gardes* elsewhere. This was partially the result of the unique class arrangements and conceptualizations in Japan, and the swiftness with which these arrangements had to attune themselves to modernity. Also critically significant was the threat to notions of Japanese identity and self-conception posed by the inundation of anomalous forms and superior technologies that came with the reopening of the country, and the rejoinder to this threat. *Avant-garde* sartorial events were at odds with general tendencies, and further, they were performed by atypical *avant-gardes*, meaning that the groups that were dressing in ways ahead of their time were different to groups in other countries because of the particular historical and social circumstances. Civil servants were producing and giving form to a modern nation state, and their clothed appearances were part of that agenda; yet the Taishō period's modern boys' and modern girls' only product was themselves. They were *avant-garde* in the displaying and the being, not in the production of works: they were existentially modern. Furthermore, and critically for modernity, they were free and responsible sartorial agents who determined their own dress development through acts of will.

There is a clear distinction between the conscious actions of the creators and the wearers of the garments of modern Japan and the long-term trends displayed by clothing, which do not appear to result from these short-term intentions. The implication is that a history of Japanese clothing would have to be very different from a history of singular events that were the outcome of individual intentions and actions. Causality in dress would, like physics, seem to operate differently at particular universal levels. Though it would perhaps be possible to formulate sartorial mechanisms in which ontogeny recapitulates phylogeny; sartorial modernity is, in general, defined by the extreme reactions against its core aesthetic agenda, and thus ontogenetic and phylogenetic properties are largely incommensurate (Haeckel 1992). The links between sartorial events and sartorial tendencies often simply reflect a relationship of sequence rather than one of causality and perhaps an understandable desire for an aesthetic dimension to the creation of aesthetic theory; finding patterns in the randomness of sartorial happenings—the beauty of those patterns being more often prescribed than inherent.

New materials

The fact that certain previously unavailable materials became available is a concrete and measurable change, as definite a change as the introduction of oil pigments was in the history of painting; and the immediate and dramatic challenge to attitudes to the body, how and when it should be covered, and whether or not clothing should echo or deny its form, are foundational to the history of Japanese sartorial modernity, and are, perhaps, anterior to other formal causalities. In all discussions of causality, free will in sartorial choice is still assumed, and the phenomenon this chapter attempts to explain is the correlation of parallel choices made by Japanese dressers endowed with free will that add up to fashions, not super-organic structures that dictate the aesthetic patterns to the wearers of clothing, nor evolutionary models, nor purely economic models (Hanks and Kroeber 1940).

Identity and its opposite—syncretic randomness—form the central, but not exclusive, narrative of sartorial causality in modern Japan. The defining factor of modernity was not any form taken by that identity, or form defined as its opposite, but the degree to which that identity became transformable. This is not to say that one could not be sartorially self-actualizing in Edo times, but rather that the scope and magnitude for it increased exponentially within the conditions of modernity, such that it can be perceived as an explicating element (Nishiyama and Groemer 1997). The way in which events were used to influence tendencies is part of the larger nation-building narrative of how modern Japan became ethnically and culturally homogeneous, or more properly, how the idea of ethnic and cultural homogeneity came to be a defining feature of Japanese national identity even in the face of manifest heterogeneity. The way in which clothing is used as a vessel for identity and its myriad variances is, in essence, a Kantian process of liberation, of movement from arbitrary to self-actualizing custom. Sartorial modernity, like modernity itself, is often defined by its extreme divergence from modernity's aesthetic agenda, as many of its dominant forms were reactionary with regard to this agenda (Mitchell 2005). The events of Japanese vestimentary modernization were thus often antithetical to the long-term tendencies that finally elucidated it, and while sartorial modernity ultimately prevailed, it was, for much of the period of modernization in Japan, a partial, minority, or elitist affair.

The traditional and the new for artisitic expression

Artists were among the first groups to engage with the unfamiliar approaches to the human form—representing and clothing it. Responsible for visualizing values, they were intensely invested in the debate over the future of Japanese culture and the place of the body within it. With the enormous wave of cultural influence that accompanied the reopening of Japan, designers of all kinds faced a choice between adapting old forms and motifs now reified as tradition, or using the new Western techniques and patterns identified with progress. Making art necessitated choosing a style, and since styles were affiliated with either Japanese or Western modes, to make art was to make a statement about culture. This same choice was experienced every day for all Japanese citizens with resources, at the moment of dressing and every time they shopped for clothing. It was not the choice faced in Western Europe between tradition and reform or within the parameters of popular fashions; it was a much more important choice at a more fundamental stage of self-identification. Isozaki Arata, the architect of the planned city, Tsukuba, in Ibaraki, said that once you make a foundational choice about what style something will be, all subsequent choices become easier as they are directed by that first choice (Miyoshi and Harootunian 1989). In choosing a sartorial style, Meiji Japan faced a similar dilemma, as did its visual artists.

The art form with the highest profile was painting, and painters were, in this period of unprecedented cultural instability, faced with a stark hermeneutic choice between two modes, based primarily on their choice of materials but also upon style and cultural affiliation. These two modes were *yōga*, or Western painting, and *nihonga*, or Japanese painting. *Yōga* artists worked in oil and watercolors, were oriented toward Europe and essentially accepted modernity as the new guiding force of artistic expression. *Nihonga* artists worked in traditional pigments and formats, taking their primary inspiration from the Japanese past, and denying the value of foreign forms and the capacity for hybrids. A handful of artists worked in both modes, but generally they were exclusive categories. Within *yōga* and *nihonga* are a welter of different affiliations and styles, ranging from the progressive to the conservative. Yet, on the whole, *yōga* was by its very nature associated with stylistic evolution and perhaps derivation, as a steady stream of young artists sought to keep pace with the *avant-garde* modes emerging from Paris (Brown and Minichiello 2001). *Nihonga*, by contrast, was inherently charged with finding, defining and refining values different from, and often existing prior to, those imported from the West. Indeed, the issue of dramatic evolution was a bone of contention in *nihonga* theorizing.

Another variable in painting choice was the subject. Standard *nihonga* subject categories include landscape, bird, and flower, and the figure, which includes historical subjects, literary themes, genre, and portraiture. Historical subjects, like portraits of famous persons, tend to favor males, especially political leaders and military heroes. Literary and genre scenes are balanced between both sexes. But females alone comprise the long-sanctioned East Asian painting category of *bijinga*, or "pictures of beautiful women." European art had, from the Renaissance, a re-engagement with humanism and the body, yet Japanese notions of the body, how it could be depicted and covered, were within *nihonga*—as perhaps with the kimono—extremely stylized.

Several artists of the *nihonga* painting elite specialized in *bijinga*, devoting their careers to representing women in stylized ways. Implicitly these artists entered the national dispute on the rise of the "new woman" (*atarashii onna*) and of feminine styles, or social roles, as indices of cultural identity where clothing was a principal battleground. Some formulated elaborate taxonomies of historical evolution and regional distinctions in canons of feminine beauty; others sought subtle variations in feminine emotions and values (Davis 2010). *Bijinga* specialists, many of whom started as illustrators, often had their work published in newspapers and magazines and reinforced conservative corporeal values in the mass media. Those with literary skills also frequently contributed essays to popular publications, debating the subject of women, largely without the influence of women themselves. And *bijinga* painters of sufficient repute even served on public committees, charged with suggesting social policy concerning women. *Bijinga* artists did not merely reflect prevailing opinions about women; they helped to craft those opinions (Sato 2003).

The representation and clothing of women

In a multiplicity of ways, women and their situation and appropriate representation were at the very core of social and cultural tension and anxiety in late Meiji and Taishō Japan. It was a common historical sentiment of the era that "women could not enter public space without arousing anxiety about their presence" (Mackie 2003). It was irrefutable that men had a self-evident stake in modernity with an equivalent sartorial expression, as a consequence of having to work in the new economy and wear the clothes appropriate to the milieu of modern employment in the factory or office. Women's participation in the project of modernization, however, was a far thornier matter. In a favorite Meiji formulation, the nation's goal was the adaptation of Western technology to preserve the Japanese spirit and the manifestation of this as clearly gendered. For the average urban male, modernization was mandatory. But for females—emblems of that native essence—westernization was inherently problematic. In the dispute over the fate of Japanese culture in the modern age, women's bodies and lives thus constituted "contested spaces."

This contest was often played out between two antithetical images of women. On one hand, the modern girl (*modan gaaru*, or *moga*)—sporting pumps, a short dress, and bobbed hair, and conspicuous in such modern spaces as cafés and urban streets—represented, at the least, an enchantment with the material surface of Western modernity. She also held the promise or threat of cultural and sexual liberation, and the possibility of militant social action (Bernstein 1991; Vlastos 1998; Clark and Tipton 2000). On the other hand, the traditional woman—championed in official ideology as "good wife, wise mother" (*Ryo sai kenbo*), and belonging to the space of the home—stood guard over conventional values sanctioned by Confucian and Victorian morality alike. These poles in the debate represent politico-cultural ideologies, aesthetic choices and even marketing strategies, all played out predominantly on the bodies of women and their clothing.

Between these compelling opposites of radical modernity and reactionary tradition was a rich and passionate middle ground, where the styles and values of the *moga* and the good wife/wise mother mingled. This culturally composite woman was largely the product of a sophisticated capitalistic society, where ideology was not simply expressed through visual style, but also could be wholly transformed into style as fashion—all the better to market it to followers who were also consumers. For instance, the June 1926 issue of *Shizeidō geppō*, published by cosmetics firm Shizeidō, included an article on the modern girl, emphasizing the coiffure, clothing, and cosmetics required to achieve the *moga* look (Shizeido 1926).

Assimilating radical difference

It is a feature common to both capitalism and fashion that they assimilate, rather than repudiate challenges to them. Anti-fashion is constantly being taken up by mainstream fashion; the rebellion commodified and neutralized. Japanese fashion does this as well: Shizeidō turning the *moga* from a dangerous challenge to female values and social position into merely a look, to be copied and then forgotten as with all fashions. There is also an element in Japanese magazines, even today, that tends to make them instructional, where it is presupposed that anyone can achieve any look, rather than expressing restrictions or exclusivity of fashions based in class envy. With a more highly developed tradition of aristocratic differentiation through clothing, the West developed magazines within Thorstein Veblen's framework of conspicuous consumption; for the aristocracy to remain visually differentiated from the rising middle classes, it had to change fashions fast enough to keep ahead of the aspirants (Veblen 1899). Japan, proudly egalitarian now—at least nominally—never had as much of a system of visual differentiation as European aristocracies. Non-samurai were simply not permitted to wear samurai clothing before the Meiji Restoration, and with the abolition of these laws in the 1870s, a new visual system was established around issues of tradition and modernity, rather than simply of class. Like the merchant classes of Europe, Japanese merchants had developed a system through which they could subtly demonstrate their wealth through items like silk linings, but they were not permitted to actually imitate their samurai superiors. Certainly, after the Restoration and the abolition of the sumptuary laws, it was only those with means who could afford the new clothing, but merchant and ruling classes wore the same thing. When Japan had a fashion trend, it was embraced universally, rather like Louis Vuitton handbags today: everyone has one, so it no longer distinguishes social class, it simply signifies luxury, but universally accessible luxury (Kyojiro 2003). Fashion was a modern desire for visual newness in Japan, not a means of class differentiation, because Japanese national identity was, and is, configured differently from identity in the West, where class was, and perhaps still is, more central.

Related to this tendency in Japanese fashion there is also a tendency to reduce threats to established order to play—a strategy of fashion and of capitalism. Sadism and masochism is called *S/M play*, the *play* part neutralizing any of the Marquis de Sade's original provocations to the norms of sex, marriage, and transgression (Krafft-Ebing and Frye 1965). In this way, foreign concepts, which could present a challenge to Japanese culture and norms, are put linguistically into an experimental, and non-serious category, where their threat is reduced. The playfulness of the terms *mobo* and *moga* hide the seriousness of their potential challenge to established order and social behavior.

Whereas the dialectics of modernity and tradition, foreign and indigenous, comprised the basic formulation for cultural criticism in Taishō Japan, there was as much of an attempt to bridge these categories as an attempt to fix or fortify them. Theoretically, the modern girl was defined in part by the difference she presented from pre- or anti-modern female styles and behaviors. Yet, because of the bridging, there was no absolute fracture between old and new, and thus the categories were not mutually exclusive but rather contingent. The concepts of modernity and tradition were hybrids, or at least heterogeneous constructs subject to modification. Not surprisingly, there were both formal efforts to deflect the potentially subversive qualities of the *moga*, by making her more like a traditional woman, and spontaneous attempts to find formal commonalities. Likewise, even as the Japanese-style woman (*wasō bijin*) was being crafted as an antidote or counterbalance to the *moga*, there were also attempts to infuse her with the vitality of the modern girl.

Kimono dynamics

Japanese clothing before the 1860s was almost entirely confined to indigenous fashions, a restriction strictly policed by the state with only a few exceptions among rich, traveled eccentrics. Essentially, the indigenous fashions consisted of many varieties of the kimono, the loosely fitted robe worn with a broad belt, made of silk, mixed silk and cotton, just cotton or linen. The kimono itself was an outgrowth of a kind of under garment called *kosode* and worn by the upper class between the eighth and twelfth centuries. This gradually became an outer garment—in a process reminiscent of the European process described by Koda and Martin of underwear becoming outerwear as social formalities evolved—and the basic style and form was fairly well set by the fourteenth century (Martin and Koda 1993). Warmth was achieved in Japan by adding layers of clothes and also by padding the garments with raw cotton or silk. Until the end of the fifteenth century, linen from flax had been the most popular fiber, but from that point on, the growing cotton industry increasingly reduced the use of linen. The silk industry developed from the end of the sixteenth century, yet silk always remained a luxury of the rich, and the sumptuary regulations—which were abolished after the Meiji Restoration—restricted its use to the samurai and noble classes, which accounted for well under 10 percent of the population (other classes, notably the merchants and rich farmers, frequently violated these regulations, using silk as a lining, and other means of subtly demonstrating growing wealth and refinement.) There is no reliable quantitative information for this period, but it is generally agreed that just before the Meiji Restoration, the average Japanese would have worn some form of cotton or linen kimono, while a rich person might have been clad in silk. At this time, woolens were very rarely manufactured in Japan—indeed, they were almost unknown (Smith 1955). Some woolen and worsted fabrics (such as Raxa and Grofgren) had been introduced at the end of the sixteenth century by Spanish, Portuguese, and Dutch merchants, but the closing of the country by Tokugawa Iemitsu, in 1639, to anything but very limited Dutch and Chinese commerce prevented this importation from developing. Until the Restoration, wool remained a luxury commodity, used only by the richest nobles for accessories—in much the way that furs might have been used in Europe (Smith 1955).

Among the first Japanese to adopt Western clothing, albeit only in the form of military uniforms, were the officers and men of some units of the shogunal army and navy. Some time in the 1850s, these men adopted woolen uniforms in the style of those worn by English marines stationed at Yokohama. Producing these uniforms could not have been an easy matter. All of the cloth had to be imported, and tailors had to be trained in the comparatively difficult art of fitting Western-style suits (Sōmuchō Tōkeikyoku and Nihon Tōkei Kyōkai 1987).

The indigenous kimono, being a loose garment, presented no particular problems of cutting and fitting, and until recently, most Japanese women were capable of putting these garments together entirely by hand. Kimonos are made from one long, rectangular length of cloth cut into eight pieces; the pattern is the same for everyone, male or female, child or adult. Every inch of cloth is used, with no waste. No matter how efficiently an article of Western clothing is cut, when fitted clothing is produced there will be pieces from which nothing can be made. No buttons or hooks or other gadgets are needed to hold the kimono on: the obi—the band or sash tied around the waist—is sufficient. This means that when the garment is put on it can be adjusted for the wearer's girth and height.

As already stated, the kimono creates a certain understanding of the body, as something to be wrapped. Western garments require a much closer individual fit, and the Japanese needed special training in order to become Western-style tailors—tailoring here meaning the English tradition of bespoke design: having the clothes customized to the particular body became the prime European male sartorial criterion. In the late 1850s and the 1860s, a few foreign tailors catered to the small foreign settlements in Yokohama and Kobe. Some of these establishments took Japanese apprentices, and they in turn became the first native entrepreneurs in this trade. By 1886, the Association of Merchants and Manufacturers of Western Suits, founded in Tokyo, already had 123 members (O.A.M.T.W.S 1930). In 1890, the first style-book (*fukusō zasshi*) was issued, designed to introduce the newest fashions of Europe to tailors and the public. Some sewing machines had been in use since the 1860s, and in 1887, a special sewing machine school was founded in Tokyo, mainly for the benefit of apprentice tailors. The Singer Co. established a school, also in Tokyo, in 1907, and here the students were largely housewives and young girls (Bissell 1999). Perhaps the most significant aspect of this early adoption of Western styles was its public origin. For quite a while the public sector remained the major champion of the new garb, reflecting the aesthetic dimension of the political agenda of modernization.

State policy on Western dress

The Meiji Restoration of 1868 established in Japan a strong central government, committed to abolishing feudalism and eager to use westernization as a model for political, economic and cultural development—the idea of development itself being the operative aspiration of modernity. These policies were reflected in the clothes in which the members of the new government chose to be seen. When the Duke of Edinburgh visited Japan, in 1869, the Imperial Court decided to receive him in formal Western dress. In 1870, navy cadets were ordered to wear British-style uniforms, while army cadets followed the French model (Harries and Harries 1991). The turn of policemen and mailmen came in 1871, and that of workers on the sole national railway line, running between Tokyo and Yokohama, in 1872.

During 1871, debate commenced as to whether the principles of sartorial reform should be extended to ministers of the central government and members of the court (Irokawa 1985). The issue was whether, to what extent and at what occasions, senior officials of the central and local government should wear Japanese or Western dress. The agenda of wider westernization prevailed, and an imperial rescript of that year reflected the official view: the court was

Figure 2.3 *Nobility in the Evening Cool*, 1887, Toyohara Chikanobu (1838–1912). The Metropolitan Museum of Art, New York.

ordered to abandon its Sinicized costumes—they were considered effeminate and un-Japanese—and courtiers and bureaucrats were urged to adopt Western clothing; it was thought that this was much more practical and would demonstrate their new alignment with Western rather than Chinese civilization (Hirano and Chen 1993). The government had the Emperor speak as follows:

> "The national polity [*kokutai*] is indomitable, but manners and customs should be adaptable. We greatly regret that the uniform of our court has been established following the Chinese custom, and it has become exceedingly effeminate in style and character [...] The Emperor Jimmu [660–585 BCE] who founded Japan, and the Empress Jingu [201–269 CE] who conquered Korea, were not attired in the present style. We should no longer appear before the people in these effeminate styles, and we have therefore decided to reform dress regulations entirely" (O.A.M.T.W.S 1930).

The emphasis was on the new adaptability that the state would require of the people in order for Japan to modernize and remain independent, and it was recognized that the reform of simple sartorial customs—the fundamental marker and means of enacting individual and collective identity—would be a crucial instrument in effecting this required malleability. The evocation of Emperor Jimmu illustrates the State's willingness to enlist and manipulate history and custom and reinvent it in the service of fostering nationalism and expedient, if untrue, collective memory.

When, in 1877, the new conscript armies of the central government faced the last internal challenge to the new regime during the Satsuma Rebellion, they were dressed in woolen uniforms while the insurgents wore the traditional cottons and silks of the samurai. The symbolic aspects of the battle were probably clear to both victor and vanquished. Thus, by the 1880s, European clothing fashions had conquered some small but symbolically important corners of the market, and their influence was spreading slowly—mainly from the top down (Hirano and Chen 1993). The higher echelons of society in Tokyo started to frequent European-style entertainments—social dances, garden parties, musicales—and the men would often appear in tuxedos, or other forms of European evening dress. At the time foreigners had extraterritorial rights in Japan, and the government believed, perhaps naively, that the rapid spread of Western manners and dress would enable it to get rid of the unequal treaties by simply demonstrating Japan's level of civilization and ability to adapt to European customs. In line with this policy, the government sponsored, beginning in 1883, a variety of nightly social affairs at the Rokumeikan, a Western-style building in Tokyo. These affairs were attended by foreigners and high-class Japanese, all in Western dress. Some department stores also opened Western-dress sections at this time (Shirokoya 1957). The Empress and ladies of the court began to be seen in dresses. During this decade, the Ministry of Education ordered that Western-style student uniforms be worn in public colleges and universities; private universities followed only at a much later date (Reischauer 1957). Businessmen, teachers, doctors, bankers, and other leaders of the new society made use of Western suits by the end of the nineteenth century, mainly at work or at large social functions, and in 1898, the total consumption of woolen fabrics reached about 3,000,000 yards, almost all imported from England and Germany (Tōyō Keizai Shimpō sha Tokyo [from old catalogue] and Ishibashi 1935).

The early twentieth century

By the early years of the twentieth century—about thirty years after the Restoration—Western dress had become a symbol of social dignity and progressiveness, an accepted symbol of civic progress. In addition, it was usually a reasonably good indication of public employment. The victory in the Russo–Japanese War (1904–5), and the economic boom associated with it, turned the eyes of Japan even more toward Europe, as the Japanese had proved to themselves and the world that they were able to defeat a European power, and somewhat broadened the narrow circle of people using wool and Western suits. It is necessary to underline how limited the use of this type of dress still was at that time. The vast majority of Japanese stuck to their own styles, within which fashion systems had begun to operate in the modern sense, and even those few who, voluntarily or involuntarily, changed to "modern" dress replaced it when they returned home, with the more (physically and mentally) comfortable kimono. Japanese interiors were impractical for Western clothing until the later trend toward European furniture. Western dress in public, and Japanese dress at home, remained the general rule for a very long time (Uenoda 1956).

At the beginning of the twentieth century, a development of much greater long-range consequence was taking place within indigenous Japanese styles. Western clothing was confined to a small elite, but the nature of indigenous clothing was also affected by the new times. From the turn of the century, woolens and worsteds showed their real gains, not in the narrow demand for Western suits but in the adoption of these materials for the kimono. Thus, the experience of sartorial modernism was, for many, not one of form, body and movement change but one of textural change. In line with the general samuraization of tastes, many adopted what the ruling class had already known about for some time.

Almost up to the time of the First World War, from the point of view of the majority of Japanese, there was no general westernization of clothes but rather a gradual adoption of a new fiber, wool, together with a continued use of silk and cotton. The people had become acquainted with wool, but there were still two enormous obstacles to the more widespread use of Western fashions: the Japanese continued to prefer their own styles, and wool remained comparatively expensive. There were always cheaper substitutes among traditional clothes. Among other things, the kimono has the advantage of lasting much longer than Western clothes. Styles—usually designs of the cloth, not designs of the clothes—change less frequently, and since the garment is loose, it can fit successive generations of wearers (Hanley 1997). Since the mid-Tokugawa period, there had been many used clothing shops in Edo, and business was so brisk that people began stealing clothing to sell it, precipitating an unsuccessful attempt to close down the market in 1724. By the eighteenth century, wholesalers of used clothing emerged; and the volume of trade was huge (Itō 1982). The standardization of the kimono made this trade much more vibrant than the trade in used clothing in Europe and America; when you can fit into anything on display, the opportunities for consumption greatly increase. This fact reduced accessibility to Western clothing through the traditional channel of traders in second-hand clothes.

Economic boom and earthquake

The Japanese economy underwent extremely rapid development during the First World War, and this was a great stimulus to the westernization of national life. Among what might be called the "smart set," the slogan *bunka seikatsu*—literally, cultured or civilized life, actually meaning a Western style of life—began to be heard. These people craved *bunka jūtaku* (cultured houses), *bunka shoku* (cultured food), and *bunka fuku* (cultured clothes), and all this meant the same thing—that European and American customs were considered superior (Clark and Tipton 2000). While this may have been the general opinion, reinforced by the arrival of Hollywood cinema and the like, the actual result was the creation of an abundance of stylistic hybrids in these areas which better suited the Japanese experience of modernity than either the indigenous or the foreign models. These tendencies continued in the 1920s, and spread considerably due to the Great Kantō Earthquake of 1923 (Jansen 1995). The disaster almost completely destroyed Tokyo and Yokohama, the largest metropolitan complex in the country, and this tragic event caused something of a turning point in Japanese fashion history. Over 700,000 dwellings were levelled, and millions lost all their possessions—including their clothes (Seidensticker 1991). Many victims replaced their clothing with a larger proportion of Western items, in part because the pattern of demand had slowly shifted to a greater emphasis on this type of fashion, and also because it was said that the kimono had proved dangerous during the quake since its long sleeves and train prevented rapid movement. Even though the latter allegation was not very plausible—after all, the Japanese had long experience with both earthquakes and kimonos—it may well have affected popular tastes. Also in the 1920s, primary and secondary school students contributed to increased westernization as, after the Great Kantō Earthquake, many of the schools adopted plain, blue serge, Western-style uniforms, and the popularity of social dancing and gymnastics intensified the tendencies to westernization.

Until the 1930s, however, the majority of Japanese still continued to wear the kimono, and Western clothes were still pretty much restricted to public, non-domestic use by certain classes. Since most Japanese women were still largely confined to the home, a large potential market was eliminated. Even when Japanese women began to appear more frequently as members of the labor force, either in industry or in service occupations, they usually remained in the kimono. It is true that the conductresses on Tokyo's municipal buses changed to Western wool uniforms in 1924, but that was an exception (Nakagawa 1986). Wherever Japanese women worked—in department stores, offices, bars, as telephone operators or factory workers—they usually performed their tasks in kimonos, if necessary covered with aprons and dusters. It was another disaster that provoked a big conversion in women's dress.

The general trend toward Western dress in the 1930s is explainable in more rational terms. By that time, most of the people had worn Western-style school or army uniforms, and presumably had acquired a kind of taste, or habit for fitted and divided clothes. From 1873, all able-bodied Japanese men had to serve three years in the army, and four years in the reserves, wearing Western-style uniforms, and living in Western-style barracks. In addition, the stature of young Japanese men and women had also changed—their very bodies had become more modern through diet and lifestyle. They had grown taller, their legs were longer and the women's busts were a little larger, and this made new styles more flattering. For example, in 1900, the average 20-year-old male was 160 cm tall and the average female 147.9 cm tall. By 1940, they were 164.5 and 152.7 cm tall, respectively (Japan. Sōmuchō. Tōkeikyoku. and Nihon Tōkei Kyōkai. 1987). Furthermore, Western fashions themselves—especially women's fashions—had changed. The skirts were shorter and the sleeves narrower, increasing the comparative advantage of dresses vis-à-vis the kimono if one wanted to lead a more active life. Western fashions for women changed, from the reaction away from modernity in the Victorian era, toward more modern forms. Meanwhile, the woolen and worsted industries had experienced considerable growth—they were now more productive and the real price of woolen textiles had declined (Smitka 1998). As a result of all these factors, by the outbreak of the Second World War, most working women in Japan, and quite a few housewives, wore Western dress. The same was true of the men working in offices or factories.

Already, in the 1920s, the Western suit had reached the upper classes in the provincial cities, and, in the 1930s, it was ubiquitous in general business circles. Male work clothes also reflected the Westernizing influences. Cotton, woolen, or worsted work clothes, following Western patterns, were used in most factories and the use of bicycles for delivery and message purposes contributed in no small measure to the wearing of pants. The group least affected by all of these changes must have been the farmers, who still made up over 40 percent of the gainfully occupied population in the late 1930s (Hirano and Chen 1993). More importantly, however, at home, in the cities and the country, most Japanese continued to relax, eat and sleep in their indigenous clothes.

Foreign fads and superficial engagement

The adoption of aspects of Western material culture was for the most part superficial and took the form of short-lived fads well into the twentieth century. The changes that occurred during the early Meiji period—carrying Western umbrellas or wearing Western shawls with traditional kimonos—were primarily changes of style and did not really constitute a radical cultural shift. It is interesting that Japan, superficially one of the most faddish nations when it comes to fashion, is also extremely slow to abandon traditions—as with "S/M play," fashions are viewed as play and are engaged with on a superficial level only, with any contexts or deeper meanings or social challenges being ignored. This argument has often been made at a linguistic level (Hogan 2003). The distance at which Japan keeps foreign influence, is also clear in the katakana alphabet used exclusively for foreign words, which are not allowed to be absorbed into the Japanese language; thus, foreign and indigenous are immediately distinguished, just as gender is immediately distinguished in European. While the argument is not without flaws and exceptions, it still has merit for demonstrating, if only partly, this phenomenon of keeping foreign influence in a separate category, to distinguish it from what is considered essentially Japanese.

Because of the early preference for the larger income of the middle and lower classes in the Meiji period to be spent on a samuraization, consumption patterns tended to favor many local products (Hanley 1997). Increases in the standard of living resulted, by and large, in a greater demand for traditional goods, and this went toward stabilizing the economy, as it meant that the producers of traditional goods did not suddenly find themselves out of work or technologically obsolete—the textile industry is a good example. The new large-scale textile factories produced cloth that was too wide for the kimono, so that, while they contributed to an increase in the consumption of cotton cloth for other purposes, they also enabled the survival of the traditional industry

Figure 2.4 *A Contest of Elegant Ladies among the Cherry Blossoms*, 1887, Toyohara Chikanobu (1838–1912). The Metropolitan Museum of Art, New York.

that produced the material for the kimono. Furthermore, consumer preference for traditional goods meant that the country did not spend its valuable foreign currency on consumer goods during the early stages of industrialization (Hanley and Yamamura 1977). This was particularly important for Japan, which not only set out on its industrialization with a somewhat lower per capita income than that of Western nations, but was also nearly a century behind England, when it began to industrialize.

The impetus for the eventual diffusion of new lifestyles and of a preference for new goods can be attributed to a large degree to the military. Just as the Sengoku Wars transformed life in the sixteenth century, the Sino–Japanese and Russo–Japanese wars, at the turn of the twentieth century, transformed life in the Meiji period. The adoption of cotton for military use by the Sengoku daimyo led to its diffusion among the population as the favored material for clothing. So, too, the soldiers' contact with Western uniforms, mainly woolen, and foods helped create a demand for such goods, when the troops returned home after the wars with China and Russia.

Conclusion

As the first non-European or non-American nation to engage with euromodernity, including modernity in clothing fashions, Japan had no model of how to navigate the dilemmas of indigenous and imported styles. The solution of essentially parallel fashion developments, a double life, was in keeping with Japan's entire approach to modernization. Japan attempted to preserve cultural aspects, while adapting foreign ideas into its modernization program. The idea that an essential Japan was being preserved, however, was an illusion, and indigenous clothing changed more than the more visible adoption of Western clothing by elites. The major movement of fashion throughout the Meiji and Taishō periods was what could be described, not as a modernization or a westernization, but rather a samuraization, with all social classes and regional variations aspiring to and gradually adopting a homogenized version of samurai clothing, previously reserved for the 10 percent who constituted the samurai social class. Underlying this, however, was the idea at the heart of fashion itself, that change for its own sake is a desirable state and the source of beauty, and it is this that really defines fashionable sartorial modernity in Japan. After the centuries of Edo period seclusion, the abolishing of feudal sumptuary laws initiated the predominant shift in tastes of early economic and social embourgeoisement and the conservative adoption of samurai tastes, previously inaccessible, financially and legally, by other classes. The availability of means to express new identities and previously dormant aesthetic impulses—was the wellspring of modernity in fashion. That change became an acceptable and preferable value was, in Japan, an example of modernity preceding modernization. The seeming contradiction that conservative vestimentary behavior was actually progressive and an act of modernism, as it denoted a social mobility in which people were self-actualizing, is a defining feature of modernity in Japanese clothing.

The Japanese example provides a clear critique of many of the assumptions of contemporary fashion theory. It shows clearly that fashion was neither a European invention nor the result of various waves of globalization. It had no single direction of influence and despite the conceptualization of a monolithic Other threatening a traditional, static cultural core, it was actually the indigenous kimono fashions that underwent the largest changes and were the subject of the biggest trends. Japan engaged with modernity on its own terms and found sartorial forms to suit its particular needs, and did not simply replay a European fashion history. All the dynamics of fashion were present; dynamics of social class, of economics, of psychology, of shifting gender relations, of technology, of aesthetics. To privilege one view, a national perspective of Japanese adoption of certain European fashions, is to miss the much larger, more complex and more interesting story of Japanese fashion and, indeed, of fashion in general.

References

Bernstein, G. L. *Recreating Japanese Women, 1600–1945*. Berkeley, CA: University of California Press, 1991.

Bissell, D. *The First Conglomerate: 145 Years of the Singer Sewing Machine Company*. Brunswick, ME: Audenreed Press, 1999.

Brown, Kendall H., and Sharon Minichiello. *Taishō Chic: Japanese Modernity, Nostalgia, and Deco*. Honolulu: Honolulu Academy of Arts, 2001.

Clark, J., and E. K. Tipton. *Being Modern in Japan: Culture and Society from the 1910s to the 1930s*. Sydney, Australia: Australian Humanities Research Foundation, 2000.

Davis, J. N. *Kitagawa Utamaro: Woodblock Prints from the British Museum*. Birmingham, London, Ikon; Gallery Ltd, 2010.

Haeckel, E. *The Riddle of the Universe*. Buffalo, NY: Prometheus Books, 1992.

Hanks, J. R., and A. L. Kroeber. *Three Centuries of Women's Dress Fashions, a Quantitative Analysis*. Berkeley, C.A.: University of California Press, 1940.

Hanley, S. B. *Everyday Things in Premodern Japan: The Hidden Legacy of Material Culture*. Berkeley, CA: University of California Press, 1997.

Hanley, S. B., and K. Yamamura. *Economic and Demographic Change in Preindustrial Japan, 1600–1868*. Princeton, NJ: Princeton University Press, 1977.

Harries, M., and S. Harries. *Soldiers of the Sun: The Rise and Fall of the Imperial Japanese Army, 1868–1945*. London, Heinemann, 1991.

Hirano, K., and Y. Chen. *The State and Cultural Transformation: Perspectives from East Asia*. Tokyo, New York: United Nations University Press, 1993.

Hogan, J. "The Social Significance of English Usage in Japan." *Japanese Studies* 23(1), (2003): 43–58.

Irokawa, D. *The Culture of the Meiji Period*. Princeton, NJ: Princeton University Press, 1985.

Itō, Y. *Edo no yumenoshima*. Tōkyō: Yoshikawa Kōbunkan, 1982.

Jansen, M. B. *The Emergence of Meiji Japan*. New York: Cambridge University Press, 1995.

Japan. Sōmuchō, Tōkeikyoku, and Nihon Tōkei Kyōkai. *Nihon chōki tōkei sōran*. Tokyo: Nihon Tōkei Kyōkai, 1987.

Krafft-Ebing, R. von, and N. Frye. *Psychopathia Sexualis; Especial Reference to the Antipathic Sexual Instinct*. New York: Bantam, 1965.

Kyojiro, H. *Louis Vuitton Japan: The Building of Luxury.* Tokyo: Nikkei, 2003.

Mackie, V. C. *Feminism in Modern Japan: Citizenship, Embodiment, and Sexuality*. Cambridge; New York: Cambridge University Press, 2003.

Martin, R., and H. Koda. *Infra-apparel*. New York, Metropolitan Museum of Art, 1993.

Minnich, H. B. *Japanese Costume and the Makers of its Elegant Tradition*. Rutland, VT: C.E. Tuttle Co., 1963.

Mitchell, L. *The Cutting Edge: Fashion from Japan*. Sydney, Australia: Powerhouse, 2005.

Miyoshi, M., and H. D. Harootunian. *Postmodernism and Japan*. Durham, NC: Duke University Press, 1989.

Nakagawa, K. *Basu no bunkashi*. Tokyo: Chikuma Shobō, 1986.

Nishiyama, M., and G. Groemer. *Edo Culture: Daily Life and Diversions in Urban Japan, 1600–1868*. Honolulu:, University of Hawai*i Press, 1997.

O.A.M.T.W.S. *Osaka Association of Merchants and Tailors of Western Suits: Nihon yofuku enkaku-shi (The History of Western Suits in Japan)*. Osaka, Japan: Osaka Yofuku Sho-Dogyo Kumiai, 1930.

Rathbun, W. J. *Beyond the Tanabata Bridge: Traditional Japanese Textiles*. New York: Thames and Hudson, in association with the Seattle Art Museum, 1993.

Reischauer, E. O. "Serge Eliseeff." *Harvard Journal of Asiatic Studies* 20 (June 1957): 11.

Sand, J. *House and Home in Modern Japan: Architecture, Domestic Space, and Bourgeois Culture, 1880–1930*. Cambridge, MA: Harvard University Asia Center, 2003.

Sato, B. H. *The New Japanese Woman: Modernity, Media, and Women in Interwar Japan*. Durham, NC: Duke University Press, 2003.

Seidensticker, E. *Tokyo Rising: The City Since the Great Earthquake*. Cambridge, MA: Harvard University Press, 1991.

Shirokoya. *Shirokiya 300-nenshi (A Three Hundred Year History of the Shirokoya)*. Tokyo: Shirokiya Co., 1957.

Shizeido. "Modern Girl." *Shizeidō geppō* (June 1926).

Smith, T. C. *Political Change and Industrial Development in Japan: Government Enterpriseize, 1868–1880*. Stanford, CA: Stanford University Press, 1955.

Smitka, M. *The Textile Industry and the Rise of the Japanese Economy*. New York: Garland, 1998.

Tōyō Keizai Shimpō sha Tokyo, and T. Ishibashi (1935). *Nihon bōeki seiran*. From catalog, 1935.

Uenoda, S. *Japan, Yesterday and Today: Sketches and Essays on Japanese City Life*. Tokyo: Tokyo News Service, 1956.

Veblen, T. *The Theory of the Leisure Class; An Economic Study in the Evolution of Institutions*. London: Macmillan & Co. Ltd, 1899.

Vlastos, S. *Mirror of Modernity: Invented Traditions of Modern Japan*. Berkeley, CA: University of California Press, 1998.

3

"FASHION" IN THE CHINESE CONTEXT[1]

CHRISTINE TSUI

Introduction

The objective of this chapter is to examine the connotations of the term "fashion" in the Chinese context. The term "fashion" itself is complex and in this chapter it is used to refer to "clothing-fashion." In this sense, the popular explanation for the equivalent Chinese term *shizhuang*[2] is "a prevalent new clothing style that fits the time."[3] This chapter primarily explores the following questions: What is the origin of the Chinese term for "fashion," *shizhuang*? What is the Chinese definition and perception of *shizhuang*? What are the primary differences between *shizhuang* in the Chinese context and "fashion" in the English context? What are the differences between *fuzhuang* (clothing) and *shizhuang* in the Chinese context? Do Chinese and Western scholars share the same understanding of "fashion"? Does fashion play the same role in Chinese and Western contexts? In this chapter, the latter, particularly, refers to the English discourse.

In order to provide a more comprehensive study of "fashion" in the Chinese context, this chapter also explores the differences between "fashion" and "clothing" in Chinese discourse. The Chinese translation for "clothing" is *fuzhuang*[4] or *yifu*.[5] The two words have little difference in connotation. *Fuzhuang* is more formal, and is normally used by working professionals, for instance, as in *fuzhuang chang* (clothing factory); *fuzhuang gongsi* (clothing company). *Yifu* is mostly used in daily life communication: for instance "please wear more *yifu* today because it is cold." I use *shizhuang* and *fuzhuang* for the Chinese terms and "fashion" and "clothing" for the English terms.

The "Chinese" in this chapter is constrained to simplified Chinese only, the common language used by mainland Chinese. In some cases, simplified Chinese may be different from the traditional Chinese used in Hong Kong, Taiwan, and/or overseas Chinese. I argue that fashion in Chinese academic discourse enjoys a less prestigious position. Research on fashion in China still mainly focuses on its material aspects. Fashion in the West is the focus of a more abstract discourse and involves a vaster scope of disciplines.

Notion of "fashion" in ancient Chinese

According to the *The Barnbart Dictionary of Etymology* (1988), a "sense of style, fashion, manner of dress" was first recorded in the year 1300. The word "fashion" itself did not come to signify "a popular style of clothes or way of behaving" until the sixteenth century (Cresswell 2009).[6] In Chinese, there are several ancient terms that signify something similar. Based on the *Etymology of Chinese* (Ciyuan 1983),[7] *shishizhuang*[8] was first introduced by the famous Chinese poet Bai Juyi (772–846),[9] and initially meant a particular makeup style for women that was in vogue at the time. The word *shiyang*[10] first appeared in a poem by Chen Shidao (1053–1102),[11] and referred to "the prevalent style fit for the time." The words *shiyang* and *shishizhuang* reveal that the Chinese people were making a distinction between "prevalent" stylish clothing, and ordinary clothing much earlier than the West.[12]

Besides the notion of a "prevalent style fit for the time,"[13] "fashion" has two other popular meanings in a Western cultural context: fashion changes,[14] and fashion as a social phenomenon[15] (social class, psychology, modernity, capitalism, identity, etc.). Although many scholars believe that fashion is a Western phenomenon (e.g. König 1974, Wilson 1985), Finnane (2008: 9) affirms that "Chinese dress in the sixteenth to nineteenth century […] shows evidences of short-term changes in urban fashions" in China. Chen (2013) argues that in Tang dynasty (618–907), both women of the royal court and outside of court used luxury silk fabrics to compete for "power" and "social status" in a period when the empire was declining and silk production expanding. In other words, "fashion" was not only a "material" but also a "social phenomenon" in the history of China. Both the explanations of the ancient Chinese words and the two cases presented by Finnane and Chen substantiate that China has had its own notion of changing trends in clothing styles for many centuries. Such a notion complies with Kaiser's argument (2012: 173) that "fashion has been historically located all around the world and that "the fact that these historical traditions of fashion are not as well-known or advertised as the European one should not diminish their value" (Riello and McNeil 2010: 4).

The origin of *shizhuang*

Shizhuang in Chinese consists of two characters, *shi* and *zhuang*. The character *shi* has been used for thousands of years and appears in the oldest set of Chinese characters available today in archeological relics (*JiaguWen*)[16] (Wei 2010). The character generally relates to "timing" or "times," "season," "on time," "immediately," "something that happens often," "fit for the time" (Zhang et al. 1996; Chi, Song, and Lu 1998: 947; Zhu 2000). It is still an active character and retains a similar meaning in China today. The Chinese character *zhuang* historically refers to clothing, traveling packages, and makeup (Gu 2003: 725; Fei and Qiu 2002), and today (when used as a noun), it denotes clothing. Therefore, the juxtaposition of *shi* and *zhuang* means "clothing fit for the time."

However, the two characters (*shi* and *zhuang*) did not converge into one word until the mid to late nineteenth century. The Chinese Etymology Dictionary *Ciyuan* collects words that were in use before the mid-nineteenth century, and *shizhuang* is not among them. Of course, the emergence of a particular word does not mean that the phenomenon did not exist—it was referred to with another term (as became clear in the paragraph "Notion Of Fashion In Ancient Chinese"). The increased use of the word *shizhuang* in the Chinese fashion industry affirms that the word emerged in the late nineteenth and early twentieth centuries, and was a result of Western influences during this period.

Documents from the Shanghai Historical Archive Center *(Shanghai Lishi Dangan Guan)* identify a "Father of Fashion" (*shizhuang zhifu*) in China—a man by the name of Zhao Chunlan.[17] Mr. Zhao traveled to the United States[18] and studied Western cutting technology[19] for women's clothing in the mid-nineteeth century. On his return to China, he cultivated a group of Chinese apprentices to continue this style. Designating Mr. Zhao as the "Father of Fashion" implies that there was no *shizhuang* before him, and, furthermore, establishes a close correlation between *shizhuang* and "Western dress." *Shizhuang* was a term that described a particular *type* of fashion, and it emerged at this time to describe a phenomenon peculiar to Western women's clothing styles, as they came to be adapted and created in China during the late nineteenth and early twentieth centuries. That is to say, the relatively recent historical emergence of *shizhuang* as a term is not a result of the relatively recent emergence of the concept of fashion per se, but rather the result of the emergence of a new branch of clothing that became fashionable as a result of China's interactions with Western modernity.

Zhao's influence continued through his students as they went on to form Hong Xiang—the first store[20] using the word *shizhuang* (fashion) in its name in China. It started out as "Hong Xiang Ladies' Tailor Shop" (*Hongxiang Nüzi Caifen*

Dian) in 1917.[21] Its founders were fourth-generation students of Zhao Chunlan. The term "ladies' tailor" was used to distinguish it from "men's tailor," as well as from "traditional Chinese tailors." Traditional Chinese tailors cut men's and women's wear in similar forms and, as a result, all historical Chinese costumes for both men and women look flat.[22] However, Zhao was not alone in introducing Western cutting techniques in China. Starting from the mid–1900s (the first Opium War 1840–2), flocks of Western merchants migrated to Shanghai. Some of them opened tailor shops that introduced new cutting technologies to Chinese tailors. The basic difference between the two cutting forms[23] at the time was that the Chinese form was flat, while the Western one hugged the wearer's body by reducing the volume differences between bust, waist, and hips. Eventually, some of the Chinese tailors switched to Western cutting methods and they were among the founders of Hong Xiang. In 1928, the shop changed its name to the "Hong Xiang Fashion Company" (*Hongxiang Shizhuang Gongsi*), while still only providing women's wear. When I asked Mr. Jin, the son of one of the founders, what made Hong Xiang choose the word *shizhuang* for the shop name,[24] he replied that the name was given by a literary friend of his father's, who understood it to mean "clothing fit for the time." This case demonstrates, again that *shizhuang* was particularly related to women's wear in its westernized form.

The nomenclature of the Chinese clothing industry from the 1920s to the 1950s[25] provides further evidence of the application of *shizhuang* in China. The Shanghai Historical Archives show that the clothing industry in Shanghai was segmented into different genres, including "new clothing" (*xinyi zu*), "normal clothing" (*yizhuo zu*), "Western men's suits" (*xifu zu*), "fashion" (*shizhuang zu*), "machine-sewn clothing" (*jifeng zu*) and "leather garments" (*qiuyi zu*). The taxonomy was based on the category of the garments and their business model.[26] Again, *shizhuang* in this context is also peculiar to "Western women's clothing" (*nüzi yang fu*[27] or *xishi nüzhuang*).[28]

From the 1950s to the 1970s, during Mao's era, *shizhuang* gradually became taboo because of its association with "bourgeois style." The word was completely eradicated from Chinese publicity during the radical Cultural Revolution (1967–76). The period in which the use of this particular word was forbidden underscores the aforementioned findings that *shizhuang* has a strong association with Western fashion. Therefore, although China possessed the notion of "popular styles or wear" 1,000 years ago, the word *shizhuang* currently used as the equivalent of "fashion" in Chinese, was a result of the gradual influence of Western fashion, starting from the middle of the nineteenth century. *Shizhuang* was initially a peculiar name for Chinese women's wear in Western form. The correlation between "women's wear in Western form" and the connotation of "clothing fit for the time" reveals that "Western women's clothing" was widely regarded as "clothing fit for the time."

Research method

To answer the research questions, I collected the definitions of "fashion" as defined by the words *fuzhuang* and *shizhuang* from three different sources: dictionaries, academic journals, and fashion textbooks, and then conducted a textual analysis of these resources and definitions.

Dictionaries

The introduction of e-libraries has facilitated quick research into the meaning of any term from numerous dictionaries. I located three popular English and two primary Chinese online resources that allow access to the multi-entries of dictionaries: Oxford Online Reference,[29] Gale Virtual Reference Library,[30] Blackwell Reference Online,[31] CNKI.net (Chinese),[32] and Apabi.cn (Chinese).[33] From the Chinese dictionaries, I collected the definitions of *shizhuang*, the English–Chinese translations of "fashion" and "clothing," the Chinese–English translations of *fuzhuang* and *shizhuang*. I then compiled the meanings of "fashion" from the English dictionaries. The search eventually identified twenty-two definitions of *shizhuang* and the same number for "fashion," dating from 1970 to 2011.[34] There are forty-five Chinese dictionaries in total that include 192 translations for the four terms. The genres of these dictionaries include general interest: TV/Film, Culture, Education, Agriculture, Military, Medicine, Accounting, Business/Trading, Economy, Politics, Clothing, Industry, Gender, Science, and Psychology.

Academic journals

I selected two academic journals to study the definitions and role of fashion in each of the two cultural discourses. The English journal *Fashion Theory* was chosen primarily because of its prestigious position in the international academic field of fashion. Although there is no equivalent of *Fashion Theory* in Chinese which concentrates on the social-cultural-theoretical aspect of clothing-fashion, the most relevant Chinese journal is *Zhuangshi*,[35] because it underpins "Chinese contemporary design practice and theory."[36] It was founded in 1958, making it the oldest academic journal in the field of Chinese design since the establishment of PRC, in 1949. It is also the core journal listed in the Chinese Social Sciences Citation Index. In order to make the research manageable, I searched the terms "fashion"/*shizhuang,* "clothing"/*fuzhuang* respectively, in the titles (as opposed to key words), then compiled the titles of the articles, their key words, abstracts, authors and years of publications into one Excel file. *Zhuangshi* has provided English translations for titles of its articles since 2002, so I used these translations to supplement my own dictionary-based translations.

By January 2014, I had located sixty-four Chinese titles that contain the word *shizhuang*, thirty-three of which have English translations; and 372 titles carrying *fuzhuang*, 239 of which have English translations. *Fashion Theory* turns out to feature fourteen titles that include the word "clothing," and 218 that use the word "fashion." After reading through the titles, abstracts, and key words of each article, I identified a list of articles that potentially included discussions of the definition of the terms. In analyzing these, I located twenty-two definitions from twenty full papers, published between 1958 and 2012 from *Zhuangshi*, and thirty-five definitions from eight papers, spanning 1998 to 2004, from *Fashion Theory,* including the citations of definitions from other resources.

Textbooks

A selection of textbooks was initially based on a search of Amazon.com in English and Dangdang.com[37] in Chinese, according to the relevance and popularity of the topic. I chose eight books in each language according to the prominence of the authors in the field, the standing of the publishers and the edition of the book (more editions usually indicate greater popularity). All of the English books had indexes, which helped me to easily locate the definitions. I also examined the introduction and/or the first chapter, as authors typically conceptualize the terms within these sections. None of the Chinese books provided an index, so I had to scan the contents of these books, then locate the sections related to connotations of *shizhuang or fuzhuang*. The search turned up eight Chinese definitions and eighteen English ones, including citations from other resources.

Findings from the research

Background of the authors

The English-language authors who write about fashion cover a wide spectrum of disciplines, including fashion research, sociology, art history and criticism, cultural studies, literature, psychology, consumer studies, and behavioral science. The Chinese publications, on the other hand, reveal that only researchers in fashion institutions are publishing on fashion topics. This implies that in the West, there is a much more diversified scholarly interest in the subject of "fashion."

The subjects

The English dictionaries cover a range of subject categories, including General, Arts and Crafts, Aesthetics, Clothing/Fashion, Body, Business, Children, Communications, Dance, Diet, Film, Sociology, World Origin, History, Literature, and Culture. In contrast to this diversity, the Chinese dictionaries converge in the General category: fifteen of the twenty-three target general readers. Additional disciplines include Arts and Crafts, Light Industry, Silk, Yu Opera,[38] and Aesthetics. Although the Chinese dictionaries also have volumes on Culture, Literature, History, Sociology, Film, Dance, Communication, Children, and Business, none of them feature the term *shizhuang.*

Findings from the textbooks demonstrate a similar outcome: a narrower range of topics in Chinese and a much wider range in English. The Chinese fashion textbooks only include Aesthetics, General Introduction of Fashion,[39] and Design Theory of Practice.[40] The English textbooks range from Fashion Communication, Cultural History of Fashion, Fashion and Identity, Fashion and Social Agenda, general Fashion Studies, and Social Theory. The variety affirms that "fashion" has much more diversified facets in the Anglophone source material. Consequently, the background of readers/authors of *shizhuang* is much narrower and unified than that of the readers of "fashion," reflecting its more specific connotations. Although *Zhuangshi* claims to be a journal of "design theory and practice," the focus of the majority of its articles is "practice" rather than "theory." Of the 1,794 key words from the 372 papers, the top-ranked 1,000 key words are almost all about the "how"—how to teach, how to cut, how to design, how to be more creative, etc. This difference reveals that Chinese scholars value "practical" components more than the "ideological" facets of fashion. A review of the full articles confirmed this result.

Definitions

In the Chinese dictionaries, fourteen of the twenty-two definitions listed define *shizhuang* as "clothing or styles fit for current time," or something equivalent. The most common adjectives used to describe *shizhuang* include "prevalent," "new," "fit for the time," "latest," "trendy," and "vogue." The data shows a high degree of consistency in the words selected to describe *shizhuang*. The form of the definition consists, in general, of repeated adjectives plus concrete nouns, of which, "clothing" and "style" are the most frequent. The results suggest that *shizhuang* has a fairly unified meaning in China and is more likely to be viewed as a material object. The English descriptions include much more conceptual diversity. Besides defining fashion as "a popular style in vogue," or something similar, these dictionaries also interpret fashion as "attitude," "communication code," "ideal," "desire," "awareness," "expression," "statement," "belief," "system of meaning," and so on. Most of the nouns used in the English dictionaries are abstract, perceptual, and spiritual. The contrast between the "concrete" and the "abstract" nouns echoes the fact that Chinese scholars attach more weight to "material" and "practical, functional, technical" than "symbolic" and "theoretical, ideological, and cultural" aspects of fashion.

The definitions offered in Chinese journal articles are also very consistent. Of the twenty-two Chinese articles reviewed, nearly half of them define *fuzhuang* as "culture" (*wenhua*), including, in one instance, amplifications of that noun: "material culture" (*wuzhi wenhua*), and "spiritual culture" (*jingshen wenhua*). Other commonly repeated definitions encompass "arts," "decorations" (of body) and "history." Not surprisingly, the English journals produce no overlaps—"fashion" means "individual freedom" (Paulicelli 2004: 4), "metaphysical overtones and aesthetic considerations" (Saisselin 1959 cited in Kim 1998: 53), and "passion for the artificial" (Baudrillard 1990 cited in Wilson 2004: 382).

Although both journals show a certain degree of resemblance or sameness, such as defining fashion as "spirit," "decoration," "economy," "language," "aesthetic," "society," "culture," "modernity," and/or "capitalism," the comparison between the two reveals that the Chinese definitions are general, vague, and highly consistent and undifferentiated, while the English ones are specific, exact, passionate, recounted, diverse, and variegated. For instance, some of the Chinese journals define *fuzhuang* as "society" or "culture," while the English ones, instead of defining "fashion" in a general way, use the expressions "character of the age" (Haas-Heye 1916, cited in Simmons 2000: 75), "the law and the codification of manners and style" (Paulicelli 2004: 4), and "dream energy of society" (Benjamin 1999 cited in Wilson 2004: 383) to paint a more elegant and delicate picture. To cite another example, some Chinese papers define fashion as "life" and/or "a lifestyle," while the English ones use "the materiality of our thoughts and memory" (Paulicelli 2004: 30) and "remembrance of its presence" (Martin 1988: 15–16, cited in Wilson 2004: 375) to specify what fashion means to "life." The variety reveals that although the Chinese researchers in the field of fashion try to entrench the symbolic meanings of fashion, their understanding of "fashion" is still of a general and undefined nature.

Vocabulary and tone

The wider choices of vocabulary demonstrate the advanced skills of Anglophone academic criticism. In addition to adopting a variety of abstract nouns, the English writers also choose metaphors and active verbs to personify fashion and endow fashion with an indispensable and polyvalent power over the gamut of daily life. When reading the English texts, I encountered active and powerful verbs like "communicate," "colonize," "construct," "deconstruct," "infiltrate," "organize," "pervert," "sweep," and "unite" next to fashion, which makes fashion appear animate and omnipotent. An example is "fashion sweeps imperiously on, conquering, infiltrating and colonizing all areas of social, cultural and (lest we forget) academic enterprise" (Radford 1998: 162). Sociology scholar Diana Crane (2000: 248) defines the role of fashion as follows in her book *Fashion and Its Social Agendas:*

Fashion and clothing, like litmus paper, offer clues to discerning links between social structure and culture and to tracing the itineraries of material cultures in fragmented societies. In the increasingly multicultural society of the twenty-first century, clothing codes will continue to proliferate as a means of expressing relationships within and between social groups and segments and of indicating responses to even more conflicted hegemonies.

Corresponding to the English texts, almost all the Chinese texts define fashion or its role in a form of "to be" verbs, i.e. *"fuzhuang is …,"*, *"shizhuang is …"* Of all the Chinese primary data that I collected, the one example that endorses fashion in the most versatile way states:

Fuzhuang is a material cultural phenomenon. It needs material […] *Fuzhuang is* an inorganic component of the human body […] *Fuzhuang is* the external "expression" of the human heart […] *Fuzhuang is* also for self-protection […] *Fuzhuang is* also about creativity, it does not always succumb to the body, (it) can quasi-modify the natural shape of the body (translation, Xu and Guan 2007: 2–3).

The use of the word "is" makes fashion feel stagnant and inanimate. Christopher Breward (2003: 9) argues that "fashion not only is something, but also functions in many ways." The "is" statement confirms that fashion for Chinese authors is a static substance and/or a passive reflection of society, rather than something that can actively shape or function in the social community. Their tones are also very different. The English papers often use "[one of] the most" to amplify fashion, for example "the most appropriate form for," "the most compelling," "the most destructive," "the most personal and most elementary," and "the most fundamental." The use of "[one of] the most" creates a determinative tone. The Chinese texts reveal very little emotion because of the use of static, plain and inanimate vocabulary. Fashion in English functions as an energetic, powerful, protean "person" that struts across a wide spectrum of fields: sociology, anthropology, politics, religion, etc., while the Chinese *fuzhuang* and *shizhuang* are banal, dull and inanimate objects.

Western scholars use the instrument of language to endow fashion with an elegant dignity. Their language use testifies to their tremendous passion and respect for fashion. Their meticulously choreographed writings elevate fashion from "material" to "spiritual," or "symbolic" levels—which makes fashion and/or clothing a "symbol" rather than a material object. As a consequence, their writings upgrade fashion in the minds of Anglophone audiences and readers. I argue that Chinese fashion researchers have not yet mastered the tactics of powerful writing; although they are aware that fashion is more than just "material," the "symbolic," or "spiritual" aspect of fashion still remains a vague concept in their minds.

Today, fashion and/or design in the West are perceived as trivial compared to other fields (Barnard 2002). However, compared to China, fashion in the West has attained a higher position in the social system as demonstrated by the increasing numbers of academic publications on fashion from different disciplines (Breward 2003: 9). Fashion in the Chinese context is usually perceived simply as a material object rather than a symbolic one. Although some of the Chinese fashion scholars agree that fashion has spiritual values, I believe the spiritual connotations remain vague in the mind of these scholars.

Differences between *fuzhuang* and *shizhuang*

Research on the translations of the four terms and applications of the two Chinese terms indicate that *fuzhuang* has a much broader usage than *shizhuang*. While *fuzhuang* has a larger scope that includes clothing, dress, fashion, costume, and garment, *shizhuang* is just a facet of *fuzhuang* which particularly means clothing that is "high-end," "in vogue/trendy," "modern," "European," "Western," "international," or "capitalist."

The following findings support how *fuzhuang* differs from *shizhuang*. By reviewing all of the translations, it is evident that *fuzhuang* translates into apparel, clothes, clothing, costume, dress, fashion, and garment.

Of all the English translations, "apparel" and "clothes" are used the least frequently. In some cases "apparel" is interchangeable with "garment," but "garment" is a more popular translation than "apparel." "Garment" is more commonly associated with "manufacture" and "technology"—for instance, "garment factory," "cutting of the garment" and so forth.

"Clothing" is the most widespread translation of *fuzhuang*. "Clothing" is often applied in a general context, i.e. "clothing and textiles," and in expressions such as "clothing, food, house, traveling" (*yishi zhuxing*), "daily clothing," and functional or special clothing like "safety clothing" and "protective clothing." "Dress" is another common English translation for *fuzhuang*. This study has revealed that the English translations "dress" and "clothing" are used interchangeably, for the most part, for *fuzhuang*. "Dress" is also used in combination with "one-piece clothing" (*lianshenqun*), "women," and "evening, party, ceremony," which is close to the English usage. "Costume" is most commonly used in association with "historical," "ethnic," "movie/film," and "opera."

"Fashion" is associated with "design" or "designer," although the Chinese version is *fuzhuang sheji(shi)* (designer) instead of *shizhuang sheji(shi)*. I ascribe this to the difference in cultural systems. In English, people speak of "fashion design(ers)" more often than "clothing design(ers)"; however, in China, the nomenclature of the education programs, which is centrally administrated by the National Ministry of Education, the program of "fashion design" is called *fuzhuang sheji* instead of *shizhuang sheji,* and, consequently, all of the Chinese titles for the fashion schools in China are *fuzhuang xueyuan* (school) instead of *shizhuang xueyuan*. *Fuzhuang* is also translated as "fashion," when the discourse relates to "vogue," "trend," "modern," "contemporary," "good quality," and "high standard" (for instance, "fashion boutiques" (*jingpin fuzhuang dian*)). Fashion is also randomly associated with terms like "advertisement," "brands," "pattern cutting," and "illustration," but these words are also connected to "clothing," "clothes," "garment," and "apparel." The translation of *shizhuang* is simply and unequivocally "fashion," although as stated above, "fashion" can be translated as *fuzhuang* depending on the context.

Research on the applications of the two Chinese terms in dictionaries, journal articles, and textbooks is consistent with the findings listed above with regard to the definitions of *fuzhuang* and *shizhuang*. *Fuzhuang* is used much more frequently and widely than *shizhuang*. *Shizhuang* is usually used when associated with certain peculiar prestige contexts: 1) representing "high-level," "high-quality," or "exquisite quality," such as *shizhuang jinpinwu* (fashion boutique), *gaoji shizhuang* (haute couture/high fashion); 2) representing "creativity," as in *chuangyi shizhuang biaoyan* (creative fashion show); and 3) when connected with fashion cities like *Shanghai shizhuang* (Shanghai fashion), *Hong Kong shizhuang* (Hong Kong fashion), *Riben shizhuang* (Japanese fashion), etc. Other applications of *shizhuang* include conventional usages, such as associated with "models," the "cat-walk," and "advertisement," for example *shizhuang moteer* (fashion models), *shizhuang guanggao* (fashion advertisement), *shizhuang biaoyan* (fashion show), *shizhuang shejishi* (fashion designer), *shizhuang zhou* (fashion week), and *shizhuang hua* (fashion illustration).

The Chinese journal papers reveal that *shizhuang* is also used in tandem with "modern" (*xiandai*), for example *xiandai shizhuang sheji* (modern fashion design), *xiandai shizhuang liuxing* (modern fashion trend) and *xiandai shizhuang tixi* (modern fashion system). *Shizhuang* is also often used to denote a time period, such as *chuantong fuzhuang* (traditional clothing), in contrast with *dangdai shizhuang* (modern fashion). *Shizhuang* is also frequently connected with the "international" domain, such as *bali shizhuang* (Paris Fashion) and *Guoji shizhuang zhidu* (international fashion capitals).

Obviously, *shizhuang* still represents the prestige of the "modern" and the "West" just as when it first emerged in China in the late nineteenth century. Apparently it is no longer constrained to "women's wear"; it generally means clothing that is fashionable. According to *The China Dictionary of Arts and Crafts, shizhuang* "[used to] mean fashionable women's wear. But now it includes men's wear, children's wear." (1999: 125).

Conclusion

Fashion, defined as "prevalent new clothing styles that fit the time" in this chapter, is an autochthonous concept in China, not a loaned one. The Chinese version, *shizhuang,* emerged alongside the migration of Western fashion and its cutting technology in the mid- to late-nineteenth century, and has not evolved much in meaning since. It originally meant "women's dress in Western forms." After the victory of the Chinese Communist Party in 1949, *shizhuang* gradually became a taboo due to its close connection with the bourgeoisie. *Shizhuang*, from the post-Mao era of liberalization and reform, is widely perceived to be clothing that is "exquisite in quality," "modern," "trendy," "vogue," "international," or "Western." The word is still associated, to some extent, with the Western phenomenon, but it no longer only refers to women's wear. It is a type of *fuzhuang* that has infiltrated academic publications and, therefore, engenders more power than *shizhuang*. This distinction approximates the difference between "clothing" and "fashion" in the Anglophone context. Although Malcolm (2002) endeavors to distinguish between the terms "clothing," "fashion," "dress," and "style" in his book *Fashion As Communication*, which discusses the definitions of and differences between each term, he also acknowledges that it is extremely difficult to distinguish all the terms explicitly. Yuniya Kawamura (2005) sees clothing as "material" and fashion as "added symbolic values." Both cases show that it is incorrect to draw the conclusion that "fashion" is a genre of "clothing" in the Anglophone context.

"Fashion" enjoys a charismatic cachet and potency and plays both active and passive roles in Anglophone discourse. It not only "is" something, but also actively influences and shapes many other aspects of society. Compared to "fashion" in the English context, "fashion" in the Chinese context earns little respect from spectators. "Fashion" in the Chinese context is banal, monotonous, parochial, and inanimate, whereas "fashion" in the Western en compasses a greater diversity of symbolic meanings, and plays a higher and more vital role than it does in the Chinese context.

To conclude, although the word of *shizhuang* was a result of influences from Western fashion, it did not naturally inherit the enriched connotations and higher roles of "fashion" in the Western context. I therefore argue that, as a result, the monotonous and material view of "fashion" in the Chinese context endows it with a lower position than in the West, resulting in a lesser development of "fashion" in China, despite the fact that the notion of "fashion" has been in existence for over a thousand years.

Notes

1   I intend to conduct additional research on the definition of "fashion" in Chinese in the context of the fashion industry.

2   时装.

3   See *Xinhua Chinese Dictionary (Xinhua hanyucidian)* (Rev. ed. 2006); *Chinese Encyclopedia: Volume of Light Industry (Zhongguo da baikequanshu: qinggongjuan)* (1992: 360); the *Encyclopedia of Aesthetic (Meixue baike quanshu)* (1990: 427–8); *Dictionary of Fashion (Fushicidian)* (2011:467).

4   服装.

5   衣服.

6   Some of the resources come from online dictionaries or encyclopedias that provide no page numbers.

7   辞源. It was started in late Qing Dynasty (1908), finished by 1915, and published by ShangwuYinshu Guan. The edition that I used for this chapter is a modified online edition produced by the same publisher between 1979 and 1983.

8   时世妆.

9   白居易, poet of Tang Dynasty (618–907).

10 时样.

11 陈师道, poet of Bei Song dynasty (960–1127).

12 Kawamura researched the notion of a "sense of style, fashion and dress" in French, English, and Latino. Based on her research, such notion of 'style" and/or "fashion" in Europe did not emerge until 1300 (2005: 3–4).

13 Doyle (2011); *Webster's New World College Dictionary* (2010); *The American Heritage Dictionary of the English Language* (2006); Calasibetta (1998); Picken & Valentine (1973).

14 Flügel (1930); Polhemus and Procter (1978).

15 Sproles and Burns (1994); Brenninkmeyer (1963); Veblen (1899/1998); Simmel (1904/1957); Spencer (1896/1966); König (1973); Baudrillard (1981,1976/1993).

16 甲骨文. Oracle Bone Inscriptions, dating from the fourteenth to eleventh centuries B.C.

17 I did not find any documents recording Zhao Chunlan's birth and death year.

18 Some of the historical sources indicate that Zhao went to the United States with a priest and learned Euro-American cutting technology in the USA. Other sources state that he learned it from a European nun in Shanghai. In either case—all documents state that Zhao was considered the "Father of Fashion" in China and learned the Euro-American cutting technology from a foreigner.

19 See the next paragraph for differences between European and traditional Chinese cutting technology.

20 According to historical data written by the son of one of the founders of Hong Xiang—Mr. Jin Taijun and Shanghai Local Annals (Shanghai difangzhi) (Mo 2011: 155).

21 According to the archives stored in Shanghai Archive Center.

22 There are several reasons why the historical Chinese costumes look flat. Difference in the traditional Chinese cutting technology is just one of the reasons.

23 The cutting form is one of the primary differences between traditional Chinese and European cutting technology.

24 The interviews were conducted for my book *Dialogues with Three Generations of Fashion Designers* (Shanghai designers only) *(Duihua Zhongguo Sandai Shizhuang Shejishi)* (2005), *China Fashion: Conversations with Designers* (2009; 2013). I double-checked this with Jin again when I saw him in July 2013.

25 This is the time when the Chinese fashion industry took shape and emerged before the Communist Party merged all the private business sectors with state-owned companies in 1956 (*gongsi heying*).

26 There were three types of business models in the clothing industry in this period. One provided full made-to-measure services that included providing materials and accessories as well as cutting, making, and trimming (*baogong baoliao*). The second type had the clients provide the fabric and accessories, while the shops only cut and made the clothing (*lailiao jiagong*). The last type represented wholesale business module, which produced garments in larger volumes (*pifa*).

27 女子洋服.

28 西式女装.

29 See www.oxfordreference.com (accessed 31 January 2014).

30 Gale is one of the brands belonging to Cenage Learning; www.cengage.com (accessed 31 January 2014).

31 See www.blackwellreference.com (accessed 31 January 2014).

32 Built in 1999, CNKI was initiated by TsingHua University and supported by the Ministry of Education, the Ministry of Technology, and the Ministry of News & Press in China. According to the introduction of the website, this is the largest electronic library in the world, its "tool books" (*gongjushu*) section contains nearly 7,000 copies of dictionaries, encyclopedias, handbooks, and other tool books. (http://cnki.net/gycnki/gycnki.htm) (accessed 31 January 2014).

33 The Apabi library was built in 2006 by a company that is part of Peking University. According to its website, "90% of the publishers in China" partner with Apabi (www.apabi.cn) (accessed 31 January 2014).

34 Due to restrictions in length, it was not possible to include the list of dictionaries, journal papers, and textbooks that I used for primary data in this chapter. Please see the References section for a complete list of dictionaries, journal papers, and textbooks used.

35 The English title of this journal is "Art & Design." I am using the Chinese title to differentiate it from other English journals with similar titles. It was founded by the first arts & crafts institute in China—the Central Academy of Arts and Crafts, which is now the Faculty of Fine Arts of TsingHua University (http://www.izhsh.com.cn/) (accessed 31 January 2014).

36 See http://www.izhsh.com.cn/magazine/24/72.html (accessed 31 January 2014).

37 Dangdang.com is the largest online bookseller in China.

38 An opera that originated in He Nan province in China.

39 In Chinese, it is *fuzhuang gailun*. The course provides fundamental concepts and an introduction to fashion as well as the fashion industry.

40 This is the theory of design practice, not of fashion theory.

References

Bai, Xiangwen. "Fashion: Between the Nationalism and Modernity (*Shilun Fuzhuang de Minzuxing yu Shidaigan*)." *Zhuangshi* (January 1984): 10.

Barnard, Malcolm. *Fashion As Communications*. London: Routledge, 2002.

Barnhart, K. Robert. *The Barnhart Dictionary of Etymology.* New York: H. W Wilson Co., 1988.

Barthes, Roland. *The Fashion System*. New York: Hill and Wang, 1983.

Baudrillard, Jean. *Seduction*. trans. by Brian Singer. Montreal, Canada: New World Perspective, 1990. Cited in Elizabeth Wilson, "Magic Fashion." *Fashion Theory,* vol. 8, 4 (2004): 375–86.

Baudrillard, Jean. *Symbolic Exchange and Death*. trans. E. Hamilton Grant. London: Sage Publications, 1992.

Benjamin, Walter. *Charles Baudelaire: A Lyric Poet in the Era of High Capitalism.* London: Verso, 1973. Cited in Elizabeth Wilson, "Magic Fashion." *Fashion Theory*, vol. 8, 4 (2004a): 375–86.

Benjamin, Walter. *The Arcades Project.* trans. Howard Eiland and Kevin McLaughlin. Cambridge, MA: Harvard University Press, 1999. Cited in Wilson Elizabeth, "Magic Fashion," *Fashion Theory,* vol. 8, 4 (2004b): 375–86.

Blakemore, Colin, and Sheila Jennett, eds, *The Oxford Companion to the Body*. Oxford: University Press, 2002.

Borrelli, Laird O. "Dressing Up and Talking About It: Fashion Writing in Vogue, from 1968 to 1993," *Fashion Theory*, vol. 1, issue 3 (1997): 247–60.

Brenninkmeyer, Ingrid. *The Sociology of Fashion*. Koln-Opladen, Germany: WestdeutscherVerlag, 1963.

Breward, Christopher. *Fashion: Oxford History of Arts*, Oxford: Oxford University Press, 2003.

Calasibetta, Charlotte M. *Fairchild's Dictionary of Fashion* (2nd ed. rev.), New York: Fairchild Books, 1998.

Chang, Ruilun, ed. *The Encyclopedia for Chinese Primary Students: Volume of Fine Arts (Zhongguoxiaoxuejiaoxuebaikequanshu: meishujuan)*, Shenyang, China: Shengyang Publishing House, 1993.

Chen, Buyun. "Toward a definition of 'fashion' in Tang China." In *Fusion Fashion: Culture Beyond Orientalism and Occidentalism,* eds Gertrud Lehnert and Gabriele Mentges. Frankfurt, Germany: PeterLang Academic Research, 2013.

Chen, Guangyu. "The Ninth International Fashion conference and the Prospect of Clothing Industry in New China." *Zhuangshi*, vol. 2 (1959): 52.

Chi, Wenjun, Song, Xulian, and Lu Hongsheng, eds, *The Encyclopedia of Shijing: Volume II (Shijingbaikecidian: zhongjuan)*. Shenyang, China: Liao Ning People's Publisher, 1998.

Ciyuan (Etymology Dictionary: The Modified Edition). Beijing: ShangwuYinshu Guan, 1983.

Cohen, Lisa. "Frock consciousness": Virginia Woolf, the Open Secret, and the Language of Fashion." *Fashion Theory*, vol. 3, 2, (1999): 149–74.

Craik, Jennifer. *The Face of Fashion: Cultural Studies in Fashion.* London: Routledge, 1994.

Craik, Jennifer. *Fashion: the Key Concept.* London: Bloomsbury, 2009.

Craine, Debra, and Judith Mackrell. *The Oxford Dictionary of Dance.* 2nd ed. Oxford: Oxford University Press, 2013.

Crane, Diana. *Fashion and Its Social Agendas: Class, Gender and Identity in Clothing.* Chicago: University of Chicago Press, 2000.

Cresswell, Julia. *The Oxford Dictionary of Word Origins.* 2nd ed. Oxford: Oxford University Press, 2010.

Davis, Fred. *Fashion, Culture and Identity.* Chicago: University of Chicago Press, 1992.

Deng, Yueqing. *Modern Fashion Design and Practice (Xiandai Fuzhuang Sheji yu Shijian).* Beijing: TsingHua University Press, 2010.

Deng, Zhifan et al. *The Chinese Rhyming Dictionary (HanyuTongyun Da Cidian).* Wuhan, China: Chongwen Book Company, 2010.

Donsbach, Wolfgang, Katherine T. Frith, and Debra Merskin. *The International Encyclopedia of Communication.* Oxford: Blackwell Publishers, 2008.

Dou, Donghong. "Fashion: Beyond the Academy *(Fuzhuang Sheji Buzhishi Xueshu Wenti).*" *Zhuangshi* (April 1987): 3.

Doyle, Charles (2011/2013) *A Dictionary of Marketing.* Oxford: Oxford University Press, 2013.

Entwistle, Joanne. *The Fashioned Body: Fashion, Dress and Modern Social Theory.* Cambridge: Polity Press, 2000.

Fass, Paula S., ed. *Encyclopedia of Children and Childhood: In History and Society.* New York: Macmillan, 2004.

Fei, Zhengang, and Zhongqian Qui, eds *Dictionary of Hanfu (Hanfu Cidian).* Beijing: Beijing University Press, 2002.

Finnane, Antonia. *Changing Clothes in China: Fashion, History, Nation.* New York: Columbia University Press, 2008.

Flügel, J. C. *The Psychology of Clothes.* London: The Hogarth Press and the Institute of Psychoanalysis,1950.

Grant, Barry K., ed. *Schirmer Encyclopedia of Film,* New York: Schirmer, 2007.

Gu, Hangkui, ed.*The Etymology of Han Character (Hanzi Ciyuan Zidian).* Beijing: Huaxia Press, 2003.

Guan, Jianming, and Rongrong Cui, eds, *The Aesthetic Study of Fashion Design (Fuzhuang shejimeixue).* Beijing: China Textile Press, 2008.

Haas-Heye, Otto (1916) "Die Mode und diese Zeit. Bruchstucke au seiner Plauderei." Graphische Modeblätter, No. 8 Cited in Simmons, Sherwin. "Expressions in the Discourse of Fashion" *Fashion Theory.* vol. 4 1 (2000): 49–88.

Hainsworth, Peter, and David Robey. *The Oxford Companion to Italian Literature.* Oxford: Oxford University Press, 2002.

Hallowell, Gerald. *The Oxford Companion to Canadian History.* Oxford: Oxford University Press, 2004.

Han, Mingan, ed. *The Dictionary of New Terms (Xinyucidacidian).* Haerbin, China: Heilongjiang People's Publisher, 1991.

Hao, Chi, Guangzhi Sheng, and Mian Dong Li, eds *The Chinese Dictionary with Words Listed in Reversed Sequence (Hanyu Daopai Cidian).* Haerbin, China: Heilong Jiang People's Publisher, 1987.

Hu, Junmin. "Modern Fashion Design Education Centered by Human's Body *(Yiren Weichidu de Xiandai Fuzhuang Sheji Jiaoxue)."* *Zhuangshi,* vol. 158 (June 2006): 26.

Hua, Mei. *The Aesthetic Study of Fashion (Fuzhuang Meixue)*. Beijing: China Textile Press, 2003.

Kaiser, Susan B. *Fashion and Cultural Studies*, Oxford. New York: Berg, 2012.

Kawamura, Yuniya. *Fashion-ology: An Introduction to Fashion Studies (Dress, Body, Culture.* 1st ed. New York: Bloomsbury, 2005.

Kent, Michael. *Food and Fitness: A Dictionary of Diet and Exercise*. Oxford: Oxford University Press, 2003.

Kelly, Michael (ed.). *Encyclopedia of Aesthetics*. New York: 2008 (online edition).

König, René. *A la mode: On the Social Psychology of Fashion*. New York: Seabury Press, 1973.

König, R. *The Restless Image: A Sociology of Fashion*. trans. F. Bradley. London: Allen & Unwin, 1974.

Lehnert, Gertrud, and Gabriele Mentges, eds *Fusion Fashion: Culture Beyond Orientalism and Occidentalism.* Frankfurt: Peter Lang Academic Research, 2013.

Leng, Yun. *China Fashion: Conversations with Designers (Zhongguo Shishang: yu Zhongguo Fuzhuang Shejishi Duihua)*. Hong Kong: Hong Kong University Press, 2013.

Li, Lingfen. (2002) "Clothing and Decorations (*Fuzhuang yu Zhuangshi*)." *Zhuangshi,* vol. 115 (September 2002): 51.

Li, Ruiquan. "The Clothing (*Tan fuzhuang*)." *Zhuangshi* (January 1958): 46.

Li, Xiaofan, ed. *The Chinese Antonym Dictionary (Zhonghua Fanyici Cidian)*. Beijing: Zhonghua Book Company, 2009.

Li, Zehou, and Xin Ru, eds *The Encyclopedia of Aesthetics* (*Meixue Baike Quanshu*). Beijing: Social Science Academic Press, 1990.

Li, Zheng. *Fashion Foundations (Fuzhuang Gailun)*. Beijing: China Textile Press, 2007.

Lin, Rongsen. "Clothing and Society (Fuzhuang yu Shehui)," *Zhuangshi* (March 1985): 46–8.

Liu, Jun. "The Values of Conceptual Fashion (*Tupojiangyu: tan gainianshizhuang de shejiyiyi*)." *Zhuangshi*, vol. 195 (July 2009): 92.

Liu, Yuanfeng, and Yue Hu, eds *The Artistic Design of Fashion (Fuzhuang Yishu Sheji)*. Beijing: China Textile Press, 2006.

Luo, Zhufeng, ed. *The Chinese Dictionary (Vol. 5)* (*Hanyu Da Cidian: Di Wujuan*). Shanghai: Chinese Dictionary Publisher, 1990.

Ma, Hong. "The Spirit of Freedom in Fashion Design (*Lun Xiandai Fuzhuang Sheji zhongde Xieyi Jingshen*)," *Zhuangshi,* vol. 230 (June 2012): 141– 2.

Marin, Richard. *Fashion and Surrealism*. London: Thames and Hudson, 1988. Cited in Elizabeth Wilson. "Magic Fashion." *Fashion Theory* vol. 8, 4 (2004): 375–86.

Martin, W. Linda, Elizibeth Ammons, and Cathy N. Davidson. *The Oxford Companion to Women's Writing in the United States*. Oxford: Oxford University Press, 1995.

McCalman, Iain, et al. *An Oxford Companion to the Romantic Age*. Oxford: Oxford University Press, 2009 .

Michelman, Susan. "Breaking Habits: Fashion and Identity of Women Religious." *Fashion Theory*, vol. 2, issue 2 (1998): 165–92.

Mo, Heng, ed. *The Contemporary Chinese Dictionary (DangdaiHanyuCidian)*. Shanghai, China: Shanghai Cishu Book Publisher, 2001.

Mo, Jianbei, ed. Shanghai Local Annals (*Shanghai difangzhi*). Shanghai, China: Editing Team of Shanghai Local Annals, 2011.

Moore, Bruce, ed. *The Australian Oxford Dictionary*. 2nd ed. Oxford: Oxford University Press, 2004.

Oboler, Suzanne, and J. Deena González, eds *The Oxford Encyclopedia of Latinos and Latinas in the United States.* Oxford: Oxford University Press, 2005.

Pan, Kunrou. "Fashion and Environmental Arts (*Fuzhuang yu Huanjing Yishu*)." *Zhuangshi.* (January 1991): 3.

Pan, Kunrou. "The Retrospective and Prospect of Chinese Fashion Design (*Zhongguo Fuzhuang Sheji de Huigu yu Zhanwang*)," *Zhuangshi* (February 1995): 4.

Paulicelli, Eugenia. "Fashion Writing Under the Fascist Regime: an Italian Dictionary and Commentary of Fashion by Cesare Meano, and Short Stories by Gianna Manzini, and Alba De Cespedes," *Fashion Theory*, vol. 8, 1 (2004): 3–34.

Picken, Mary B., and Claire Valentine. *The Fashion Dictionary: Fabric, Sewing, and Apparel as Expressed in the Language of Fashion* (Revised and Enlarged). New York: Funk & Wagnalls, 1973

Polhemus, Ted, and Lynn Procter. *Fashion & Anti-fashion: An Anthropology of Clothing and Adornment.* London: Thames and Hudson, 1978.

Radford, Rober. "Dangerous Liaisons: Art, Fashion and Individualism," *Fashion Theory*, vol. 4, 2 (1998): 151–64.

Ren, Chaoqi, ed. *Xinhua Chinese Dictionary (Xinhua hanyucidian).* Wuhan, China: Chongwen Publishing House, 2006.

Ren, Wendong, and Xiang Wang. "The Role of Body in Fashion Design" (*Lunrentizuowei Fuzhuangsheji de Diyiyaosu*). *Zhuangshi*, vol. 184 (June 2008): 101.

Riello, Giorgio, and Peter McNeil, eds *The Fashion History Reader: Global Perspective.* New York: Routledge, 2010.

Ruan, Zhifu, and Zhongxin Guo, eds *The Modern Chinese Dictionary (XiandaiHanyu Da Cidian)*, Shanghai, China: Shanghai Cishu Publisher, 2009.

Saisselin, Remy G. "From Baudelaire to Christian Dior: The Poetics of Fashion." *Journal of Aesthetics and Art Criticism*, XVIII (1) (1959): 110–15. Cited in Sung Bok Kim, "Is Fashion Art." *Fashion Theory*, vol. 2, 1 (1998): 51–72.

Simmel, Georg. "Fashion," *The American Journal of Sociology*, vol. 62, no. 6 (May 1957): 541–58.

Simmons, Sherwin. "Expressions in the Discourse of Fashion." *Fashion Theory*, vol. 4, 1 (2000): 49–88.

Spencer, Herbert. *The Principles of Sociology*, Vol. II. New York: D Appleton and Co., 1966.

Sproles, George B., and Leslie D. Burns. *Changing Appearances: Understanding Dress in Contemporary Society*. New York: Fairchild Publication, 1994.

Steams, Peter, ed. *Oxford Encyclopedia of the Modern World*. Oxford: Oxford University Press, 2012.

Stearns, Peter N., ed. *Oxford Encyclopedia of the Modern World*. Oxford: Oxford University Press Print Publication, 2012.

Stein, Marc, ed. *Encyclopedia of Lesbian, Gay, Bisexual and Transgendered History in America*. New York: Scribner, 2004.

Sun, Tao (2001) "'Decoration' and 'Design Form' ('*shi de puchen*' yu '*xing de shengcheng*')." *Zhuangshi*, vol. 208 (August 2001): 115.

Tao, Yi. "The Thinking Processing of Fashion Design (*Guanyufuzhuangsheji de Siwei Guocheng*)," *Zhuangshi.*, vol. 154 (February 2006): 47.

The American Heritage Dictionary of the English Language. Boston, MA: Houghton Mifflin Co., 2006.

The Vocabularies of English–Chinese Textile Industry. Beijing: China Textile Press, 1979.

Tsui, Christine. *China Fashion: Conversations with Designers*. Oxford: Bloomsbury Academic, 2009.

Veblen, Thorstein. *The Theory of Leisure Class*. Amherst, NY: Prometheus Books, 1998.

Waite, Maurice, ed. *Oxford Paperback Thesaurus*. 4th ed. Oxford: Oxford University Press, 2012.

Wang, Xiangfeng, ed. *Aesthetic Handbook for Youth (Qingnian Shenmei Shouce)*. Shenyang, China: Liaoning People's Publisher, 1988.

Wang, Yong. "The Influence of Social Factors to Fashion Styles (*Shehuiyinsu dui Fuzhuang Fengge de Yingxiang*)" *Zhuangshi,* vol. 120 (2003): 40.

Webster's New World College Dictionary (2010) Ohio, CL: Wiley Publishing, Inc.,

Wei, Li, ed. *The Etymology of Frequently Used Han Character (Changyong Hanzi Yuanliu Zidian)*. Shanghai, China: Shanghai Cishu Publisher, 2010.

Wilson, E. *Adorned in Dreams: Fashion and Modernity*. London: Virago, 1985.

Wilson, Elizabeth. "Magic Fashion," *Fashion Theory,* vol. 8, (2004): 375–86.

Wu, Fan. "The Value of Non-main-stream Culture to Fashion Aesthetic Trend (*Tan Feizhuliu Wenhua dui Shizhuang Chaoliu zhi Shenmei Daoxiang de Yiyi*)." *Zhuangshi,* vol. 137 (September 2004): 90.

Wu, Shan, ed. *The Dictionary of Chinese Arts and Crafts (Zhongguo Gongyi Meishu Dacidian)*. Nanjing, China: Jiang Su Fine Arts Publishing House, 1999.

Wu, Zicheng, Jianguo Wu, and Mian Zhao, eds *The Chinese Yuju Dictionary (Zhongguo Yuju Da Cidian)*. Zhengzhou, China: Zhongzhou Historical Books Publisher, 1998.

Xiao, Qiongqiong, ed. *The Theory and Practice of Fashion Design (Fuzhuang Sheji Lilun yu Shijian*. Beijing: Beijing Polytechnique University Press, 2010.

Xie, Feng. "The Nature of Fashion (*Lun Shizhuang zhi Benzhi*)," *Zhuangshi* (April 1987): 5.

Xu, Hairong, ed. *The Dictionary of Chinese Costumes (Zhongguo Fushi Dadian)*. Beijing: Huaxia Publishing House, 2000.

Xu, Hongli, and Zhikun Guan. *The Textbook of Fashion Aesthetics (Fuzhuang Meixue Jiaocheng)*. Beijing: China Textile Press, 2007.

Yang, Yueqian, ed. "Shizhuang." In *The Encyclopedia of China: Volume of Light Industry (Zhongguo da Baikequanshu)*. Beijing: Encyclopedia of China Publishing House, 1992.

Yuan, Ze. "The Role of Silhouette in Fashion Design (*Lun Fuzhuang Sheji zhongde Zaoxingxian)*," *Zhuangshi* (January 1986): 45.

Zhang, Jiatai, and Che Xu, eds *The Modern Chinese Dictionary of Commendatory and Derogatory Terms (Xiandai Hanyu BaobianYongfa Cidian)*, Shenyang, China: Liaoning People's Publisher, 1992.

Zhang, Weiyuan, and Chuanming Wang, eds *Dictionary of Fashion (Fushi Cidian)*. Beijing: China Textile Press, 2011.

Zhang, Yaheng. "The Aesthetic Taste of Fashion (*Shilun Fuzhuang de Shenmei Tezheng)*," *Zhuangshi* (June 2002): 13.

Zhang, Yali (2006) "The Spiritual and Emotional Accent in Fashion Design (*Fuzhuang Sheji Yishuzhong de Jingshen Benzhi yu Qinggan)*," *Zhuangshi* vol. 157 (May 2006): 104–5.

Zhang Yujin, et al., eds *Dictionary of Xuci of Ancient and Modern Chinese (GujinHanyuXuci Da Cidian)*. Shenyang, China: Liaoning People's Publisher, 1996.

Zhu, Hongxi, ed. *Dictionary of Ancient Chinese (Gudai Hanyu Cidian)*. Chengdu, China: Sichuan Cishu Publishing House, 2000.

Websites

www.oxfordreference.com (Oxford Reference online) (accessed 31 January 2014).
www.cengage.com (CENGAGE Learnning EMEA) (accessed 31 January 2014).
www.blackwellreference.com (Blackwell Reference online) (accessed 31 January 2014).
www.cnki.net (the largest e-library in Chinese) (accessed 31 January 2014).
www.izhsh.com.cn (official website of journal *Zhuangshi*) (accessed 31 January 2014).
www.apabi.cn (e-library in China) (accessed 31 January 2014).

Acknowledgments

The author would like to thank her supervisor Professor Louise Edwards, and the editors of the volume, Professor Jennifer Craik and Dr. Angela Jansen, for their invaluable feedback on this chapter.

PART II

THE COMMODIFICATION OF CULTURAL HERITAGE

4

BEING FASHIONABLE IN THE GLOBALIZATION ERA IN INDIA: HOLY WRITING ON GARMENTS[1]

JANAKI TURAGA

Introduction

India is a perfect example of the fact that fashion is not a recent development of globalization; on the contrary, it is deeply rooted historically, as well as connected to the rest of the world. Fashion in India, like anywhere else, is simultaneously a materialization of internal social, cultural, political, and religious developments, and also a reflection of external influences. In the last two decades, India has seen the emergence of a fashion trend, which consists of an amalgamation of sartorial sensibilities of the urban Indian youth and international fashion trends. A common fashion and lifestyle statement is being made by young people through wearing religious and spiritual symbols and mantras on their garments. Religion and spirituality have become fashionable, and are proclaimed not only on commonly worn garments such as T-shirts, *salwar-kameezes*, and shirts, but also on couture garments. Traditionally, sacred cloths, which ranged from plain to written to pictorial, were the esoteric preserve of the initiate, and were worn only in culturally prescribed sacred contexts in various parts of India. The modern garments with holy writing and symbols are worn in non-sacred contexts and primarily used to make fashion and lifestyle statements.This chapter examines this burgeoning of the modern day "secularized sacred" fashion across India since 2000, and analyzes both internal and external (both Eastern and Western) factors that have resulted in a decidedly post liberalized and globalized phenomenon. It questions what makes the wearer cross the traditional rules of engagement with the sacred, taking elements of it to the non-sacred domain, which ironically, proclaims the fashionableness of the wearer, while at the same time proclaiming and underscoring his or her underlying religious and spiritual beliefs. It is argued that this era is characterized by the critical rethinking and interpretation of nearly all elements of life and society, and the redefining of the value systems that structure lives and lifestyles. This critical, recasting process is reflected in the more visible areas of religion, fashion, and modes of articulation in the realm of popular culture. In clothing and fashion, there has been a sea change in the clothing styles of communities and people that reflects clear negotiation between tradition and modernity, a marked transition from traditional to modern, and multiple fashion trends.

India is witnessing a commodification of elements of culture, whereby religious iconography is applied to fashion. This chapter deals with the holy writing fashion trend, primarily in the context of Hindu religious texts and sacred cloths, but Jain and Buddhist sacred cloths and holy writing fashion are also included in the larger schema, wherever there is commonality.[2] The social lives (Appadurai 1988) of the extant sacred cloth traditions and the contemporary fashion are very different and distinct with independent cosmologies of meanings and signs besides their praxis of production and consumption.

Being essentially a recent urban fashion trend, the data for this research was collected through fieldwork conducted between January 2013 and July 2014 in New Delhi, and more specifically in *Dilli Haat*, an urban *Haat,* where craft producers come from all over India to sell holy writing fashion garments directly to consumers.[3] The sacred cloth traditions of India are used as the reference point and cultural counterpoint of holy writing fashion because they break all the rules of the traditional sacred enclaves, also the rationale and point of departure for its sociological interrogation. Holy writing fashion is conceptualized in this chapter as "secularized" sacred fashion. It is a product of popular culture that has emerged from the processes of liberalization and globalization. Its contextual framework is new age spiritualism and religion, the urban middle class (encapsulating both the old and the new), and popular culture.

Holy writing is defined as the written names of deities, mantras, and symbols of Hindu religious and spiritual heritage, such as *"Om,"* which is written both as a symbol and as a mantra, depending on how it has been visualized and conceptualized, or the *Gayatri mantra,* considered to be the supreme mantra of Hinduism.[4] The concept of "secularized" sacred has been defined in this chapter as an element of the sacred (object, image, text, verse, and so on) that despite being desacralized, still retains in its new "secular" avatar, some of its sacredness, which functions as its identifying marker. The sacred is exclusive, while the secularized sacred is more inclusive, with unrestricted usage and open accessibility to all in the public domain, which gives it the secular identity marker. The traditional sacred cloths which are conceptualized within the framework of great and little traditions and "s*anskrit*" and "*Prakrit*" traditions, constitute the reference point for the modern enclaves of the "secularized" sacred garments, not only because the latter are independent of the former, but also because they transgress all cultural conditions that govern the usage of the former. The following sections examine the production and socio-cultural usage of holy writing garments in juxtaposition to the traditional written sacred cloths.

Traditional enclaves of the sacred cloths

Sacred cloths with holy writing, images, and symbols of deities are part of the cultural and religious traditions of India. Traditional sacred cloths can be divided into two categories: those that are worshipped (such as Andhra Pradesh's *Srikalahasti Kalamkari*, Gujarat's *Mata ni-pachedi*, Rajasthan's *Nathdwara Pichchwai*, Assam's *Brindavani Vastra*), and those that are not worshipped but worn by the worshipper for ritual use, for the duration and time of worship and within the geographic space of worship such as a household shrine. In the category of sacred cloths that are worn, there are two distinct categories. There are the plain ones, with or without a small border, either in silk, cotton, or a mix of cotton and silk, in shades of white, ecru, yellow (*pitambar*), and saffron. In South India, bark cloths made of agave in shades of natural green and murky brown were used extensively by the priests and *brahmins* during ritual use. Banana rayon cloths are now currently used in shades of white and ecru for ritual use. Their usage and production are nearly similar with minor regional differences. Then there are the illustrated ones, which include writing, symbols, and pictures of deities like "*Namavali*"[5] sacred cloths, as well as *common sacred cloth*s, which are also illustrated, but are of a lesser quality, and whose usage and production are limited to certain parts of India.

The "*Namavali*" sacred cloths belong to the great and "s*anskrit*"[6] tradition, while the common sacred cloths belong to the "*Prakrit*"[7] tradition. Further, the usage of the written sacred cloths, whether the *Namavali* sacred cloths or the *common sacred cloths*,[8] varies, but both are, in general, geographically limited to North and East India (for *Namavali* sacred cloths see Pathak 2008). The *Namavali* sacred cloths are worn by a niche of worshippers,[9] and are woven with precious fibers such as silk and *Pashmina* wool, as well as printed. These are the luxury cloths worn by rich people who can afford expensive fabrics and the high cost of labor. By contrast, the common sacred cloths with multiple local traditions have a more widespread usage, and are worn by common people including priests and worshippers. Often, both kinds are also worn by worshippers during *puja*, depending on the socio-cultural context of the region as well as the worshipper.

The *"Namavali"* sacred cloths[10] used to bear the names of a single deity, repeated a specific number of times. These cloths were the esoteric preserve of the initiate and worn only in culturally prescribed sacred contexts in varied parts of North and East India. They were worn as upper garments only, as shawls, caps, turbans, and a stitched upper garment known as *kurta*. These traditional sacred cloths with holy writing were worn by priests and worshippers, typically male, only during the worship of the deity and meticulously removed on completion of *puja*. Women were generally not allowed to wear them. The culturally conditioned rules of engagement with the sacred words or the *"paddhati"* were usually not breached by both the wearer (consumer) and the weaver/printer (producer). For example, one was not supposed to sit on these garments, and the garment had to be kept off the floor at all times to prevent desecration of the names of the gods. The producers of these holy writing garments were mainly weavers and hand block printers working with silk and cotton, who took care to weave and print correctly, and in complete form, the name of the deity. Incomplete, incorrect, and incorrectly-written names of the deity were considered a mistake and inauspicious both for the creator and the wearer. Therefore, weavers and printers took great care to ensure accuracy of spelling and adhere to the exact number of repetitions of the names and the design pattern of the *Namavali*.

Common sacred cloths belonging to the little, *"Prakrit"* tradition are mainly prevalent in North India, where they are part of popular culture and in the hands of common people. The usages governing these are more varied and flexible. The producers are dispersed, and varieties of cloths are produced for different local traditions and markets. The conformity to local traditions remains intact as long as the local market remains stable and insists on the same products done in a specific way. Since they are produced according to the shifting market demands, they are more flexible and fluid, reflecting the trending preferences of its consumers. With the expansion of markets especially through distant and floating populations of pilgrims and spiritual tourists, more generalized products have emerged that cater for a mass market. Therefore, in recent years, many such holy writing cloths have appeared with incomplete or incorrect names that do not adhere to the traditional system of printing of holy names with reference to the number, sequence, and arrangement. These are mainly screen printed and mass-produced. The general template is a yellow or ochre, or saffron field with red or maroon print, which at once indicates a spiritual and religious cloth. On this background, any kind of printing of any spiritual or religious sect is done like *Shirdi Sai Baba*, for example. Many of the new fangled religious gurus of minor sects/cults get custom-made cloths with mantras and images specific to their sect/cult, which are worn by the followers as a display of their membership to the sect/cult, especially during public events.

The consumption base of these little traditional *"Prakrit"* sacred cloths is vast, dispersed, and more extensive than the traditional constituency of the great tradition sacred cloths. Traditionally, the "*Prakrit*" tradition holy cloths culture is strong in holy places and pilgrim destinations mainly in North India. Today, these cloths are commonly available in neighborhood shops that sell items for worship as well as in and around temples. Although a certain ethics and rigor used to govern the production of these shawls with holy writing, even as recently as the 1980s, today there is a marked laxity in their production. These cloths are typically bought as souvenirs by tourists, as well as pilgrims to these sites. The hippie subculture that flourished in the late 1960s and 1970s included many spiritual seekers and explorers from abroad who could be seen sporting the holy upper garments, printed with the holy names of *Krishna* and *Rama*, while wandering about pilgrim centers. The blockbuster Hindi film *Hare Rama Hare Krishna* (1971) captures the flower power and hippie culture in India and Nepal, and some of its cast wear clothing inscribed with the holy writing of *Hare Rama Hare Krishna*.

Modern enclaves of the "secularized sacred" cloths: holy writing fashion trend

The first decade of the twenty-first century saw the emergence and widespread acceptance of clothing inscribed with holy writing in urban areas, where cultural mores and taboos were less distinct and more diluted. This fashion trend is not only independent of the written sacred cloths tradition, but also seems impervious to the cultural prescriptions and proscriptions that affect and restrict the production and consumption of traditional written sacred cloths. The holy writing here consists primarily of the names of deities and all kinds of identifiable and unidentifiable mantras and holy verses besides "*Om*", like the *Gayatri Mantra*, for example. They are seen on daily attire such as T-shirts, shirts, *kurtas, dupattas, salwar-kameez* suits, stoles, shawls, saris, *Bandee/Sardaree* (the traditional Indian style jackets), and casual trousers styled according to the latest fashion, as well as on yardage used to produce ready-made garments.

This present-day fashion trend fundamentally differs from both the *Namavali* and the *Prakrit* traditions of sacred cloths in terms of content, nature of usage, context, producer, consumer, production, and consumption, and is the inverse of the written sacred cloths tradition. These holy writing "secularized" sacred fashionable garments hinge on design and aesthetics, which is a very important aspect which gives them their uniqueness, and distinguishes them from the written sacred cloths. The design repertoire and color palette is also different from the traditional sacred cloths. A fine line is walked by the designers as a design and color palette misjudgment renders their garments non-marketable in the fashion segment. Saffron color, which is the traditional holy color of spirituality, is used creatively with other colors so that the fashionable garments are not visually perceived as traditional sacred cloths by the consumer. Given the popularity of these garments, especially among the urban youth, it is clear that they have defied all prevailing usages of holy writing on garments, and also transgressed cultural rules and traditions.

Holy writing fashion garments, including their site of production and consumption, are rooted in the non-sacred, and are secularized because of their use in non-sacred contexts, as well as their accessibility to people of all religions and sexes. Their consumption base is vast and dispersed, and is more extensive than the traditional constituency of the sacred cloths, which is culturally conditioned and restricted. Furthermore, they do not represent a transition from traditional sacred textiles to modern sacred textiles, since traditional holy textiles have continued to remain in their traditional enclaves, while the modern fashion trend of holy writing on textiles is a contemporary phenomenon, whereby elements of religion are commodified. The producer–consumer matrix of these two independently coexisting niches is different: the production base of the written sacred cloths tradition is primarily the block printers and weavers of North India, while holy writing fashion is designed and produced by both screen printers and block printers in urban and rural areas across India.

A necessary condition for mantras to be printed onto fashion garments was the freedom from religious and social sanctions, which was created due to the commodification of religion and mantras (see page 87). When religion became commodified, the hitherto culturally restricted mantras were deliberately brought into the public domain by various religious *pandits* (scholars) who advocated them to people approaching them as a sure fire, quick panacea and cure for all kinds of problems. Mantras began to be used everywhere, such as in body art (tattooing) and clothing. Beginning with *Om,* which is a traditionally popular mantra, and also the most commonly tattooed motif in India, the range of mantras has extended over time from the common to the unfamiliar and esoteric.

The prime originators of this fashion trend are the graphic artists and designers (visual artists), who creatively reappropriated and reframed elements of culture for consumption in popular culture (see page 88). High-profile fashion designers have actually played a limited and minor role in this fashion trend, primarily because they have been facing criminal complaints and public protests from right-wing organizations, forcing them to withdraw from engaging openly with this fashion trend. In 2006, both fashion designer Dipen Desai and a store in Ahmedabad that was selling his garments, printed with the Jain *Navkar* mantra and Hindu *Gayatri* mantra, faced criminal complaints by the police, under Section 295(c) of the Indian Penal Code, based on the complaints by Hindu and Jain organizations on the grounds of (i) "hurting religious sentiments," and (ii) that the clothes insulted Hindu and Jain religions.[11] The incident was reported on the

India Fashion Week's website,[12] as well as discussed in Jain discussion forums on the Internet. It acted as a deterrent to fashion designers wanting to venture into designing holy writing garments. Furthermore, in 2007, in Gujarat, a Member of the Legislative Assembly of the right-wing conservative Hindu party Bharatiya Janata Party, along with his followers, confiscated holy writing garments printed with *Navkar* mantra, *Gayatri* mantra, and *Om* from helpless local vendors and stormed a police station in Ahmedabad, complaining that these garments not only injured the religious sentiments of the people, but also that unholy acts are performed by boys wearing these fashion *kurtas*.[13] This backlash from politicians and right-wing organizations has dissuaded fashion designers from bringing out fashion collections on holy writing. In areas of cultural conservatism, holy writing fashion functions at best at a subterranean level.

The travel trajectory of holy writing fashion began with a Western garment—the unisex T-shirt that has been integrated into Indian clothing tradition—and progressed to indigenous garments. The T-shirt is the most favored site of creative expression of the youth. The nature of production of the T-shirt, which is smallscale, dispersed, unobtrusive, and highly profitable, has enabled the production and consumption of "Yoga" and Buddhist holy writing garments. These products are sold in the major markets in New Delhi, frequented by the youth (and especially foreign tourists), as well as in upmarket craft markets such as *Dilli Haat* and elite boutiques. E-commerce sites such as www.amazon.com, and www.myntra.com, for example, have emerged as significant market places, ensuring anonymity and freedom from any backlash from right-wing organizations. The expansion of the Internet on mobile phones has facilitated the mushrooming of e-businesses, which offer these garments with a wide range of designs throughout India, facilitating the spread of this fashion trend both in diverse anonymous production centers, as well as consumer bases. Innovative use of new textile fashions such as Srikalahasti Kalamkari (which itself is a derivative of the traditional sacred textile tradition), as well as holy writing fashion, are seen in products sold on e-commerce sites such as www.exoticindiaart.com.

The availability of digital printing and machine embroidery facilities has enabled customized individual designs (particularly Buddhist), which are popular on tourist markets in India. Every year new trends occur in terms of extension to other garments, such as *Bandees* (a cotton sleeveless jacket), and trousers, the addition of new holy writing mantras, innovative design templates, and color palettes. In early 2013, saris (see Figure 4.1) and *salwar-kameez dupatta* sets (see Figure 4.2) were introduced, with *Shiva* and *Om* mantras, interspersed with the sun motif, and using a black, saffron, and maroon color palette. In early 2014, yardage, with holy mantras interspersed with the sun motif, were stitched into unisex *sardarees/bandees,* as well as on tourist-market casual trousers (see Figure 4.3). They became highly popular among tourists and, more selectively, among the Indian urban youth.

Figure 4.1 Sari with holy writing. Sari with Om, Shiva, Hare Rama Hare Krishna mantras and other illegible mantras in 2013, being sold at Dilli Haat, INA, New Delhi. Photograph by the author.

Figure 4.2 Salwar-kameez dupatta sets with holy writing. Salwar-kameez dupatta sets with different legible and illegible mantras being sold in a handloom stall at Dilli Haat INA, New Delhi in 2013. Photograph by the author.

The geographic locus of consumption is limited to areas of cultural tolerance and cosmopolitanism such as urban spaces. It is neither tolerated nor sanctioned in tradition bound, culturally conservative regions, and rural areas and specific urban neighborhoods. Within cities, it is restricted to parts that are amenable to this fashion. Furthermore, fashion dynamics, levels of cultural tolerance, and cosmopolitanism, all determine its prevalence and popularity in each metropolitan city. Mumbai is considered to be the most culturally tolerant and cosmopolitan, followed by Bengaluru (formerly Bangalore), which is one of the centers of the global Information Technology (IT) economy. Conservative cities like Chennai (formerly Madras) and Hyderabad, for example, are now changing. Kolkata (formerly Calcutta) has always been artistically inclined and is culturally tolerant. Smaller cities like Ahmedabad and Visakhapatman, for example, have low levels of cultural tolerance and cosmopolitanism.

Figure 4.3 Touristy casual trousers. These trousers, popular with foreign tourists, are inscribed with partly legible mantras. Photograph by the author.

The consumer base is both niche and geographically widespread. This niche is further nuanced with multiple non-exclusive sub-niches which are also geographically widespread. Of the middle classes, those that are professionally linked to the global economy are the primary constituency. This category is the prime mover as exposure to other cultures—within India, as well as outside the country, both East and West—has expanded the middle class's own level of cultural and religious tolerance. Members have also been influenced by other (both East and West) perceptions of Hinduism. Bought at boutiques and aesthetically designed by designers trained in fashion or otherwise, these garments are favored by them and are considered "high status." For this niche, displaying these garments on their bodies is meant to show that they have the perfect combination of materialism and spiritualism with an aesthetic fashion sense. The sub-niche of the youth, considers wearing these holy writing garments as "cool," but these are only one kind of the many fashionable garments worn by them, and are not ubiquitous like jeans and T-shirts. Part of secular India, they are often unaware of the cultural taboos regarding the usage of sacred elements in daily life. They favor T-shirts, *kurtas*, shirts, touristy trousers; the latter are more popular among foreign tourists. Foreigners in tourist sites such as Goa and headquarters of the new age spiritual gurus such as those found in Bengaluru and Coimbatore are the major buyers of these garments. Another sub-niche is that of young adults who have graduated from wearing T-shirts to shirts, *kurtas, dupattas, salwar-kameezes,* and *saris*. The older-age group of men and women in their 40 to 50s also provides a consumer base for these *kurtas* and *saris*. Lastly, there are the pilgrims undertaking pilgrimages, who wear these garments, in lieu of the traditional sacred cloths, when they go to the temple to pray to the gods. The rich upper-class segment sources its holy writing fashion garments from high-end boutiques, and also commissions fashion designers to create for them. The middle-class segment sources its holy writing fashion garments from a more diverse set of producers spread across India, such as small clothing businesses which stock the designs of graphic artists and designers (visual artists), independent craft producers, and others.

Buyer and seller mindscapes: Negotiating around the edges

Actual production is a closely guarded business secret, and producers and sellers are reluctant to reveal the actual place of production, the selection of mantras, the designing of the garments, and so on. The producers are small scale and dispersed, including block makers, hand block printers and screen printers, who do not advertise their work; neither do producers and sellers. In order to address varied consumer demands, producers experiment and innovate to bring out new designs and mantras in varied color palettes. Test marketing of new mantras is continuously done. Unknown mantras with low sales that have to be repetitively explained to the customers are discarded. Obscure and sometimes unintelligible mantras or verses are also sold without any qualms or explanation. It is common to see incomplete and incorrectly sequenced mantras, as well as unknown mantras that make no sense. The accountability of the mistakes is passed on by the producer to someone else in the production chain such as the designer or the block maker. But despite these mistakes, which traditionally would have been perceived as sacrilege, these garments are popular.

The cultural matrix governing the use of mantras impacts the producers and sellers, too, who make a distinction between personal choice and business. A lady producer and seller confessed that while neither she nor her family members would wear these garments, she produces them nevertheless because it is business. Some producers make a deliberate choice not to produce garments that clothe the lower part of the body such as trousers and *salwars*, for example, instead, focusing on creating garments that clothe the upper part of the body. However, some producers choose to treat the production of lower garments inscribed with holy writing as a purely business venture and produce trousers that are highly popular with foreign tourists.

Many block printers and producers chose not to print mantras, mainly due to their adherence to the cultural restrictions governing the use of mantras in daily life. Some producers of yardage and garments printed with the scripts of regional languages, refused to print holy words onto their products because it was against their cultural sensibilities and practices. One Sikh producer whose popular products include *kurtis, kurtas*, and stoles, beautifully conceived and executed based on the interplay of two great Punjabi traditions—*Phulkari* embroidery and *Gurmukh*i script—did not allow any holy words or scripture from Sikh religion to be printed on his garments as it went against the basic tenet of Sikhism. Similarly, a traditional hand block printer and an entrepreneur businessman from Rajasthan, did not print any holy writing fashion garments as it was against Rajasthani culture and textiles tradition. Instead, he preferred to produce fashion garments with vernacular language alphabets that are hand block printed on cotton fabric. Dastkari Haat Samiti's "*Akshara*"[14] initiative, which was designed to bring literacy to illiterate crafts people through the creation of products that incorporate the alphabets of vernacular languages, decided to steer clear of needless complication to its literacy project by not including holy writing, especially as both Hindus and Muslims produced goods for each other's communities.

The typical buyer's perception involves an entirely different set of criteria that come into play while buying a holy writing garment. The set of criteria primarily involves the interrogation of the written elements on the garment, assessment of its suitability by examining its connotative meaning in his/her syncretic cultural matrix, and, finally, determining whether it is useful in the creation of the desired image of oneself. A college-going urban student, who is part of secularized India, is often unaware of the cultural taboos, and views them merely from a fashion and aesthetic point of view. But a woman aware of the cultural taboos of her socio-cultural matrix, has to take into account the cultural proscriptions of her family's cultural background, and, if married, that of her in-laws, her social circle, and her workplace. Similarly, she must figure out ways to negotiate the cultural proscriptions—for instance, that one should not sit on holy writing and gods' images, not go to the toilet wearing any sacred clothing, not wear any sacred clothing while menstruating, as well as other notions and practices involving purity and pollution—while still going about the business of daily life. The management of these multiple minefields determines her choice of whether or not to buy a holy writing fashion clothing item, where to wear it, and how often.

The classic fashion dispersal model is the top down trickle model from the higher social classes and cognoscenti, to the middle classes, and finally to the lower classes, as well as from the fashion designers to the imitators at lower rungs (Simmel 1904), but this does not apply to holy writing fashion. Rather, it trickles across disparately located groups with similar consumption trajectories and levels. It emerges from the middle classes, spreading horizontally and verti-cally within that group. Its spread to upper and lower social classes is limited as it is determined by multiple factors such as the nature and content of the holy writing, and its engagement with conservatism in different locales, both geographical and cultural. The fashion model most applicable is the populist model, where multiple groups belonging to varied cultures, socio-economic status, location and age groups have created this fashion trend. This is explained by the fact that the middle classes are the locus of production and consumption. The primary producers were, and are, graphic artists and designers (visual artists who are often professionally trained), who creatively interpret the various elements of Indian religion and culture onto garments. Simultaneously, the vast burgeoning middle class constitutes the consumer base.

Contextualizing holy writing fashion: societal changes in globalization era

The post-liberalization and globalization era has been characterized by large-scale social changes which have led to both structural changes, such as the emergence of new middle classes, and socio-cultural phenomena, such as new age spiritualism and religion, and popular culture. These provide the template for the emergence and spread of holy writing fashion, which is uniquely placed at the juncture of these three contexts. This section examines these social changes in the context of the genesis and trajectory of holy writing fashion.

The urban middle class

Holy writing fashion decodes, as well as articulates the middle class's[15] urban psyche, that is its economic and socio-cultural situation; what it seeks, wants, needs, desires, fears, expresses, and articulates, as well as its self conceptualization and self-construction. The socio-cultural contexts of holy writing fashion lie in the larger internal changes brought about by the post-Independence development agenda in India. These have seen an increase in literate professionals who form the exponentially expanding middle classes, both old and new[16] which largely inhabit India's metropolitan cities. Wider processes of urbanization, education, industrial growth, and development policies created a highly skilled labor pool, not just for India's domestic economy, but also for the world economy, many of which migrated to Indian cities, as well as abroad. Today's educated middle-class India is more exposed to the rest of the world than any other generation in the history of the country; it inhabits a truly global world. This process has intensified, deepened, and accelerated due to forces of liberalization and globalization in the late 1990s—particularly as a result of the development of the IT and communication sector (mobile, Internet, and satellite direct to home TV), which has had a profound and far-reaching impact on modern India.

This has resulted in the extension of the secular, which, in turn, has given rise to a certain kind of generalization of worldviews and consumption patterns across the Indian middle classes.[17] The rising aspirational expectations of the expanding middle class have given rise to increasing consumerism. Therefore, a mobile and educated middle-class India has been critically revisiting many of its ancient cultural practices, as well as its spiritual and religious notions. This concurrent rediscovery of its rich and diverse heritage, on the one hand, and the ever increasing exposure to global developments and worldviews, on the other, has given rise to multiple frames of reconstruction of the self by objectifying some elements of culture, reframing and appropriating them. This postmodern encounter with a middle-class Indian has been a two way engagement where the middle-class Indian has not merely brought his or her own understanding of modernity to negotiate with the multiple modernities that he or she encounters (Breckenridge 1996), but also created a postmodern template where things, events, cultures, and personal and professional growth are framed and contextualized. The postmodern urban middle-class Indian identity is continuously self-constructed, as well as a pastiche of various styles (Berger 2010), with multiple-identity constructions for each kind of encounter, with various kinds of modernities. This critical reevaluation has not only resulted in a very vigorous popular culture, and the open articulation and expression of anxieties and conflicts brought about by rapid changes in both personal and socio-cultural milieus, but also in the increase of new age spiritualism and religiosity. As a result, the hidden and private aspects of spirituality and religiosity in general as well as personal terms have been brought out into the open. The integration of a spiritual and religious anchor or belief into one's life is often publicly displayed by holy marks and clothing, in this case holy writing fashion. The urbanized middle class is the locus of the holy writing fashion trend's genesis, production, and consumption. The old is the site of cultural production, while the site of consumption of holy writing fashion is both the old and new middle classes.

New age spiritualism and religiosity

The internal and external changes have created conditions of existence where the old order and paradigm are no longer valid, but a new order is not yet in place. The resultant loss of moorings, both cultural and socio-economic, a feeling of rootlessness, and that of not belonging have created a vacuum and a space for a renegotiation of the self. The modern Indian suffers from *lebensangst* (an unwillingness to face up to life's problems) and searches for *lebensraum* (living space).The spiritual and religious presents itself as something universal and available. However, the dipping into spiritual and religious is not confined to Hinduism, but rather concerns all spiritual and religious traditions.[18] Elements of religion have been commodified to make not merely lifestyle statements, but also assuage an underlying *lebensangst* brought on by continuous shifting life situations and contexts and the gradual disintegration of old expectations and established behavioral patterns. The new age spiritual and religious Gurus' primary constituency is thus these vast burgeoning middle classes seeking personal moorings. They are offered different packaged brands, which are designed to strengthen, deepen, and widen the consumerist lifestyle without its side effects, but with an added perquisite of spiritual benefits.[19] Religion and spirituality are commodified and repackaged as tools for contemporary living.[20] This explains the rise and proliferation of new age spiritual gurus, the bulk of whose followers come from the middle classes.

The depth and extent of the widespread need to resort to the spiritual and religious realm to resolve the existential dilemmas of all classes of Indians is manifested through:

a) an emergence of numerous religious and spiritual TV channels and programs which specifically provide solutions to existential problems of the common people;

b) films that make gods more accessible to people by recasting them as friends of the people, such as *My Friend Ganesha* (Rajiv S Ruia: 2007)—in which the god is deliberately cast as a cute child, thus reinforcing the idea of him as a friend—and *My Boss Bajrang Bali* (Krishna Vamsi: 2004);

c) the proliferation of religious magazines which offer with nearly every issue, a holy item (such as a *Rudraksha* bead) guaranteed to aid in solving problems; and

d) an increase in numerous religious popular culture products, such as images of gods set in contemporary settings, for example, Ganesha working on a computer.

The reappropriation of selective elements from spiritual and religious spheres is most visible in the proliferation of popular culture products. In the last decade, many such products have been available on the market across India, and numerous graphic artists and designers have played with holy symbols and images in various lifestyle products. It is now common to find fridge magnets or flying kites with "*Om*" inscribed on them, small plates featuring the *swastika* symbol, or laptop skins with gods and holy symbols on them. Specialized shops have emerged which sell products such as cushion covers, coasters, and other lifestyle products featuring images of gods that have been playfully interpreted and depicted.

Popular culture as a site for holy writing fashion

In today's integrated India, where people from different walks of life, communities, and cultural and social backgrounds converge and intermingle in the same working arena, the individual requires incredible skills to negotiate this minefield of conflicting morals and cultural frameworks. Popular culture is a safety valve and an avenue for the expression of this *lebensangst*. It functions as *lebensraum*, as a site for expressing existential fears. The proliferation of religion and spirituality in popular culture is an eloquent commentary on the present state of Hindus, who are increasingly seeking a religious/spiritual intervention, repackaged to address their issues and dilemmas. It tells of a deeply fractured psyche riddled with existential dilemmas, unwilling to compromise on anything, but seeking to have it all—seemingly a most materialistic attitude of existence. The fun religious popular culture products have effectively prepared the ground for the short but significant leap from popular culture products to the emergence and wider acceptance of holy writing garments.

The holy writing fashion's popularity and acceptance is also due to the specificity of popular culture. In India's rapidly changing society, popular culture has mediated changes in culture, and the major areas of negotiation include dressing styles, cultural icons, and spirituality. It has allowed and provided space for articulation of thoughts, feelings, responses, and action without disrupting and creating havoc in the existing system. More significantly, it has sanitized the revolutionary potential of the new and emerging interventions. It has incubated and developed popular resistance to all kinds of hegemonies, often in a humorous, non-threatening manner, and has allowed space for critiques of the social system to become part of the traditional, mainstream society. This kind of change is insidious and very sly, but yet "in your face," out in the open, and non-threatening to the established order. This version of religion in popular culture, which is continuously metamorphosing according to the market demands, is seen for the first time in India's history and that, too, on a large scale.

A further impetus to the growth of this trend has been the intensification, since 2000, of Western interpretations and adoptions of Indian spiritualism and religion into their lifestyle, as witnessed by the prolific use of holy symbols like *Om* and the *Gayatri* mantra in clothing used as yoga and meditation accoutrements, and the designer lines depicting Indian deities and gods. India, in its turn, has partly mirrored this Western fashion trend of incorporating Indian spiritual/religious heritage in clothing.

Since 2000, there has been an emerging trend of indigenous appropriating and reclaiming of local cultures, visible especially in advertisements. Graphic artists, designers, and advertisement professionals, catering to a contemporary India, have revisited aspects of Indian culture in order to create products relevant to Indian customers. Thus, today we have two perspectives—the Self and the Other—each interrogating Indian spirituality from within and without, in a non-exclusive, interactive manner.

Holy writing fashion and the individual: the making and remaking of the self

The recent trend of mixing and matching elements from different cultures is only part of a larger historical trend of religious and spiritual syncretism, which is characteristic of India. In a plural heterogeneous society, its multiple groups have their own codes, daily life practices, ways of living, sexuality, bodies, and the "cultural" meanings and myths connected to the cosmos, spiritual world, and the material world. New contemporary meanings are generated through the interplay of combining various elements, at times conflicting, from one's own and others' culture. In postmodern India, where metanarratives have failed and are failing, individual narratives are being constructed to make sense of one's own life. These personal narratives involve accessing multiple cultures that function as resources from which the individual picks and chooses elements to construct his or her own individual and unique narrative.

Holy writing fashion, then, is only one template upon which a transient individual narrative is based, and is discarded by another template over the course of time. It provides one kind of a social skin which is constructed and put on for an occasional display in a certain context in which it functions as a code for unique and distinct membership. This social skin is subsequently shed in order to create another narrative in a different context. In the course of the day, an individual in today's urban India inhabits many such social contexts that are constituted by the people with whom he or she engages, be it family, relatives, colleagues, friends, peers, or others, and thus that individual constructs and sheds many social skins depending upon the number of social contexts that constitute the day.

Garments function as multiple social skins that are peeled off and put on in the habitus of these varied contexts of daily or occasional engagement. A person wearing holy writing fashion garments communicates to his or her reference group, as well as to others, that he or she is fashionable, spiritual, hip and cool, and has great taste, as well as aesthetic and syncretic sense. This public face of the wearer also reflects the private face of the wearer. The intention of the wearer could thus be a declaration of any or all of the following: his or her inner spiritual tendency, membership to a reference group, fashion and aesthetic sensibilities, fashionability, and/or to create a personalized protective armor for self protection.

Conclusion

The fashion trend of holy writing on garments is symptomatic and reflective of the transformation that Indian society is undergoing due to its transitioning economy. The resultant large-scale societal changes have given rise to a vibrant popular culture, an extension of the secular, and the commodification of various elements of culture, notably religion and spirituality. This fashion is essentially indigenous, reflecting and articulating an indigenous perspective and engagement with the changes in society. This new gaze is neither wholly Western, nor wholly traditional or indigenous, but rather a synthesis, a mix of the modern and the traditional, reflecting the mindset of the modern urban—which is curious and flexible, prone to continuously reinterpret, adapt, and recast its cultural and religious heritage. Partly fueled by the emergence of neo-spiritualism which caters again to a lifestyle that induces stress and diseases, the present generation seeks to make sense of its existence through instant nirvana fixes available on the market. Rooted in the middle classes, who are the backbone of the transitioning economy, it is located in popular culture, which has allowed the emergence of new syncretic cultural matrixes that permit a seamless integration of diverse and conflicting elements of culture. It is one of the many fashion trends of present day India with a populist fashion model and a trickle across a fashion dispersal model that emerge from the middle class. Two trends have enabled the fairly widespread geographic niche acceptance of holy writing fashion garments: firstly the cultural appropriation of foreign cultural influences into one's own, making it an integral part of one's constructed identity; and secondly the resolving of personal insecurities, *lebensangst*, through spiritual and religious (fashion) products within the template or context of popular culture. Individuals create multiple-identity constructions to function in today's society, whereby these holy writing garments provide not only a talismanic succor but also a social skin that the consumer wears in specific contexts.

Traditional culture matrixes do not allow the buying and wearing of these fashionable holy writing garments, but new syncretic cultural matrixes provide scope for seamless accommodation of this fashion into a person's life. Its success lies in the dominance of new syncretic cultural matrixes over the traditional ones. Holy writing fashion symbolizes the negotiation of cultural heritage for self-construction, the negotiation and resolution of varied minefields and complexities in one's lifestyle, and the articulation of one's public and private self. It is the articulation of one's spiritual inclinations, as well as sartorial sensibilities. It is a modern fashion phenomenon that has emerged due to large-scale internal changes, as well as external influences that impinge upon individuals as they encounter and negotiate multiple modernities that are both local and international. It functions as a tool for negotiating complex changes and is ever evolving and responsive to change. Having been in existence for more than a decade with numerous avatars, this fashion trend is here to stay, although it is not clear what forms the holy writing on garments fashion may take in the future.

Notes

1   I am thankful to Dr. Vijayalakshmi Shankar, Dr. Anamika Pathak, Dr. Lotika Varadarajan for fruitful discussions during the course of this independent research project. Finally, I am deeply grateful to Professor T. Desiraju, who motivated me to continuously engage with the world with an open, curious, and questioning mind.

2   The trend of holy writing on fashionable clothing is non-existent in Christianity, Islam, Zoroastrianism, and Sikhism, but exists at a subterranean level in Jain and Buddhist religions. Jain and Buddhist religions are minority religions, but as offshoots of Hindusim, they partly share the broader notions of cultural prescriptions and proscriptions such as the theory and praxis of dealing with sacred things and objects, for example.

3   *Dilli Haat* attracts a regular, but wide and disparate consumer base from all over
    the country, ranging from the young to the old. It is much frequented by the college
    students who provide a pan-Indian fashion platform reflective of the local popular
    markets. It also provides a space where one can interact with buyers and sellers, as
    well as producers. Interestingly, very often the seller and the producer are one and
    the same. In addition, the pan-Indian validity of the findings were validated through
    a research of Internet news reports, debates and discussions, e-commerce sites.
    as well as telephonic interviews with consumers from other Indian metropolitan
    areas.

4   The study excludes other visual symbols such as the feet of Vishnu, the Sun, or
    the *Trishul* of Shiva because they are visual symbols.

5   The Hindu deities have numerous names, and 108 different names of a deity
    generally constitute a *Namavali*. However, higher counts do exist and the
    worshipper has the choice between the basic 108, or more.

6   *Sanskrit* tradition in this context is referred to as the great tradition which is
    the preserve of the few, with possible Aryan origin such as *Sanskrit* language,
    brahminical Puranas, Vedas, and so on. *Prakrit* tradition, often referred to as
    the little tradition, is the preserve of the rest, and is indigene with numerous
    local traditions, vernacular languages, folk tales, non-brahminical, and others.
    The *Sanskrit/Prakrit* binary opposition is like other binary oppositions used to
    understand the incredible diversity of India such as *Marga/Desi, English language
    (colonial, alien and now dominant)/ Bhasha (vernacular), India/ Bharat*.

7   We do not know the exact origin of *Namavali* cloths whether they originated from
    the great-*sanskrit* tradition or from the little-*prakrit* tradition. It is suggested that
    the template for the development of *sanskrit* and *prakrit* traditions came from an
    already existing template which was in the public domain and which subsequently
    evolved into *sanskrit* and *prakrit* traditions. It might still survive in a niche market
    and usage, accessible to few who insist on the age-old *paddhati*.

9   Typically, the rich and the royal as only they could afford the expensive silk
    and pashmina wool fabrics. The painting in National Museum, New Delhi,
    from Raghogarh, Central India, (circa AD 1795, Paper, 30.5x44 cm, Acc. No.:
    51.71/218) perfectly illustrates this point. It depicts Raja Balwant Singh (1770–97)
    of Raghogarh with his son, Jai Singh, worshipping the idols of Rama and Sita
    and others on a swing. Raja Balwant Singh is wearing *Namavali* cloths, while the
    attending priests wear the regular plain sacred cloths.

10 The production of these luxury garments has by all accounts ceased a long time
    ago, though a one-off commissioned item may still be produced at the numerous
    production centers in North India, but a contemporary piece has not yet come
    into the public domain. The name/s of the deity was either printed or woven onto
    the cloth, the material ranging from cotton or silk to a mix of silk and cotton. The
    name/s of the deity is written 108 times, either as the repetition of only one single
    name, such as *Hare Rama* or *Hare Krishna* or *Jai Shree Devi Durge* or as 108
    different names of the deity. The design of the *Namavali* sacred cloth primarily
    encapsulates the written word, symbols, and images of the deity such as *Sri
    Rama, Krishna, Durga*, and *Siva*. Technically, *Namavali* consists of numerous
    names of one single deity, which often are the celebrated attributes of the deity
    chanted during *puja*. So, while the original *Namavali* has both multiple names and

single name of the deity, the textiles derivative of *Namavali* repeats only one name, possibly due to the technicalities associated with weaving.

11 http://ibnlive.in.com/news/religious-text-on-clothes-offending/17902-15-1.html (accessed 20 August 2014).

12 http://www.indiafashionweek.com/news/26165.html (accessed 21 August 2014).

13 http://www.jainsamaj.org/rpg_site/ahimsa_times_show.php?id=123 (accessed 21 August 2014).

14 Interview with Jaya Jaitly, Dastkari Haat Samiti, who conceived the Akshara project, on January 15, 2014.

15 In this chapter, the concept middle class is used to denote both the old and the new that coexists in India. The old is not yet a part of the global economy, while the new middle classes are firmly integrated into global economy, especially Information Technology.

16 Leela Fernandes defines the "new" middle classes as "a distinctive social and political identity that represents and lays claim to the benefits of liberalization" (2006: xviii).

17 Pavan Varma (2007) explains the overt homogeneity of a very heterogeneous class as being the result of the same educational pattern, work atmosphere, increased mobility, media expansion, and consumption patterns whether it be food, fashion, cinema, music, or others.

18 The popularity of feng shui in India is phenomenal and it is now pervasive on TV channels, and in the proliferation of shops in urban areas that are widely patronized by all sections of society.

19 Edward Luce gives a perfect example of an Infosys employee represented by a typical new middle-class urban Indian who is a migrant from the village, is a follower of a prominent new age spiritual guru and displays his photograph in his office cubicle. He follows the new age spiritual guru's branded package of tools for living that will help him acquire a higher self-esteem, and become more Indian (2006: 306).

20 For a more detailed examination see the article online at: http://indiatoday.intoday. in/story/stereotype-of-saffron-clad-sadhus-are-out-new-age-gurus-are-trendy-young-people/1/206030.html.

Glossary

Bandee a traditional cotton Indian jacket worn by commoners to royals.

Churidar stitched lower garment of North India, trouser-like, fitting the legs and gathered at the ankles akin to bangles on arms, hence, the name churi in Hindi which in English means "bangles."

Dupatta a woven cloth used to cover the shoulders and upper part of the body, part of the salwar-kameez ensemble.

Haat a traditional informal market in India.

Kameez typical upper garment stitched top of North Indian girls and women. The kameez, along with salwar, the lower garment, and dupatta, an unstitched length of cloth that is used to cover the head and the bosom by draping it over the kameez, is the typical dress of Punjabi women, but has now become a pan-Indian dress code. The Pakistani Pathan suit is the male variation of salwar-kameez.

Kurtas upper garment of women worn over trousers/jeans and salwars and churidars.

Kurtis a fitted and shorter version of kurta. The kurta was reinvented as a kurti by a fashion designer post in 2000.

Namavali garland of names; etymological meaning of Namavali: Nama-names, Vali- garland.

Paddhati established systems of, rules and regulations, or ways of doing something that are culturally conditioned rules of engagement.

Pitambar the yellow color of Lord Vishnu's garments.

Prakrit the low-brow, common traditions of the remaining castes, includes folk culture.

Puja ritual worship of the deities.

Salwar typical lower garment stitched somewhat like gathered trousers, and worn by women of North India, but with specific styles for both sexes.

Sanskrit the great, highbrow and pure tradition of the upper castes.

Sardaree made of wool fibers, this is a traditional Indian jacket worn by anyone from commoners to royals.

References

Appadurai, Arjun. *The Social Life of Things: Commodities in Cultural Perspective.* Cambridge: Cambridge University Press, 1998.

Berger, A. A. *The Objects of Affection: Semiotics and Consumer Culture.* New York: Palgrave Macmillan, 2010.

Breckenridge, Carol A. *Consuming Modernity: Public Culture in Contemporary India.* New Delhi: Oxford University Press, 1996.

Craik, Jennifer. *The Face of Fashion: Cultural Studies in Fashion,* London: Routledge, 2005.

Geertz, Clifford. *The Interpretation of Cultures: Selected Essays*. London: Fontana Press, 1993.

Fernandes, Leela. *India's New Middle Class: Democratic Politics in an Era of Economic Reform*. Minneapolis: University of Minnesota Press, 2006.

Jain, Jyotindra, ed. *Popular Culture: Iconic Spaces and Fluid Images*, Mumbai: Marg, 2007.

Kasbekar, Asha. *Pop Culture India! Media, Arts, and Lifestyle.* Oxford: ABC Clio, 2006.

Luce, Edward. *In Spite of Gods: The Strange Rise of Modern India*. London: Little, Brown, 2006.

Moti Gokulsing, K., and Wimal Dissanayake, eds *Popular Culture in a Globalized India*, London: Routledge, 2009.

Nandy, Ashis. *An Ambiguous Journey to the City*. New Delhi: Oxford University Press, 2001.

Pathak, Anamika. "Siva-Parvati Woven Namavali Shawl." *Kala: The Journal of Indian Art History Congress,* vol. xiii, 2007–8.

Simmel, G. "Fashion." *International Quarterly* 10 (1904):130–55.

Turner, Terence. "The Social Skin." *Journal of Ethnographic Theory* 2 (2) (2012): 486–504.
Varma, Pavan K. *The Great Indian Middle Class*. New Delhi: Penguin Books, 2007.

5

EXOTIC NARRATIVES IN FASHION: THE IMPACT OF MOTIFS OF EXOTICA ON FASHION DESIGN AND FASHIONABLE IDENTITIES[1]

JENNIFER CRAIK

Introduction

The idea of the exotic has been central to the history of fashion design and its reception as innovative, unique, or outstanding. But while there are many references to the exotic and exotica, it is rarely defined, especially in relation to how the term is used in relation to fashion and design. The idea of the exotic implies a sense of magic, something that is recognized but intangible—something out of the ordinary. Despite that, an element of the exotic is a central part of how cultural identity is formed and defined. The exotic is also shorthand for the divide between the persistent distinction made between inspiration in Western "fashion" and non-Western symbolism in "dress," since non-Western exotica is the recurring and deeply embedded basis of Western fashion. Above all, an examination of the use of the exotic in fashion reveals the mutual dependency and synergies between fashion sensibilities in all cultures and historical moments. In other words, there is a convergence between Western and non-Western fashion, as contemporaneously illustrated in the case of China and India, which have demonstrated their success at engaging with Western (or Eurocentric) fashion, while retaining their distinctive symbolism and stylistic registers as producers, consumers and increasingly as cutting edge designers. This chapter explores the case of the incorporation of the exotic in Australia indigenous fashion design.

Elsewhere, I have explored the ways in which three distinctive types of exotica have constructed narratives of national identity in Australian fashion, namely, outback or rural dress, swimwear, and Australiana-themed fashion (Craik 2009). More recently, a fourth type of national identity has recurred as a form of fashion inspiration, namely, motifs of Australian indigenous culture. Since European settlement, the place of indigenous culture has been contested with the consequence of ambivalent references in discourses of national identity. This has been reflected in different cultural narratives including tourism, film, photography, art and craft, sport, and music. But it has also featured in fashion and, as the assertion of indigenous identity has become more prominent in recent years, so, too, has the visibility of indigenous themes in the design of textiles and garments. Increasingly, references to indigeneity are becoming the leitmotif of discourses about national identity and culture and thus, too, in national dress codes and fashion. The exotic in Australian fashion is, therefore, increasingly indigenous. This chapter explores specific indigenous fashion narratives, and contrasts surface (2-D) references to the exotic—for example, in textiles—with structural (3-D) manipulations of the exotic in the design process—for example, in the shape, form, and construction of garments.

Defining exotica

To begin, it is necessary to define the term "exotica". A range of definitions can be found in dictionaries and glossaries, including phenomena that are: curiously unusual or excitingly strange; foreign, unfamiliar, strange, or rare; a fusion of something foreign with local or indigenous culture; something introduced from abroad, but not fully naturalized; and something having a strange or bizarre allure, beauty, or quality. To summarize, exotica refers to something or a quality that is not embedded in a particular culture, but to which the culture relates or responds, or with which it resonates.

In relation to fashion inspiration, I have argued that exotica is integral to what is regarded as cutting-edge design. In other words, exoticism and fashion go hand in hand such that references to cultural motifs are a foremost inspiration in fashion. So, what is it that exotic motifs add or contribute to design? Here, I argue that exotic references create narratives of difference and distinctiveness both for the designer and the wearer. This includes allusions to motifs, objects, customs, and aesthetics from other cultures in fashion, as well as well-known cultural tropes from the art, history, and popular culture of one's own culture.

In an earlier publication (Craik 1994), I proposed that there were three forms of exoticism in fashion:

1   Techniques of dress and decoration in non-Western cultures. Examples include: saris in the subcontinent; kimonos in Japan; hanbok in Korea; tunics, robes, and pigtails in China; veiling in Islamic cultures; and tattooing as a symbol of status or role.

2   Adaptations of traditional (customary) dress within Western fashion. Examples include: the salwar-kameez in diasporic Indian cultures, saris with cardigans or coats in cold climates, and leggings under dresses and skirts with headscarf for Muslim schoolgirls in Western societies.

3   Appropriation of "exotic" elements in Western fashion. Examples include: the inclusion of North American Indian fringing or feathers in mainstream fashion; the reproduction of Aboriginal paintings as textiles for use on T-shirts, or other fashion; and the periodic appearance of the "cheongsam" in Western fashion.

To this I have added a fourth form, namely, the appropriation of Western fashion in non-Western fashion. Examples include: the combination of denim jeans with customary dress; the global proliferation of baseball caps as sporting and leisure wear; and the normative status of sneakers as the default footwear of choice when they were originally designed as sports shoes. While we recognize inspirations and references like these, almost without thinking, we are also conscious of a set of tensions and oppositions that are embedded in such cultural borrowings and adaptations. There are three sets of oppositions:

1   Indigenous versus exotic motifs and references;

2   Contrived versus appropriated motifs and references; and

3   Authentic versus inspirational motifs and references.

While these overlap, and sometimes may be synonymous, an indigenous motif refers to something that is specifically and uniquely embedded in a particular culture (e.g. the myth of the rainbow serpent, or representation of a turtle totem), as opposed to a generic, but design-imbued representation of something commonly associated with exotica (e.g. a boomerang, handprint, or kangaroo). Often the difficulty is establishing whether a certain motif has a specific "ownership," or belongs in the sacred, rather than the profane domain—and who has the authority to designate it in one domain or another.

The second tension relates to the act of using motifs. In a contrived use of exotica, a motif, image, or theme is deliberately used and manipulated to achieve a particular design outcome while appropriation refers to the deliberate borrowing or reusing of a motif or image, often in a different context, and with little regard for the ethics of use (e.g. permission, licensing, collaboration).

The third tension is to some degree a judgment as to whether a motif appears as an authentic design usage versus the creation of a design that has been inspired by, but is not a direct translation (rip-off) of a motif or an image.

These tensions and oppositions run through the discussion and reception of exotic imagery in textiles and fashion with scant regard to the issues raised by such practices, in particular, that Western cultures draw on the exotica of non-Western cultures and past cultures (e.g. folk cultures, traditions, historical cultures) to add an element of frisson to everyday culture and imbue the everyday with a special—almost magical—quality. Non-Western cultures, by contrast, tend to have grounded connotations and relationships with exotic motifs in their cultures that convey quite specific social meanings and implications. Mixing these two registers lies at the heart of fashion for exotica, but in so doing raises many questions about the links between Western and non-Western as codified symbolic and communicative realms.

The following discussion looks specifically at how the idea of the exotic has been used in and shaped by the development of a distinctively Australian sense of fashion.

How has Australian fashion design been shaped by exotica?

Exotica has long been a motif in Australian fashion, as traced by Margaret Maynard (2001). Throughout the twentieth century, exotic motifs, including Aboriginal, Polynesian, Indonesian, Hawaiian, and Indian inspirations, have "been plundered for women's leisure clothing (although not exclusively) to stimulate and titillate the jaded tastes of consumers" (Maynard 2001: 153). As well as using exotic motifs in Australian fashion design, garments and fashions from non-Western cultures have also been incorporated into what has become termed "ethnic chic."

Maynard outlines the use of exotica in Australian swimwear in the 1920s (such as oriental designs, and garments such as the kimono, as well as references to the cultures of antiquity), Polynesian and Hawaiian influences in the interwar years (especially in textile designs, such as hibiscus, palm trees, and pandanus), and Islander and Indonesian influences from the 1940s (with sarongs and batik fabric), while Indian garments, fabrics, and accessories dominated the youth fashions of the 1970s, and have recurred in subsequent fashions. Alongside these diverse forms of exotica, the use of Aboriginal motifs has also occurred, for example, in the textiles of Olive Ashworth, from the 1950s, in her efforts to counter the craze for what she called "mock Hawaiian, pseudo Spanish and phoney Polynesian" motifs circulating in fashion (Maynard 2001: 154; Williamson 2010: 117). This was the start of an ongoing fascination with Aboriginal motifs in fashion and textiles, in a cyclical process of acclamation, followed by renunciation, coinciding with periods of nationalistic fervor (Craik, forthcoming).

Since Ashworth, many other designers have continued to make explicit links between Aboriginal culture and leisure wear, emphasizing the problematic links between women at home and as objects of fantasy. At times the exotic is stressed through generalized Australiana motifs, not simply Aboriginal designs (Maynard 2001: 154). Prominent among these motifs are: Australian flora and fauna (such as waratahs, gum blossoms, Sturt Desert Peas, koalas, kangaroos, cockatoos, and reef life); landscape and the colors of the outback, especially the desert (the mythical heart of Australia); images and symbols derived from well-known examples of Australian art (for example, the textile designs of Florence Broadhurst's wallpaper, "pop" artist Ken Done's colorful depictions of Australiana, and artist Del Kathryn Barton's popular culture symbols); icons and clothing typifying rural Australia (such as R. M. Williams' moleskins and boots, Akubra hats, Drizabone coats, and ug/ugg boots); images that allude to Australia's climate and surfing-cum-swimming lifestyle and culture (such as images of elements of beach culture, sunsets, sharks, and thongs); and motifs associated with indigenous identity and national identity (x-ray artworks depicted on T-shirts, "dot" painting style designs, ochre palette colorways representing the soil of the outback).

The heyday of the uptake of Australiana in fashion was the 1980s. Australiana references have been prominent in the design of successive uniforms for Australian sporting teams at international events. For example, in 1984, prominent fashion designer Prue Acton designed the opening parade uniforms for the Australian team in the Olympic Games, choosing wattle yellow wool dresses (for women) and shirts (for men) depicting koalas, emus, and wombats. While ridiculed by the Australian media and public, the team won the best-dressed award for the opening ceremony (Williamson 2010: 107; Berry 2012: 91). In 1988, athletes wore yellow Drizabone-style coats and Akubra hats; in 1992, khaki shorts with Australiana patterned shirts; and, in 2000, Mambo-designed colorful ironic Australiana shirts and jackets (which subsequently became collectors' items). In *avant-garde* fashion, designers such as Jenny Kee and Linda Jackson popularized the sophisticated blending of indigenous and Australiana inspirations in colorful textiles, fashion, and artwork, epitomized by their Flamingo Park boutique and catwalk parades, as well as collections with names such as Bush Couture and Opal (Maynard 1999, 2000, 2001; Craik 2009; in press). Other notable designers included Jenny Bannister, Bronwyn Bancroft, and the fashion label Balarinji. A number of indigenous collectives also emerged during this period, including Tiwi Designs, Desert Designs, Ernabella, Utopia, and Bima Wear (Williamson 2010: 115–19).

Fashions inspired by Australiana became mainstream during this period as Australians proudly wore colorful, nationalistic clothes that reflected a newfound sense of national pride. As Berry observes:

In simplifying Australian landmarks and animals as symbols of national identity, designers simultaneously created garments that appealed to tourists as souvenirs and conveyed postmodern irony in the local context. (Berry 2012: 54)

The underpinning of this period was the desire to create a new sense of national culture in order to reconcile the traditional myth of Australian identity as the bush and the outback with the recognition of a modern urban culture fanned by the energy of youth and popular culture. While an earnest pursuit at one level, this quest also embraced an irreverent and rebellious "larrikin" sensibility with irony, juxtaposition, critique, and spoof central to the emergence of a contemporary design language and discourse (Gray 2010: 152).

As well as achieving popularity as mainstream fashion, the work of these designers also resonated with developments in the art world and galleries and museums acquired examples for their collections. An increasing number of galleries have held fashion exhibitions drawn from their own collections or touring shows. This demonstrates that the incorporation of Australiana and indigenous motifs in fashion has resonated with a new sensibility and homegrown aesthetic in Australian art. Indeed, with no gallery dedicated solely to fashion or costume in Australia, examples of fashion from this period are almost exclusively found as "artefacts" and examples of "material culture" in art galleries and museums (such as the Powerhouse in Sydney, National Gallery of Australia, and National Gallery of Victoria) rather than in other collections. But are they there because they are fashion, art, craft or design? Berry (2013) has traced the fraught and ambiguous uptake of Australiana fashion as the craft versus art embodiment of national cultural identity.

Another development during this period was the politicization of indigenous culture and recognition of the sovereignty of Aboriginal people. As a result, the use of Australiana motifs—especially indigenous ones—has become increasingly tinged by the overt and implicit politics of inspiration and appropriation. Aboriginal activists used Australiana clothes such as T-shirts as effective forms for advertising and promoting their causes, alongside the more benign proliferation of indigenous-themed fashions of the day. Such concerns have become even more prominent in recent years.

One of the underpinnings of the classification of Australiana motifs in textiles and fashion is the form these take, in particular, whether exotic references and inspirations take the form of surface (2-D or two-dimensional) representations and translations of depictions of Australian-ness, for example, in textiles or as surface decoration on T-shirts or jumpers; as opposed to molded forms (3-D or three-dimensional) which involve the manipulation of shape, contours, and construction, for example, in creating silhouettes and embellishing the body–clothes relationship through how a garment fits on the human form. While 2-D examples of Australiana fashion have been treated as artwork—akin to paintings—3-D Australiana fashion tends to be classified as craft, decorative art, or high-end design creations. Equally, 2-D Australiana is generally more suited to the mainstream fashion (mid to low) as well as the tourist market. This is what fashion designer Roopa Pemmaraju describes as the "cliché of Aboriginal art being limited to 'dot paintings or cheap $2 merchandise'" (quoted by Sutton 2013).

Australian fashion designers using exotic inspirations

In the contemporary fashion context, a number of designers have been playing with exotic inspirations in their designs. However, there are a number of different sources of exotica and different cultural identifications of designers incorporating exotic motifs. In particular, indigenous-inspired fashion is developing a sophisticated visual language and interplay between 2-D and 3-D forms.

Table 1: Typology of exotic inspirations for Australian fashion designers

Ethnicity of designer	Source of inspiration	Mode of production
Non-Australian	Culture of origin Australian design icons	Customized niche clientele High-end artisans Couture market
Australian non-indigenous	Global cultural exotica	Collaborations with non-Australian textile artisans High-end market
Non-Australian	Australian indigenous artworks	Collaborations with Australian indigenous communities and artists Textile and garment production by non-Australian artisans Mid-market
Australian non-indigenous and indigenous	Australian indigenous exotica and culture	Collaborative "fusion" design Australian business model Collaborations between indigenous and non-indigenous production Niche "eco" market
Australian non-indigenous	Global cultural exotica, Australiana, and popular culture references	Collaborations Niche fashion-forward clientele Fashion-art fusion

Drawing on the above typology, examples of these designers can be distinguished and contrasted as follows.

Non-Australian inspired by another culture and iconic Australian design inspirations

In many ways, it has been easier for non-Australian designers to find a voice to articulate the spirit of national culture than Australian-born designers. This may be because they remain observers looking on from the fringes at the national obsession with claiming a unique identity. A prominent recent example is Japanese-born, Sydney-based fashion designer Akira Isogawa who has achieved recognition of excellence both in Australia and abroad. Migrating to Australia in his 20s, Akira's' grounding in Japanese culture created an interesting fusion with the prevailing Australian cultural zeitgeist of the 1980s. According to Parkes:

> His design is informed by a multicultural background and a respectful inter-action with other cultures; he seeks the approval of Europe, but is conscious of nurturing the local market; he remains obsessed with the quality of crafts-manship and materials used in his work; he is not constrained by the limits of his field (designing rugs, homewares, costumes for dance etc), and is a committed collaborator; and he has embraced iconic elements of Australian identity within his work. (Parkes 2006: 21)

Akira's design inspiration has been shaped by his nuanced understanding of traditional Japanese costume and textiles, adapted for a relaxed Australian aesthetic in order to produce exquisitely crafted clothes that are also wearable. The designer's long-standing success rests on his ability to subtly combine his Japanese cultural heritage and symbolism with a deep understanding of Australian aesthetics and cultural heritage, which, as a migrant, he sees with new eyes. However, his cultural references are not confined to merely Japan and Australia, instead drawing widely on other cultural references and motifs from the arts and crafts of Asia, and elsewhere. He seeks out handcrafted textiles, and employs specialist craft artisans to produce textiles, as well as to embellish surfaces through beading, embroidery, and smocking. The results are stunning combinations of exquisitely chosen textiles and embellishments from different cultural traditions and forms (from commissioned silks to home furnishing fabrics) to create garments that embody a blend of multicultural references in sophisticated and elaborate yet wearable garments (www.akira.com.au).

Collaborations and close working relationships are central to the designer's production process. His aim is to make garments that are "timeless," yet individual. The result is complex constructions (often incorporating origami-folding techniques) that make innovative use of textiles, and feature detailed finishes in natural fabrics. According to Akira: "The designs are quite specific, but in that way they are timeless and quite individual" (quoted by Oakley Smith

2010a: 18). His work has featured in a number of exhibitions, notably solo shows at the National Gallery of Victoria, in 2005, and Object Gallery, in Sydney, in 2001.

Collaborations with global artisans

In contrast to Australian designers who rely on Australia-specific inspirations or alternatively eschew that for an "international" or global source of inspiration, the label Easton Pearson draws on multiple exotic references that are interpreted in a specifically Australian design context. Like Akira, Easton Pearson shows in Paris, as well as in Australia.

Friends Pamela Easton and Lydia Pearson established the label in Brisbane, in 1989, capitalizing on their close proximity to Asia to draw on "a melange of Asia Pacific cultures through a manifestation of techniques and fabrics and the relationships built through commerce" (Oakley Smith 2010b: 111). By extensive travel and collaboration with artisans, Easton Pearson focuses on custom-designed textiles as the source of inspiration exhibiting color and embellishment. As the designers explain:

> There is a very artisanal feel to the clothes we make. It's about decoration, color and interesting construction. And we design with a lot of different "someones" in mind [...] It seems that the people attracted [to the clothing] are those that can make it their own (Oakley Smith 2010b: 113).

Through the combination of commissioned textiles and collaborative hand-craft finishes via long-standing partnerships with Indian craftspeople, Easton Pearson has achieved acclaim in the fashion industry and recognition. Tony Ellwood, director of the Queensland Art Gallery, says that their 2009 exhibition at the Gallery of Modern Art in Brisbane (Wallace, McNeil and Teliga 2009) highlighted:

> their sourcing and production of ideas and sources, from the history of art and dress, literature, film, books and music, that distinguishes much of their work. Art museums world-wide [now] consider fashion design a part of a contemporary visual culture. (Tony Ellwood, director, Queensland Art Gallery, quoted in GOMA 2009)

Indigenous inspirations in Western fashion design

Another non-Australian designer who has had an impact is Roopa Pemmaraju, who came to Australia from India in 2007 with her engineer husband. Trained in fine arts, and with considerable experience as a fashion designer in her native Bengalaru (Bangalore), as well as having a mother who owns an apparel production factory, Pemmaraju was well placed to take advantage of her skills and connections when she entered the Australian fashion industry. Captivated by the vibrancy of Aboriginal art, she sought to collaborate with an Aboriginal art collective to work on creating textiles based on Aboriginal designs that could then be styled as ready-to-wear fashion for the mainstream market. After receiving a number of rejections, the Warlukurlangu Artists Aboriginal Corporation in Yuendumu (in central Australia) agreed to cooperate with the designer. The first collection was launched to acclaim in 2012, and was bought by department store David Jones.

Pemmaraju selects the designs for textiles that are manufactured using a variety of traditional craft-based processes utilized by her mother's factory. Skilled artisans produce the silk garments and embellish the clothes with delicate hand finishes. Pemmaraju's collections are now a staple of fashion shows, and also stocked by Australian department store Myer, as well as sold through various stockists and online.

The hallmark of Pemmaraju's label is the recognition of synergies between the traditions of Indian artisans and Aboriginal artists, while ensuring fair trade and sustainable protocols in her dealings with indigenous people. Royalties of 10 percent are paid to the Aboriginal community, and Indian workers are paid considerably higher than in other peer apparel factories (Sutton 2013). Pemmaraju separates the inspirational aspect of her exotic inspiration from the political issues, saying:

I love Aboriginal art because it's pure, it's natural, it's ethical. I don"t care about the politics. I care about the artists, what's their inspiration, what they see around them, what's their tradition. It is the same way I see my artists in India. (Quoted by Breen Burns 2012.)

Creatively, the designer's aim is that: "Dreaming narratives are imbued with themes of cultural memory, voyage and ancestry and challenge traditional perspectives on Aboriginal art" (quoted by Sutton 2013). Each garment has a tag attached to it that tells the concept and story associated with it:

The connection with Aboriginal art seems to have been a tactic of assimi-lation. Fashion has allowed her to weave two cultures into one; the intricate patterns of Aboriginal artists manufactured with the careful skill of Indian craftsmen. (Brient 2013)

According to Pemmaraju, the artists and artisans in both communities are pleased with the collaboration because it enables them "to engage with the wider world" via "a positive interaction with the rest of the world" (Cecilia Alfonso, Warlukurlangu manager, quoted by Brient 2013). Despite her success and high profile, Pemmaraju has had difficulty establishing a viable business model. Although stocked by major department stores as high-end fashion, sales of her designs have flagged, and the costs of maintaining collaborations, and of design, manufacturing, and distribution have not proved viable. Pemmaraju has sought partnerships with start-up creative entities to develop the concept behind the brand.

Figure 5.1 AKIN Collection 2012 collaborative fashion project: Top designed by Shea Cameron; pants designed by Georgia Grainger; textiles designed by Napoleon Oui; photography by Michael Greves. Courtesy of QUT Creative Enterprise Australia.

Australian indigenous and non-indigenous collaboration in design, production, promotion, and distribution

The AKIN collaboration is, in some ways, a continuation of the collaborations of Jenny Kee and Linda Jackson with Aboriginal communities and artists. In this case, the Creative Enterprise initiative of the Queensland University of Technology paired five indigenous artists[2] with five emerging fashion designers[3] through KickArts in Cairns (McBrierty 2013). The aim was to produce a catwalk collection from which to develop business models to take the collaborations further and ignite "an ongoing platform for indigenous artists and the Australian design community to work together" (Arts Queensland and Brisbane City Council 2013). The project grew out of concerns about previous use of Aboriginal motifs in fashion:

> There is a history of indigenous artists in Australia being treated unethically; by misappropriation and misrepresentation of their work, inequity of payment for their creativity and little acknowledgement of their cultural contribution to collaborative fashion products sold globally. This has created an atmosphere of bad press for fashion, as well as a fear for emerging designers to include/collaborate with indigenous artists for textile prints. (McMahon, Morley, and Macnee 2012)

The result has been that many designers have looked outside Australia for sources of inspiration such that collaborations with indigenous designers and communities outside Australia have been easier and more successful. Not only does this undermine the potential for Australian indigenous fashion to "brand a truly unique Australian label in the international marketplace," where fashion labels have engaged in collaborations, this has generally involved adapting "indigenous prints, for collections that have little acknowledgement of the artist's contribution and strong branding for the label and/or fashion designer." (McMahon, Morley, and Macnee 2012)

In order to redress this situation, the AKIN project sought to create an overarching brand that presented the collective work of the designers and in which each received equal payment and recognition. As part of the process of designing a collection, participants were trained in supply chain logistics, costing, time management, collection "ranging," and textile-printing processes. The outcomes were well received by the media and public, and have produced "an ethical template for other indigenous artists and emerging designers to create fashion collections that offer a unique aesthetic that could position and brand Australian fashion in the international marketplace" (McMahon, Morley, and Macnee 2012).

The result was a collection of distinctive fabrics featuring indigenous-inspired prints which could mix and match in outfits that combined "classic tailoring techniques and loose form silhouettes" with the resulting collection being

Figure 5.2 AKIN Collection 2012 collaborative fashion project: Top and pants designed by Shea Cameron, and textiles by Tommy Pau; coat and visor designed by Monique White, and textiles by Arone Meeks; photography by Michael Greves. Courtesy of QUT Creative Enterprise Australia.

"wearable, functional and full of modern Australian heritage" (McBrierty 2013). The AKIN collection became a centerpiece of the inaugural Australian indigenous Fashion Week, in 2014, and it was subsequently invited to show in a fashion event in Indonesia. The result has been judged as successful and as "an equal exchange between indigenous artists and Non-indigenous designers" (Arts Queensland and Brisbane City Council 2013).

Figure 5.3 AKIN Collection 2012 collaborative fashion project: Shirt, shorts, and scarf designed by Hayley Elsaesser; textiles designed by Sharon Phineasa; photography by Michael Greves. Courtesy of QUT Creative Enterprise Australia.

Australian non-indigenous designers inspired by global exotic and popular culture references using diverse collaborations with artists, designers, and cultural workers

The final example is the label Romance Was Born, a collaboration between Anna Plunkett and Luke Sales. In some ways, this is both a return to the heady Australiana days of the 1980s and also a new level of combining indigenous with a kaleidoscope of other cultural exotica and inspirations (English and Pomazan 2010; Romance Was Born 2014). Launched in 2005, the designers have been inspired to push the boundaries of fashion by creating vivid and outlandish theatrical pieces for collections, which have been launched in spectacular promotional shows and installations.

These non-indigenous Australian designers are inspired by a myriad of cultural references, motifs, images, and icons including a strong connection with kitsch Australiana. By the use of craft techniques ranging from the simple to the complex, and intrigued by the theatricality of costume, Romance Was Born collaborates with artists, singers, designers, and celebrities to produce distinctive one-off pieces that are outlandish yet wearable:

> We like to think Romance Was Born has its own style or signature, with its own prints and cuts and shapes, and sometimes people find it hard to translate this when buying in a shop. (Quoted by M. Oakley Smith 2010: 274)

Although a niche label, by aligning themselves with the art world and performance events, the label has attracted national and international acclaim being included in diverse exhibitions, winning awards and being stocked in Australian and overseas fashion outlets. In 2014, they were commissioned to produce the children's program to accompany the Jean-Paul Gaultier Exhibition at the National Gallery of Victoria (Story and Harvey 2014). In an earlier collaboration with fashion guru Jenny Kee and textile maverick Linda Jackson, the cultural currents of the 1980s fused with the spirit of the 2010s to create an invigorated revival of cultural Australiana and a projection of yet another phase of national cultural identity.

Australian indigenous Fashion Week 2014

Recognition that Australian indigenous fashion design has reached a new plateau came with the staging of the first Australian indigenous Fashion Week (AIFW), in Sydney, in April 2014. Although there had been indigenous designs and designers represented in previous fashion weeks and events, this was the first dedicated fashion event specifically to showcase an emerging generation of indigenous Aboriginal textile and fashion designers as well as models. The event was a signal that the fashion world was acknowledging the rich cultural and creative potential as inspiration for fashion design. As one commentator reflected:

> Australia's indigenous people are synonymous with a rich cultural palette that is both elusive and enchanting. Their intensely spiritual stories of the Dreamtime, vibrant music and eclectic artistry, pay homage to the world's oldest enduring culture [...] However, when it comes to that small, cultural signature we call fashion, far less is known about the native flare of Aboriginal Australians. But that is about to change. (Willis 2012)

This was a new chapter in indigenous design. Indigenous motifs have recurred in Australian design historically and contemporaneously, most notably in the Balarinji-designs painted on Qantas planes in the 2000s, and the recent reinvention of the craft of making possum skin cloaks, which have become a feature of Aboriginal elders during the openings of sporting and parliamentary opening ceremonies. However, these have been exceptions and symbols of indigenous identity rather than as part of the grammar of Australian design more generically: "What is more difficult is determining the nature of the relationship between contemporary indigenous designers and the design world at large" (Cook 2014). Russell Cook argues that the Bauhaus heritage in design practice marginalized Aboriginal design to the point where it "is hardly ever referred to as such, and is often dismissed as craft or art" (Cook 2014).

The advent of AIFW has been welcomed as an important step in the recognition of the legitimacy of contemporary Aboriginal design as a legitimate art form and creative practice alongside its inclusion in the "art world" as paintings, ceramics, and textiles:

> The recent shift in the fashion world towards supporting contemporary Aboriginal designers is a powerful step in the right direction. AIFW will further raise the profile of Aboriginal designers and Aboriginal fashion models—not as a cultural curio but as engaged with design and fashion as anyone else working in the industry.

> What was until now seen as a customary creative practice can today be accepted as a dynamic modern fashion movement. (Cook 2014)

Under the tagline, "It's not just dots," AIFW showcase the designs of established and recent designers and labels including Desert Designs (and Jimmy

Pike), Grace Lee (sophisticated silhouettes with indigenous-inspired fabrics), Mia Brennan (Mimi Designs featuring silk and leather dresses in indigenous-inspired fabrics), Lucy Simpson (Gaawaa Miyay Designs creating textiles and fashion), Shaun Edwards (Wild Barra swimwear, shorts and T-shirts), Letticia Shaw (Ticia label), Lyn-Al Young (silk sheaths and leather harnesses), and the AKIN collection (Behrendt 2014). The resulting show presented a:

> smorgasbord of styles reflect[ing] the diversity of indigenous cultures across Australia. Indigenous design and handicrafts inspired bold prints, chunky knotted and woven fabrics, carved and painted soft leathers and references to the *dhari*, the striking ceremonial headdresses of the Torres Strait Islands. (Behrendt 2014)

The best known of the designers was Desert Designs, a collaboration between non-indigenous design teachers Steve Culley and David Wroth, and Aboriginal prisoner and artist Jimmy Pike (Wells 2011). Established in the 1980s, it has become a fixture in embodying the mainstream fashion and interior design possibilities of indigenous inspiration by translating artworks into textiles for fashion, accessories, and interior design (such as carpets and rugs). The inspiration has been the interpretation of the culture and visuals of landscape in vibrant colors which have been commercialized to provide economic return to Pike and other collaborators.

The brand has recently been revitalized by a new generation of directors (notably Jedda-Daisy Culley and Caroline Sundt-Wells) and a group of Aboriginal artists with new licensing agreements (Chandra 2013). The success of the label has stemmed from the strength of the artwork: "Jimmy Pike's designs were vivid, dynamic and ground-breaking in their use of non-traditional colors" (quoted in Wells 2011). The collection shown at AIFW was perhaps the most outstanding show revealing the depth of inspiration that this label had achieved. Overall, the event was judged a success.

The aim of the AIFW was to take indigenous fashion from a "cottage" industry to the "next phase" of mainstream fashion by mentoring emerging indigenous fashion designers and introducing them to the mainstream industry and its business practices with the aim of taking "one step closer to a moment when indigenous fashion is a central element of Australian style" (Behrendt 2014). It is now expected to become an annual fixture depending on sponsorship.

Reactions to AIFW were generally positive, although fashion retail experts cautioned that indigenous artworks as the basis of design was not sufficient to create marketable fashion garments. Rather, designs also had to offer consumers something distinctively different in terms of fashion language. As David Bush, former GM of David Jones, commented: "There's plenty of lovely art, but art doesn't necessarily translate into fashion" (quoted by Lobban 2014).

Spelling out what this meant, fashion cognoscenti Nancy Pilcher, former VP at Condé Nast (Asia Pacific), reflected:

> "From my perspective, I think the print is one thing but the design is vital [...] There's no doubt the prints are amazing, but if it's done in a way that doesn"t suit the fashion trends, no one is going to buy it [...] There is a future here. There is a story and the Indigenous know how to tell a story through their art [...] There has to be a plan to take it forward. These Indigenous designers have to be guided. It has to be fashionable. It needs to have the edge that makes it interesting for the global fashion world." (Quoted by Lobban 2014)

Nonetheless, the consensus was that the event succeeded in creating a new and distinctive design language for indigenous fashion. As founder of AIFW Krystal Perkins put it, the catwalk collections combined traditional story telling with indigenous skills to create fashion garments with a strong emphasis on sustainability of culture and fashion. Although the event was deemed a success, the AIFW subsequently went into liquidation with significant debts and a repeat fashion week seems unlikely in the near future.

The cultural politics of exotic fashion and inspiration

This chapter has demonstrated that Australian indigenous fashion design has a strong creative potential that challenges dichotomous and linear assumptions about the domain of fashion as exclusively Eurocentric versus "dress" practices in other cultures, times, and places. Instead fashion sensibilities are global as well as being nuanced to simultaneously incorporate global trends while incorporating specific themes, symbols and cultural references that are unique to each locality. Understanding global fashion, therefore, involves unpacking the interplay between the global and the local in the production of multiple and competing fashion systems that exhibit hybridity, cultural borrowing, invention and reinvention.

To begin that process, future researchers need to investigate some key questions that dog the rich state of indigenous fashion design. These include: How should we define innovation in fashion design as compared with revivals and reworkings of previous designs? Where is the dividing line between inspiration and appropriation with regard to the use of indigenous motifs, designs and themes? Why are some indigenous designs regarded as generic symbolism and thus "available" for use as inspiration and manipulation while other motifs and designs are deemed to have specific owners with rights over intellectual property and thus the use of these images? While these issues are specifically related to design protocols and cultural integrity, they are embedded in wider issues of sustainability and ethics. These involve a myriad of complex pressing concerns about the politics of fair trade, ethical and environmentally friendly sourcing and supply chains, strategies of licensing, collaborations, codes of conduct, codes of authenticity, and the outsourcing of specialist skills to subcontracted artisans in developing countries.

Conclusion

This chapter has traced the narratives of Australian culture and national identity through the changing references to, and uses of, exotic motifs and themes in fashion design. It has shown that fashion design is now structured by narratives of relational and transnational fusions that reflect new cultural alignments and assertions. These stem from new cultural politics that underpin deeper issues than just body-clothes relationships in the global fashion wardrobe and, in the case of Australia, have changed the conceptual basis of national identity to place indigenous culture at the heart rather than on the periphery.

Notes

1 A version of this chapter was presented at the 3rd Fashion in Fiction Conference, City University of Hong Kong, Hong Kong, June 12–14, 2014.

2 Arone Meeks, Napoleon Oui, Sharon Phineasa, Tommy Pau and Margaret Mara.

3 Monique White, Georgia Grainger, Hayley Elsaesser, Shea Cameron and Samantha Delgos.

References

Arts Queensland and Brisbane City Council. "The AKIN Collection," *The Fashion Archives*, October 22, 2013. Available online at: http://thefashionarchives. org/?pieced_together=akin (accessed 5 February 2015).

Australia Government (2008). "Australian National Dress." Available online at: http:// australia.gov.au/about-australia/australian-story/austn-national-dress (accessed 30 August 2014).

Australian Indigenous Fashion Week (2014) http://www.aifw.com.au/ (accessed 30 September 2014).

Behrendt, L. "Indigenous Fashion Week: Putting the Bush into Boutiques," *The*

Guardian, April 15 2014. Available online at: http://www.theguardian.com/
fashion/2014/apr/15/Indigenous-fashion-week-putting-the-bush-into-boutiques
(accessed 4 September 2014).

Berry, J. "A Uniform Approach? Designing Australian National Identity At The Sydney
2000 Olympic Games," *Journal of Design History*, 26 (1) (2012): 86–103.

Berry, J. "Relational Style: Craft As Social Identity In Australian Fashion." *Craft + Design
Enquiry*, 5 (2013): 49, Available online at: http://craftdesignenquiry.blogspot.com.
au/2013/05/relational-style-craft-as-social.html (accessed 30 September 2014).

Breen Burns, J. "Colour That's Hard To Ignore," *The Age*, July 21, 2012. Available online
at: http://www.theage.com.au/action/printArticle?id=3470536 (accessed 30 August
2014).

Brient, T. "Roopa Pemmaraju: Outback Fashion Aesthetic Using Indigenous Australian
Art," *Issimo Magazine*, November 20, 2013. Available onine at: http://www.
issimomag.com/2013/11/20/roopa-pemmaraju-outback-fashion-aesthetic-using-
Indigenous-australian-art/ (accessed 15 September 2014).

Chandra, S. "Desert Designs' Dream Time," *Broadsheet Melbourne*, July 24, 2013.
Available online at: http://www.broadsheet.com.au/melbourne/fashion/article/desert-
designs-dream-time (accessed 15 September 2014).

Clements, K. "The Kind Of Magazine Cover Australia Barely Ever Sees," *Mamamia*,
April 16 2014. Available online at: http://www.mamamia.com.au/style/australian-
Indigenous-fashion-week/ (accessed 18 April 2014).

Craik, J. "Exotic Impulses in Fashion." In *The Face of Fashion*. London: Routledge,
1994.

Craik, J. "Is Australian Fashion Distinctively Australian?," *Fashion Theory*, 13 (4) (2009):
409–42.

Craik, J. "From Iconography To Inspiration: Australian Indigenous References In
Contemporary Fashion." In *Communicating Transcultural Fashion*, edited by A.
Peirson-Smith, J. Hancock, and V. Karaminas. Bristol: Intellect Publishing (in press).

English, B., and L. Pomazan. "Contemporary avant-garde: Cutting Edge Design."
In *Australian Fashion Unstitched*, eds B. English and L. Pomazan. Melbourne:
Cambridge University Press, 2010.

Gallery of Modern Art. "Easton Pearson, 22 August—8 November 2009, Brisbane."
Exhibition Media Kit. Brisbane: Gallery of Modern Art/Queensland Art Gallery, 2009.

Gray, S. (2010) "The Australiana Phenomenon In Australia," In *Encyclopedia of World
Dress and Fashion, Volume 7: Australia, New Zealand and the Pacific Islands*, ed.
M. Maynard. Oxford and New York: Berg, 2010.

Gray, S. "Relational Craft And Australian Fashionability In The 1970s–80s: Friends,
Pathways, Ideas And Aesthetics." *Craft + Enquiry*, 4 (2012). Available online at:
http://press.anu.edu.au/apps/bookworm/view/craft+%2B+design+enquiry%3B+
issue+4,+2012/10031/ch01.html (accessed 30 September 2014).

Healy, R. "Making Noise: Contemporary Australian Fashion Design." In *Freestyle: New
Australian Design for Living*, ed. B. Parkes. Sydney: Object: Australian Centre for
Craft and Design/Melbourne: Melbourne Museum, 2006.

Leong, R., and K. Somerville. "Beyond The Boundaries: Australian Fashion from
the 1960s to the 1980s." In *Australian Fashion Unstitched*, ed. B. English and
L. Pomazan. Melbourne: Cambridge University Press, 2010.

Lobban, J. "As Industry Craves Authenticity, Aboriginal Fashion
Week Takes Flight," *Business of Fashion*, April 15, 2014.
Available online at: http://www.businessoffashion.com/2014/04/

industry-craves-authenticity-aboriginal-fashion-week-takes-flight.htm (accessed 20 April 2014).

Maynard, M. "Grassroots Style: Re-Evaluating Australian Fashion and Aboriginal Art in the 70s & 80s." *Journal of Design History*, 13(2) (2000): 137–50.

Maynard, M. *Out of Line. Australian Women and Style*. 1st ed. Sydney: UNSW Press, 2001.

Maynard, M. "The Red Centre: The Quest For 'Authenticity' In Australian Dress," *Fashion Theory*, 3(2) (2012): 175–96.

McBrierty, G. "AKIN Available To Order at The Fleet Store," (2013). Available online at: http://www.creativeenterprise.com.au/fashion/articles/AKIN-available-to-order-at-the-fleet-store (accessed 20 April 2014).

McMahon, K., J. Morley, and C. Macnee. "Akin Collection: Curation Of A Collaboration Between Indigenous Artists And Fashion Designers To Create A Retail-Ready Luxury Fashion Label," (2012). Available online at: exhibition/event, http://eprints.qut.edu.au/55431/ (accessed 20 April 2014).

Oakley Smith, M. "Akira. Akira Isogawa," In *Fashion Australian & New Zealand Designers*. Fisherman's Bend, Victoria: Thames and Hudson, 2010a.

Oakley Smith, M. "Easton Pearson. Pamela Easton and Lydia Pearson," In *Fashion Australian & New Zealand Designers*. Fisherman's Bend, Victoria: Thames and Hudson: 2010b.

Oakley Smith, M. "Romance was Born. Anna Plunkett and Luke Sales." In *Fashion Australian & New Zealand Designers*. Fisherman's Bend, Victoria: Thames and Hudson, 2010c.

Oakley Smith, M. *Fashion Australian & New Zealand Designers*. Fisherman's Bend, Victoria: Thames and Hudson, 2010d.

Ongley, Hannah. "Australian Indigenous Fashion Week Isn't Just Pretty Prints," *The Fashion Spot*, April 18 2014. Available online at: http://www.thefashionspot.com.au/tag/australian-Indigenous-fashion-week/ (accessed 20 April 2014).

Parkes, B. "Foreword." In *Freestyle: New Australian Design for Living*, ed. B. Parkes. Sydney: Object, Australian Centre for Craft and Design/Melbourne, Melbourne Museum, 2006.

Pemmaraju, R. "Our Community, Our World," (2014). Available online at designer's website:, http://roopapemmaraju.com/pages/ethos (accessed 30 April 2014).

QUT. "Indigenous Artists Take On High Fashion," *Media Release*, October 4, 2012. Available online at: http://eprints.qut.edu.au/55431/57/Indigenous_artists_take_on_high_fashion32_copy.pdf (accessed 20 April 2014).

Romance was Born. "About," (2014). Available online at: http://romancewasborn.com/about (accessed 13 September 2014).

Russell Cook, M. "A Hot New Model At The Inaugural Australian Indigenous Fashion Week," *The Conversation*, April 10, 2014, Available online at: http://theconversation.com/a-hot-new-model-at-the-australian-Indigenous-fashion-week-25389 (accessed 15 April 2014).

Storey, R., and N. Harvey. "Romance Was Born Rejects Fashion Week To Create Kaleidoscopic Exhibition With Rebecca Baumann," ABC Arts, *Australian Broadcasting Corporation*, April 10, 2014. Available online at: http://www.abc.net.au/arts/blog/Video/Romance-Was-Born-rejects-Fashion-Week-to-create-kaleidoscopic-exhibition-with-Rebecca-Baumann–140408/default.htm (accessed 11 April 2014).

Sutton, A. "The Reverent World Of Roopa Pemmaraju," *Broadsheet Melbourne*, October 2, 2013. Available online at: http://www.broadsheet.com.au/melbourne/fashion/article/reverent-world-roopa-pemmaraju (accessed 15 April 2014).

Wallace, M., P. McNeil, and J. Teliga. *Easton Pearson*. Brisbane: Queensland Art Gallery, 2009.

Wells, K. "Jimmy Pike and Desert Designs in Ningbo," *Craft Australia*, March 2011. Available online at: http://www.craftaustralia.org.au/library/review.php?id=jimmy_pike_desert_designs (accessed 20 April 2014).

Williamson, L. "Interlaced: Textiles for Fashion." In *Australian Fashion Unstitched*, ed. B. English and L. Pomazan. Melbourne: Cambridge University Press, 2010.

Willis, L. "Native Flare." *The Genteel*, September 2012. Available online at: http://www.thegenteel.com/articles/society/native-flare (accessed 20 April 2014).

PART III

SELF-ORIENTALISM OR NATION BRANDING?

OTTOMAN COSTUME IN THE CONTEXT OF MODERN TURKISH FASHION DESIGN[1]

ŞAKIR ÖZÜDOĞRU

Introduction

In the context of early globalization theory, it has been argued that the spread of European fashion on a large scale would result in the disappearance of so-called non-Western fashions. Within the Eurocentric discourse in fashion studies, clothing styles outside of Europe have been depicted as static and traditional, as opposed to dynamic and modern European fashion. However, Turkish fashion designers have been successfully using their cultural heritage (traditions) as a source of inspiration to create distinctive design identities. On the one hand, in a globalized world, it allows them to differentiate themselves on the highly competitive international fashion market, while on the other hand, on a national level, it makes them successful as a result of a general revaluation of local cultural heritage as a counter reaction to cultural globalization. Therefore, this case study meets the general theme of this volume in that globalization is not leading to cultural homogenization, but, on the contrary, stimulates cultural heterogenization through the (re)invention of, and emphasis on, local cultural heritage and vestimentary traditions as a powerful means of distinction.

Following a number of state development plans initiated by the Turkish government in the 1960s and 1970s, Turkey became an important manufacturing center for European and North-American confection companies; production was cheap and of high quality. Additionally, in the 1980s, the rapid spread of a liberal economy in Turkey made it possible for the country to compete in the international market. As a result of the Customs Union Agreements with the European Union in the 1990s, textile and clothing export expanded, but this growth required more effort in order to be competitive. On the one hand, Turkey had to compete with low-cost contract manufacturer countries, such as China and India and on the other hand, the country was up against developed countries like Italy, France, and England, which were strong on design, while using the Third World for their production. Therefore, Turkish companies which aspired to become international, could no longer solemnly focus on production, but rather had to transform themselves into innovative and creative design enterprises. As such, Turkish companies and their fashion designers started to turn to local cultural heritage for inspiration in order to create a distinctive design identity that was able to stand out, and differentiate itself in the international market. This cultural heritage helped them to establish a design authenticity that would play a central role in their branding strategies abroad. Not only did the legacy of the Ottoman Empire have a strong reputation abroad, but also its richness enabled a large variety of styles and identities.

From that moment on, Turkish fashion designers began to develop collections that merged European fashion aesthetics with Ottoman clothing elements. These collections became collages of European fashion and Ottoman traditions and varied from Ottoman decorations, produced with modernized techniques, to pieces of traditional Ottoman clothing, adapted to European silhouettes. The main aim of this chapter is to examine how contemporary Turkish fashion designers have been incorporating Ottoman cultural heritage in their designs, and particularly how this heritage is being used in a self-Orientalist manner as a promotional tool to gain recognition on the international fashion scene. In this chapter, four contemporary Turkish designers' collections and discourses are analyzed in order to demonstrate how they position themselves on the international fashion scene through the eyes of outsiders. At this stage, it is important to underline that all of the fashion designers discussed received their fashion training in Europe, and/or are trained in European fashion design, and that their primary aim has been to become successful in Europe and/or in the United States besides Turkey. Cemil İpekçi, who was trained at the Royal Academy of Arts in London, for example, is well-known for both his "ethnic designs" and haute couture dresses, and has his own couture house in İstanbul. Atıl Kutoğlu is one of the most influential fashion designers on the Turkish fashion scene, while also being successful in Austria, where he presented his work initially. He opened his first flagship store, which is especially successful among middle- and upper-class Turks, in Turkey, in 2009. Nedret Taciroğlu, who specialises in haute couture, has designed two lines, the "Nedo Collection" and "Nedret Taciroğlu Collection" for the Turkish market. Dilek Hanif, in her turn, was the first Turkish fashion designer to have presented during the official Paris Haute Couture Week in 2004. She created the ready-to-wear brand "Dilek Hanif" in Turkey in

2011, and has collaborated with various international brands since. This chapter focuses on these four Turkish fashion designers and their design approaches.

A brief history of Ottoman costume

Anatolia, which hosted various small and large civilizations from the prehistoric ages to the present, has been the motherland of the Turks since 1071. In 1299, the Turks established the Ottoman Empire, the boundaries of which covered three continents. These boundaries comprised a cultural mosaic of diverse ethnicities, religious beliefs, and traditions, resulting in a hybrid cultural identity over time. Interestingly, this cultural mosaic entailed both the so-called "East" and "West," and both seemingly opposing cultural traditions blended in Ottoman's rich vestimentary heritage. But, between 1876 and 1922, the Ottoman Empire, during the Reformation Period (not to be confused with the European Reformation), turned more to Europe in terms of both culture and politics, and European fashion came to influence Ottoman clothing particularly during this time. After the collapse of the Empire in 1923, the Turkish Republic was established, and characteristic Ottoman garments like the *fez* and the black chador were banned because of their notoriety as symbols of reactionism and conventionalism. Wearing this apparel in public was forbidden, while European fashion, as a symbol of cultural modernization and secularism, came to dominate the public sphere.

Throughout the history of the Turks, it can be noted that there have not been significant transformations in dress until the introduction of Islam in the eleventh century. Until then, Turkish clothing consisted of nearly the same garments for both men and women (Barbarosoğlu 2009: 97), namely a type of long shirt and loose trousers. Both men and women wore a waistcoat over their shirt, as well as a belt and a headpiece. They also wore a *caftan,* a long T-shaped garment with long sleeves, a round collar, and open in the front, and shoes or sandals. The most significant transformation in Turkish clothing with the introduction of Islam was that women adopted a *yaşmak*, a two-pieced-headscarf (Sezer Arığ 2007: 9), but for the most part the garments remained nearly the same until the Reformation Period in the nineteenth century.[2]

Later, Ottoman clothing changed slowly through interaction with Europe. According to Muhaddere Taşçıoğlu (1958: 21–5), the first appearance of a European-style gown in the Ottoman Palace was in the sixteenth century, during the period of Süleyman the Magnificent. After this period, differences between women's and men's wear developed, and many styles were banned for women in public places. The acclaimed historian Cemal Kafadar (1993: 256–8) states that in local and foreign art works representing the Ottomans in the sixteenth century, a long and loose topcoat, a two-pieced-headpiece, and a face-covering material can be seen. In the early years of the Ottoman Empire, between the fourteenth and eighteenth century, the social life of women was confined predominantly to the private domain. They only had access to public life in the company of their husbands or close male relatives. In the eighteenth century, women enjoyed a period of emancipation, and gained access to public places, which resulted in a transformation of their clothing from a veiling instrument to a form of adornment. For example, the two-pieced-headscarf, mentioned above, was now made from a thin see-through fabric, ornamented with gems. Also, long, loose topcoats became fitted to the body and their collars were expanded. Additionally, a new kind of topcoat that clearly showed the lines of the body was introduced, but these were banned by the Sultan's imperial order (Taşçıoğlu 1958: 52–4).

By the eighteenth century, lost wars and territories necessitated some transformations in the state structure of the Ottoman Empire, and, in the last decades of the eighteenth century, ideas of modernization from Europe were implemented, and Ottomans started to adopt European fashion. Aspects of euromodernity were first introduced in the army, with Selim III completely reorganizing the army according to European standards. In addition, he separated the realms of education, law, and politics.

In the beginning of the nineteenth century, ambitions of euromodernity were expanded and especially under the reign of Mahmut II, many reforms and regulations were introduced. New schools for medicine, military education, and music were opened, and Mahmut II introduced new clothing regulations that were inspired by Europe. For example, a European style jacket and trousers were introduced in the army, and the sultan banned the male Ottoman headdress, which strongly referenced Islam, replacing it instead with the male headpiece called *fez*. According to Ayten Sezer Arığ (2007: 23), these regulations became equally imposed on the civil population, whereby the frock and religious headdresses were only allowed for religious men, while wearing a *fez* became mandatory for all male civilians. In this period, European fashion was also increasingly adopted by women, but exclusively by members of the palace.

After the declaration of reforms in 1839, European fashion became more widespread and progressively mixed with local fashion. It was increasingly introduced and promoted by magazines and tailors and by now adopted widely by Ottoman women, especially in İstanbul. Adopting all the latest fashion trends from Europe, including hairstyles, women would adorn them with characteristic Ottoman silver thread decorations. A garment that became characteristic for the Reformation Period is the *istanbulin*, which was worn by officers. Although the frock coat had become the official attire for civil servants during this time, some older men did not feel comfortable wearing a starched shirt, collar, and tie; these clothing items also made it difficult to perform religious necessities, such as *abdest* and *namaz*. Thus, the *istanbulin*, an Ottoman version of the frock coat, was introduced. Since the chest of the *istanbulin* was totally enclosed, the tie and the starched cuffs became unnecessary (Özer 2006: 329).

The Ottomans were not only affected by fashion trends from Europe, however; they also adopted fashion trends from the East. For instance, the *fez* came from Morocco, while the characteristic black outer garment for women, the chador, was adopted from the Middle East. Due to the chador's widespread use in public, it transformed, over time, into a hybrid form merging Western and Eastern influences. For example, in the last years of the nineteenth century, it was split into two pieces: a skirt and a gown. Then, the skirt part was shortened and gloves came to cover the arms. The last version of the black chador was a sort of pelerine placed on a tailleur, while a tulle piece covered the wearer's face. An European-style umbrella was added as a fashionable accessory to this outfit. According to Muhaddere Taşçıoğlu (1958: 54), this version of the black chador was more a fashion statement than a means of modest covering. Although still accepted as daily attire for women in the last years of the nineteenth century, by the beginning of the 1920s, the black chador had been banned under the new Republic.

It must be emphasized that the transformations that are mentioned above did not necessarily apply to all of society. Some appeared at different times and places, while others never made it to the rural areas. Conversely, while people living in the palace were usually the first to adopt new fashions, the black chador was never adopted, even though it became widespread among the rest of the population. The palace and privileged classes tended to adopt European fashion first, before it trickled down into the everyday lives of the lower social classes, but new fashions needed considerable time to replace old ones. Thus, while some segments of the population had already adopted European fashion, others continued to wear local fashion.

The Republican period and the modernization of dress

The Republic of Turkey was officially founded on October 29, 1923. Reforms in daily practices were almost immediately introduced, including changes to holiday dates, measurements, the calendar system, the alphabet, and also clothing. The founder of the modern Turkish Republic, Mustafa Kemal Atatürk, gave speeches that emphasized the importance of clothing in the modernization of Turkey. He described the modern Turkish costume as: "low-cut shoe, pants, vest, shirt, tie, jacket and, of course, as a supplement of these, a European style headdress" (Sezer Arığ 2007: 38). After Atatürk's famous speech on hats on August 27, 1925, the wearing of the *fez* was banned, and the wearing of a European-style hat became mandatory by law. Therefore, the hat became a symbol of modernity in the Republic of Turkey (Şeftalici 2004: 4–5). At the same time, the wearing of the black chador by women was banned in the early 1930s, in order to force women to adopt a European lifestyle. Both the banning of the *fez* and black chador, and the imposing of European garments did not go without resistance. For example, women would attach a headscarf to their gown under the chin. This style, called *sarma baş,* was very close to today's veiling style of traditional Muslim women.

During the first years of the Republic, Atatürk himself promoted European fashion among the people by wearing suits, pullovers, vests, coats, penguin suits, tuxedos, and so forth. He always wore appropriate hats with his suits and sported European-style accessories, such as handkerchiefs, walking sticks, and chain watches (Sezer Arığ 2007: 43). Atatürk also educated people in European fashion, and established training institutions because education had a primary role in the adoption of European fashion aesthetics in Turkey. The Girls Art Institute, for example, was founded in 1927, with the aim of manufacturing European style clothes for modern life in Turkey by teaching students European tailoring skills. In addition, Evening Art Schools were established with again the primary subject being clothing (Şeftalici 2004: 15–18).

Further stimulus came, following the 1929 economic depression, which deeply affected the Turkish economy. In order to help the economy, the government decided to support local textile production, while installing radical limitations on imports. In 1933, the Sümerbank was founded with the aim of managing the official factories, improving the industries, establishing art schools, and giving out scholarships. With the establishment of Sümerbank, and the limitations on imports, most of the national textile demand was covered, but at the same time, textile production came totally under state control, as well as clothing manufacturing—from its production to its consumption (İnalcık 2008: 152).

To summarize, in the first decade of the Republic, the introduction of euromodernity was orchestrated meticulously by the state as a social engineering project in every aspect, from its political regime to daily life. During these years, European fashion became a symbol of modernity. While the new government banned local dress, European dress became common attire through both restrictions and education campaigns. Nevertheless, the wearing of European fashion was limited to the Kemalist elites as a symbol of modernity, while it was largely criticized and rejected by the conservatives. This separation became the visual evidence of the political debate between Kemalists and conservatives focused on secularism, which can still be seen through clothes, even today.

Contemporary Turkish fashion designers

Turkish sociologist, Fatma Karabıyık Barbarosoğlu (2009: 144), divides the history of Turkish dress into five main periods. The first stretches from the Huns, which is acknowledged as the first state established by nomadic Turks living in Middle Asia around AD 370, until the adoption of Islam by Turks in the tenth century. She determines the second period as extending from the acceptance of Islam until the early decades of the nineteenth century. The third period begins in the nineteenth century, and ends with the instauration of the new Republic. The fourth period, she describes as going from the instauration of the Republic to the 1960s. Finally, the fifth period is described as going from the 1960s to current day. The history of a large part of the second period and the whole of the third period is also the history of the Ottoman Empire. According to Barbarosoğlu, the period of the Republic is divided into two periods. The first begins with the declaration of the Republic and ends in the 1960s, because in this period the textile sector was the engine of industrialization in Turkey, and most of the textile production was state-controlled, aiming to meet national demand. The second period went from the 1960s to the 1990s and correlates with the superiority of the private sector over state-controlled textile production. Although I agree with this periodization, I think the period from the 1990s until today should be differentiated since in the 1980s, the textile sector focused on importation, and in the 1990s Turkey started to be a significant player in the international market. According to Senem Kozaman Som (2011: 94), in this period, the contract manufacturing-based market approach was transformed into enterprises focusing on branding, and, thus, Turkish firms needed to transform themselves into firms offering novelty and creativity, in order to compete in the international market. The number of Turkish brands known internationally subsequently increased.

Students, who were sent to Europe after the declaration of the Republic to learn European tailoring, returned to Turkey in the 1930s to open the first European tailoring ateliers. They introduced the latest European fashion trends, particularly haute couture. Simultaneously, the textile sector reached an important production capacity by this time, and, thus, Turkey could supply most of its own textiles from 1932 to 1962. Girls Art Institutes organized numerous fashion shows, both in Turkey and in several European countries in the 1950s (Şeftalici 2004: 15–19). In the 1960s, it was particularly the ready-to-wear sector that developed. The period also witnessed an important transition in the country, from a totalitarian regime to a multi-party regime, as well as a liberalization of politics. As a result, private equity in the textile and ready-to-wear sector became larger than the state's.

Due to the prevalence of ready-to-wear, the concept of designer started to emerge. Turkish fashion design can be read as an evolutionary process that began with imitations of European designers in the 1920s, European design, and Turkish production in the 1930s, and the development of Turkish fashion design and production in the 1960s. The concept of fashion designer, however, which implies designing unique and innovative items, did not become widespread until the 1980s. In these years, through the removal of limitations on import, Turkey managed to position itself on the global market due to the expansion of consumption culture in Turkey, whereby foreign companies opened retail shops in the centers of large Turkish cities. Simultaneously, through the Customs Union Agreements, Turkey entered the international market as an important manufacturer. However, an essential factor in aiding Turkey to compete in the international market was the transformation from contract-based manufacturing to offering innovation and creativity. Thus, Turkish firms and fashion designers developed various strategies in order to strengthen their position (Kozaman Som 2010: 95–6). One of the strategies was to modernize characteristic local garments such as the *caftan*, the şalvars, and the *entari*s by designing hybrid styles, merging Western and Eastern clothing traditions. References to elements of Ottoman clothing, and distinctive motifs and colors of Ottoman decorative arts became rich sources of inspiration for Turkish fashion designers. However, reinventing and modernizing Ottoman garments, and creating hybrid designs in an eclectic manner, resulted in diverse ideological, political, and social discussions. Turkey is a hybrid space on the crossroads of East and West, and modernization is an ongoing contradictive process, not only in politics, but also in daily life and clothing. According to Fred Davis (1992: 17), fashion came into existence, as a system drawn upon certain recurrent instabilities in the social identities. Although he makes this statement based on European fashion, the symbolic meaning of clothing in Turkey is a materialization of uncompromising tensions between Eastern and Western influences on Turkish society. Since the first interactions between Old Europe and the Ottoman Empire, westernization has been a controversial topic. There have been endless debates between modernists and conservative thinkers, and the discussion is still very much ongoing today.

Simultaneously, Turkish women's lifestyle magazines were introduced in the last years of the Ottoman Empire, featuring the latest fashion trends in female attire. Here, too, while some people claimed that imitating Europe was damaging local identity and culture, others defended the Europeanization process in all formal and informal institutions, including the army, education, management, and clothing (Barbarosoğlu 2009: 143–60), claiming that westernization had to be introduced in all aspects of life, and not just in technology. According to these supporters, following European fashion trends was a distinctive sign of being modern (Göle 2008: 66). In terms of politics, Georgeon (2006: 11) states that the uniqueness of Turkish modernization comes from the fact that it is a country that has a substantially Muslim population, as well as a secular state. Simultaneously, he emphasizes that a part of the Turkish intellectuals criticizes Atatürk for having caused a break in

Turkish identity, which resulted in an identity crisis. According to Georgeon (2006: 11–12), this discourse is not aimed at defending Islam, but rather at praising tradition. In clothing, this tension resulted in a wide variety of hybrid clothing styles and fashion trends, ranging from Ottoman-inspired European fashion to Islamist consumerism and conservative-liberal clothing styles.

A group of fashion designers has been materializing this tension by merging Ottoman fashion elements with European fashion aesthetics since the 1980s. Of the first generation of Turkish fashion designers, Cemil İpekçi, for example, played an important role because he defended the politics, beliefs, and clothing of the Ottoman Empire through his designs, speeches, and attitudes. He was born in Istanbul, in 1948, and studied textile design at the Royal Academy of Arts in London. After working as a ready-to-wear designer in France between 1972 and 1975, İpekçi went onto establish his own brand, "Tzagne," before returning to Turkey in 1984. He became famous for his references to Eastern influences in his designs, and his collections reflect a wide variety of Seljuk, Ottoman, and Arab influences. Although he is known as an ethnic designer, his collections are generally based on European-style silhouettes, with reference to characteristic Seljuk and Ottoman clothing.

Joanne B. Eicher and Barbara Sumberg (1995: 296) argue that ethnic dress emphasizes group identity, and separates the wearer from others. İpekçi uses elements from various periods of traditional Seljuk and Ottoman craftwork and clothing history in combination with European cuts, offering new designs season after season. For example, in his fashion collection "Seljuk," presented in 1984, he combined Seljuk motifs and decorations with European silhouettes. He applied abstract flower motifs from the artworks of the Seljuk Empire on loose fitting two-pieced suits, tailleurs, and gowns, but instead of respecting the Seljuk's rich color pallet, consisting of claret red, turquoise, green, and purple, he used contrasting black and white. This collection implied the Orient by its decoration, but referenced the Occident by its cuts and colors.

In 2006, İpekçi found inspiration in traditional Turkish ceramics, i.e. çini for his fashion show "Kütahya." The art of ceramics has a long history in Anatolia, but the most impressive objects were produced in the Seljuk and the Ottoman periods. In his 2006 collection, he presented corsets with loose fitting dresses, waists wrapped with sashes, and women's trousers. Tinsels, which are very characteristic components of Ottoman clothing, were used as decoration. Motifs of the typical ceramics were embroidered or painted on the fabrics, emphasizing a hybridization of Eastern and Western elements. By 2000, İpekçi started integrating both Ottoman daily wear, as well as court and *harem* dress in his designs. In his *Harem* collection presented in 2000, for example, he used Ottoman clothing as his inspiration, and the collection was presented in different Turkish cities, including Antalya, İstanbul, and Bursa. Interestingly, he does not only consider the Ottoman Empire as a period of visual opulence, but he also claims that Turkey should take the Ottoman Empire as a model for democracy. According to him, the Ottoman Empire was a democratic state in its own time, and after the declaration of the Republic, the pluralistic social structure of the Ottomans was lost as a consequence of state politics. He auto-identifies himself as Ottoman, and not as Turkish. An example of this is when İpekçi remembers an incident from his days in France:

> When I was in Nice, Grace Kelly opened a music hall that was named after her. At the opening ceremony, there was a recital by a Turkish pianist. I was invited as a protocol member and I was sitting close to the first row. Grace Kelly, Princess Caroline and Stephanie were sitting in the first row. I attended the opening wearing my black şalvar, gown, long black boots and my jacket embroidered with traditional motifs like a marshal. I will never forget how all of them turned and looked at me and when they asked "Monsieur, where are you from?," I answered "I"m an Ottoman" and then I saw that they looked at me in wonder. When you say you are Turkish especially in a Western vesture, they think you are inferior to them." (in Dirlik and Yaman 2011: n.p.)

This statement not only reflects the designer's pride in being an Ottoman, but also a longing for investigating and reintroducing Ottoman traditions. For his fashion collection "Sait Halim Pasha," presented in 2006, he redesigned traditional Seljuk and Ottoman clothes by combining Western and Eastern clothing elements. Blouses, loose fitting dresses, and jackets were combined with *caftans*, şalvars, and sashes. Seljuk and Ottoman decorations, as well as precious stones were used as supplements to the garments. This collection can be read as an investigation of an intermediate-form, a sphere where boundaries between East and West are challenged. Another interesting example from İpekçi is his 2010 collection, named "The Ottomans." This collection directly referenced both daily Ottoman clothes, as well as attire worn by the palace, but represented modern interpretations of them. Men's wear, for example, consisted of *entaris* and şalvars. Paint, in various colors, was sprayed on the clothes randomly like a tableau of action painting, while sashes and military belts were used in harmony. Women's wear consisted of characteristic Ottoman clothes, such as şalvar, *entari*, and *caftan*, but were combined with long dresses, trousers, *bustiers*, and balloon skirts, made of tulle, and decorated with Ottoman motif prints. Another contrast in the collection was the juxtaposition of characteristic men's wear consisting of *caftan*, *entari*, and şalvar with high-waist trousers and a transparent blouse for women. İpekçi keeps the tension between East and West alive in his unique combinations. Regardless of whether these creations are successful, it should be emphasized that his designs represent an inter-zone between the East and the West.

Another Turkish fashion designer, Atıl Kutoğlu, was born in Istanbul, in 1968, and studied in Vienna, where he graduated from the Department of Management.

Although he did not study fashion, he was awarded "the best fashion designer of Austria" in the WOOLMARK competition in 1993. Since 1994, he has been presenting at fashion weeks in Milan, Paris, and New York, and also won the famous "Salzburg Prize." While living in Vienna, he has presented his collections in different countries including New York, Milan, Paris, and İstanbul. Kutoğlu calls his Ottoman-referencing-style "silent luxury," and identifies it as a mixture of architectural and geometric elements in an Oriental style. He stresses that his main inspiration comes from Ottoman and Turkish culture, but translated into modern and contemporary clothes (McLoughlin 2012: n.p.). In 1999, he presented his "Ottoman Collection" in honor of the seventh centenary of the establishment of the Ottoman Empire, in the Yıldız Palace, in İstanbul. Kutoğlu argues that this collection was largely designed for Europe by applying Ottoman patterns and motifs to European-style-clothes. His Ottoman–based inspiration was mostly visible in modernized models of şalvar for men, as well as characteristic patterns and decorations used in minimalistic ways. He says that after the introduction of the modernized şalvar in "The Ottoman Collection," foreign fashion designers also started designing these forms:

> John Galliano and Dolce & Gabbana have also featured the şalvar in their collections. Of course, as a Turkish designer, I think I use the şalvar better. I am a man of this culture and these lands. That's why I reflect these motifs more consciously and with more love in my creations (in Özarslan 2010: n.p.).

In addition, in 1999, Kutoğlu presented a collection in Vienna in support of the earthquake victims in Turkey. In this collection, Ottoman clothes were modernized, and accessories, such as bags and high heels, were used. Nudity was emphasized by the use of wide décolletés, and transparent fabrics in contrast with veiling. In his 2006–7 Autumn/Winter collection, which was presented during the New York Fashion Week, he found inspiration in Mozart's *Il Seraglio* and its relation to the Ottomans. His collection was a mixture of Ottoman motifs and Mozart's baroque period, presenting asymmetrical *caftan*s, draped dresses, printed jackets, and şalvars decorated with prints of Ottoman motifs. The designer's 2006–7 Spring/Summer collection, named "Ottomania," was in the same spirit, including asymmetrical *caftan*s made of silk and chiffon, hooded tops, and long dresses, decorated with Ottoman motifs. "Ottomania" refers to the easy and free spirit of rock 'n' roll, whereby Kutoğlu attempted to convey an American lifestyle mixed with Ottoman clothing.

Kutoğlu is a member of the Turquality project, which was initiated in 2004 to strengthen Turkish firms' competitiveness in the international market, and to create brands that can establish international fame. The project aims to both increase exports by supporting Turkish firms with an international reach, as well as strengthen the image of "Turkish goods" and Turkey, in general (Turquality

2007: n.p.). Kutoğlu has been using inspiration from the Ottoman Empire in his collections since the 1990s, but, unlike İpekçi, his designs have mainly European silhouettes, and the Ottoman elements are only a visual vocabulary. He aspires to be successful in Europe and the United States, and his use of Ottoman inspiration is largely a promotional strategy (Özarslan 2010: n.p.). His fashion show, during the New York Fashion Week, was supported by the Turquality project and, after the "Ottomania" show, Kürşat Tüzmen, the Minister of the State said that it not only promoted Turkish fashion, but also Turkey, in general (Karaağaç 2005: n.p.). Similarly, Kutoğlu stated, after his 2006–7 Autumn/Winter collection show, that he wanted to represent the quality of Turkish design to the whole world (Hürriyet 2006: n.p.). Kutoğlu embodies the strategy of Turquality very well and his collections show how Ottoman heritage can be reinvented and merged with European fashion aesthetics or vice versa (see Figure 6.1).

Figure 6.1 A piece from Atıl Kutoğlu's more recent fashion show, held on March 24, 2014, in İstanbul, Turkey. In this collection, he used printed abstract Ottoman floral motifs on long dresses combined with boleros and jackets. Photograph: Vittorio Zunino Celotto/Getty Images.

Dilek Hanif, who started her fashion career in 1990, presented her fashion collection "Ottoman Fairytale," in 2009, during the Paris Fashion Week. She portrayed the elegance of European women of the 1950s through silk-draped dresses, boleros, waistcoats, and Ottoman decorations; long dresses decorated with handwork strongly contrasted with evening gowns with large décollétes, emphasizing the contradictions that lay behind the clothes. Decorative elements of Ottoman dress were set against the plain and simple cut of European dress, and the nudity of the models strengthened the tension between these two clothing styles. In this collection, Ottoman clothing was merely treated as a visual source embodying the Orientalist point of view from the West. Inspirations coming from Ottoman clothing and combining with European fashion can be traced to Hanif's recent collections. For example, in her couture show, presented during Paris Haute Couture Week in 2012, she showed a stylized caftan, cut in European lines and decorated with tinsel floral motifs (see Figure 6.2).

Figure 6.2 A piece from Dilek Hanif's Haute Couture Show held on January 23, 2012, in Paris, as a part of the Paris Haute Couture Week. In this piece, tinsel floral motifs were applied to a dress that seems to be an intensively stylized caftan. Photograph: Victor Virgile/Getty Images.

The Turkish fashion designer Nedret Tacıroğlu, who started in the 1980s, describes herself as a "fashion ambassador of Turkey." She, too, often uses Ottoman motifs and decorations in her collections. In 2008, she attended the New York Fashion Week with her collection "City of Sultans," and according to Tacıroğlu, her inspiration for this collection came from the flamboyance of the Ottoman Empire, combining the historical and the modern. However, it is difficult to trace the "spirit" of the Ottomans in Tacıroğlu's designs for she uses *tughra*s of sultans and Ottoman jewels on European-style, loose-cut, and bright-colored dresses. In the "City of Sultans" collection, she merely used Ottoman heritage as a visual source, neglecting religious and political connotations.

The number of fashion designers who use Ottoman heritage in their collections has increased considerably since the 2000s, but these designers mainly use it as a powerful marketing strategy in order to become successful in Europe and the United States, as well as in Turkey. These newcomers include fashion, jewelry, and hat designers, such as Merve Bayındır, Gülin Girişmen, Tuvana Büyükçınar, and Sedef Çalarken. Like their predecessors, they do not necessarily acknowledge the social, spiritual, and/or religious ideologies bound to these vestimentary traditions. In Turkey, Ottoman clothing has had symbolic values since the eighteenth century, signifying conservatism and Islamic values. High-fashion designers mostly employ Ottoman heritage as a visual source instead of its ideological and religious value. While Ottoman clothing is a powerful tool for contemporary Turkish fashion designers by which to differentiate themselves on the international fashion scene and in the media, its socio-cultural, and political connotations are ignored.

Conclusion: self-Orientalism in Ottoman-inspired fashion design

Inspiration from local/national and so-called traditional cultural heritage has permeated the international fashion scene since the 1990s. According to anthropologist Ted Polhemus (2005: 91), there are three reasons why local clothing styles have appeared in global fashion. According to him, the foremost reason is the increasing interest in cultural alternatives to the globalized world. The second is the need to look at "the Other" after a long age of Western arrogance. The third reason is the disappearance of Western dominance in the fashion system. So-called "exotic, traditional, and authentic" cultures have inspired European fashion designers since the nineteenth century. However, contemporary fashion designers from different cultures have questioned and rejected the dominant European fashion system and they mixed it with their own design history (Teunissen 2005: 19–21). Nevertheless, the dominant fashion capitals of the West have maintained their positions. These capitals acknowledged and allowed non-Western fashion designers to present their collections, often if they merged characteristic local clothing styles with European fashion aesthetics in their design approaches.

According to Yuniya Kawamura (2004: 97–100), who conducted ethnographic research on the position of Japanese fashion designers in Paris, being in the city strengthens the designer brand's image among Japanese consumers both in Japan and in Europe. Japanese fashion designers explain that the reason why they run their business from Paris is because, in order to be internationally successful, it is a necessity to be successful in that city. Issey Miyake, for example, explains that these designers are the first generation to grow up after the Second World War with a true mixture of Japanese and Western culture, the first generation that have had to look in another direction in search of a new identity. Although they respect European fashion traditions, they believe they do it better (Kawamura 2004: 97). For the European consumers and gatekeepers, however, the most significant component of their image is their Japanese identity. Consequently, being in Paris not only guarantees their cultural capital, but also their symbolic and social capital.

According to Mike Featherstone (2007: 93), certain cities are accepted as cultural capitals due to their rich artistic and cultural pasts, and these cities are the places where cultural capital transforms into economic capital. Moreover, these cities have great potential to gain social capital. Kawamura's research shows that Japanese fashion designers have a stake in being in Paris in that they can reach the educated and skilled creative networks, as well as the international fashion media. Besides which, newcomers can link themselves to established and influential designers in Paris. On the other hand, although Japanese fashion designers claim that their designs are not related to their Japanese identity directly, and that they design in a universal manner, European media emphasize their Japanese identity (Koren 1984: 80). As Lisa Skov (1996: 151) remarks, "one of the meanings of 'Japan' in Western consumer culture seemed to be an 'otherness' inside people's minds, made visible through austere dress." In fact, Japanese designer designs can neither be positioned in the European fashion system, nor directly within Japanese vestimentary heritage. They have created a hybridized form of European and Japanese fashion.

Yet, Aijaz Ahmad (1992: 68-69) states that proponents of cultural hybridization ignore the economic power of Western capitalism. Under such circumstances, the symbolic capital created by the French fashion system should be considered, because the creators of the French fashion system designated the conditions of acceptance to the system, and also accepted Japanese fashion designers publicized by European fashion media. Therefore, it is not easy to claim that the Western dominance of the fashion system has totally disappeared as Polhemus (2005: 91) stated. Even now, accepting Japanese fashion designers, the French fashion system opened itself to the Other while trying to assimilate the Other. Through this process, the French fashion system became witness to the critics and reinterpretations of itself. Jan Nederveen Pieterse (1994: 64) states that hybridization is not a process that creates static hegemonic relations, but a process in which these relations are restated continuously. In the context of Turkish fashion, throughout Turkey's Republican period, in which European fashion has been implemented through state politics, debates on dress have constantly taken place. In order to differentiate the new Turkish Republic from its religious past, dress politics have been employed to turn European fashion into a symbol of secularism and modernism. However, with the rise of fashion designers and ready-to-wear consumption, Selcuk and Ottoman heritage have become significant tools by which to differentiate Turkish fashion on the international fashion scene. Thus, the relation with the past has shifted from rejection to inclusion and acceptance in regard to its discursive and inspirational power.

Those Turkish fashion designers, who have showed in influential fashion capitals, have incorporated references of characteristic Ottoman clothing in their collections as a strategy to become successful in Europe and the United States. The styles of these designers usually merge Ottoman iconography with European-style dresses almost as collages, either as pastiches of the past, or ultramodern forms in which the past is purely ornamental. In this respect, Dorinne Kondo (1997: 58) uses the concept of the "auto-exotic gaze" for Japanese designers who look at their culture and present their products by making them exotic. This concept can also be applied to Cemil İpekçi's designs, whereby, in an interzone between the West and the East, Ottoman clothing elements are transformed into a pastiche. While Japanese designers interrogate the European fashion system aesthetically and structurally (Kawamura 2004: 164), clothing elements that belong to the East and the West come together as if they unite on a *tabula rasa* in Cemil İpekçi's collections. In the interview mentioned above, Cemil İpekçi emphasizes that his Orientalist approach is a deliberate choice (Dirlik & Yaman 2011). He imagines a utopian democratic Ottoman Empire in which all religious beliefs can exist and live in peace. In a similar fashion, in his designs, all forms, colors and styles from Seljuk and Ottomans to European fashions can be combined without any restraint. His images have been taken from Turkish and European history randomly, and shaped in forms of historical costumes or modern fashions. He erases the boundaries of time and place. Yet, his ruling state is Ottoman, and he celebrates Ottoman glory and is proud of being an Ottoman, at least in his discourse.

The work and discourse of İpekçi call into mind Ulrich Beck's concept of "cosmopolitanism." According to Beck (2000: 88–9), in our times "everyone has to locate himself in the same global space and is confronted with challenges, and now strangeness is replaced by the amazement at the sameness." Beck poses the remarkable question about coexistence: "How can coexistence in multi-religious, multi-ethnic and multi-cultural societies work?" As for institutionalization of culture and cultural exchanges, Beck (2000: 98) implies that cosmopolitanization does not indicate one cosmopolitan society, but an "interactive relationship of de-nationalization and re-nationalization, de-ethnicization and re-ethnicization, de-localization and re-localization in society and politics." Through the hybridization of Ottoman, Seljuk, Arab, ethnic Turkish, and European clothing styles, the work of İpekçi creates an imaginary cosmopolitan zone where all historical connotations and cultural influences coexist instead of dictating binary oppositions, such as West/East, traditional/modern, and so on.

Designs by Atıl Kutoğlu, Dilek Hanif, and Nedret Taciroğlu are mostly dominated by European clothing styles with Ottoman motifs and decorations. In their designs, oppositions between elements associated with respectively the East and the West such as veiling/nudity, handcraft/industrial, and adorned/plain are striking, and are clearly used in a "self-Orientalizing" way. Teunissen argues (2005: 13) that in European fashion, designers first look at the history of other cultures for inspiration instead of searching their own past. This, however, applies just as much to the three designers mentioned above. Therefore, they belong to the European fashion system, whereby they attend Western fashion weeks in Paris, New York, and Milan, sell their products mostly to Western consumers, and look at their past and cultural heritage through Western eyes, as well as mythologizing it as such. According to the concept of "self-Orientalism," the West not only creates an "exotic" image of the East, but the East recreates this image and internalizes it (Dirlik 1996: 100–5). Thus, the West–East binary is maintained just as much by the East, and operates in two ways: firstly, the unique aspects of the East are mythologized into a national identity that is then promoted on the global market. As Masafumi Monden (2015: 12) writes, "'us' versus 'them' logic is often constructed in order to serve a particular purpose, to define their identity and achieve a feeling of 'superiority' over other cultures." Simultaneously, this mythologized identity shapes "a form of collective expression" (Mears 2010: 142). Secondly, cultural formations are transformed by referencing the West, and once these cultural formations are shaped in Western lines, old cultural formations are slowly effaced. Eventually, their cultural repertoires are transformed into new ones, but only as images and narratives (Yan & Santos 2009: 298).

Although self-Orientalism is often presented as a way of accepting Western hegemony and internalizing it, one should keep in mind, however, that the same ideology could serve as a process of self-empowerment. While writing on exotic appeal of Oriental luxury on Westerners since the Crusades, Getrud Lehnert and Gabriele Mentges (2003: 7–8) emphasize that even though "in the 16th century, Europeans started to imitate and copy the quality of the imported textiles," and "the knowledge about these objects increased," the "fantastic images" of these objects written by European travelers has remained. At the same time, these "fantastic" images of the Other always have a strong impact. These images can also serve as a platform of dialogue in/between cultures. Ignoring the fact that Islamic fashion trends have been spreading among European middle class women, as well as Turkish, Middle Eastern and African women (Abaza 2013: 72–3) this may result in overlooking multi-directional hegemonic relations and hybridization processes between cultures and societies as Lehnert and Mentges (2003: 9) ask: "what does oriental fashion mean to the European bourgeois lady wearing a Turkish style head scarf or coat?" By imitating the look on himself/herself, while creating his/her self-presentation and self-formulation, one can reveal the unique sides of this self-presentation and self-formulation, and also expose the hegemonic relations and exchanges between the seer and the seen. As Nederveen Pieterse (2009: 140) puts it, "hybridities are braided and interlaced, layer upon layer, to the point that it may be difficult to decide which is which." This understanding of self-Orientalism can protect us from a Eurocentric conceptualization of fashion and present a way of exchanging glances.

The way those three designers have applied Ottoman heritage to their designs has been a means to create a mythical Ottoman man/woman. Kutoğlu, for example, revisits the imperialist politics of the Ottomans in Europe as a designer living and working in Europe. Hanif, in her turn, presents the Ottoman Empire as a fairy tale land by exoticizing it. Taciroğlu, then, claims that her inspiration comes from the glory of the Ottomans, but she never explains what exactly this (imaginary) glory means, or to what it refers. In these works, the Ottoman Empire functions merely as a décor that is appealing to the international market and fashion scene. As Ted Polhemus (2005: 93) puts it, to create a national brand in the global village, design is the central element, and the most preferred way of differentiating the Self from the Other seems to be through referencing national identity and cultural history. However, in their way of referencing, the Ottomans ignore the origins of the political and religious tensions between the pro-modernists and Islamists and transform cultural and historical pasts into a visual presentation aroused by an "exotic" Ottoman scene.

To sum up, for contemporary fashion designers in Turkey, referencing Ottoman heritage has become a powerful marketing tool to gain recognition in the international market. While referencing Ottoman heritage, the Ottoman Empire is generally seen through Western eyes in a "self-Orientalizing" way. These self-Orientalizing fashion collections not only provide recognition for fashion designers, but also benefit the image of contemporary Turkey. In the near future, the fashion scene in Turkey seems set to become a platform for symbolic struggles between the Kemalists and the Islamists due to the shifting political balance; and hopefully one can claim that upcoming fashion designers will show us the new ways of interrelating the cultural and historical past by covering its religious and political controversies and transforming them into new narratives. These narratives can avoid utilizing the fashion phenomenon as "participatory narratives" of countries "in the light of recent socio-economic achievements, their 'convergence' with the rich West and their successful engagement with fashion as consumers and producers" (Riello and McNeil 2010: 5), and expose unique local fashion developments independently or in-between exchanges of cultures, even worldviews.

Notes

1 The author would like to thank Osman Şişman, İsmail Özgür Soğancı, A. Emre Cengiz, and M. Angela Jansen for their helpful comments on the manuscript.

2 Although this description of Turkish clothing generally includes main clothing items —caftans, headpieces, belts, etc.—used by Turks throughout the pre-Islamic period, it fails to acknowledge the transformation in clothing between different Turkish states and communities. It also fails to explain the differences between the local clothing styles, so-called traditional clothes. It needs to be enriched by detailed historically- and anthropologically-oriented studies in order to understand the effects of the exchanges between pre-Islamic Turk communities and Asian societies and the rest of the continent. As Jennifer Craik (1993: 4) states, fashion is not a phenomenon that only belongs to Western modernism and capitalism. People live in either open or closed societies, present themselves to others, and the ways of self-representation and self-formation change in time. Susan Kaiser (2012: 173) claims that fashion has been historically located all around the world, however "Euromodern representations of hegemonic fashion" have marked European upper-class-women's apparel as the site of newness, since the rest of the world was described as static and fixed. Even today, in Turkish cities, local clothing styles, so-called traditional clothes, change in color, shape, construction methods and so on. I do not focus on these exchanges in/between cultures and societies, since my aim in this chapter is to focus on the relationship between Ottoman clothing and contemporary Turkish fashion design. Hence, a historically anthropologically inspired study of this kind extends beyond my thematic boundaries. Throughout this chapter, I refer to characteristic items of apparel such as caftans, şalvars, headdresses, pants, jackets, skirts, and decoration by the term "clothing." And by the term "fashion," I refer to the exchanging, borrowing, merging, adopting, and mutating of these clothing items, and their materials, colors, shapes, construction methods, etc., as well as their being as the site of newness and transformation of them.

References

Abaza, M. "The Motahajiba in Cairo, Inter-Arab Islamic Chic, Adaption, Hybridity and Globalization." In *Fusion Fashion: Culture beyond Orientalism and Occidentalism*, eds G. Lenhert and G. Mentges. Frankfurt: Peter Lang, 2013.
Ahmad, A. *In Theory: Classes, Nations, Literatures*. London: Verso, 1992.
Barbarosoğlu Karabıyık, F. *Moda ve Zihniyet*. İstanbul: İz Yayıncılık, 2009.
Beck, U. "The Cosmopolitan Perspective: Sociology of the Second Age of Modernity," *The*

British Journal of Sociology [Electronic], vol. 51, no. 1 (2000): 79–105. Available online at: http://web.b.ebscohost.com/ehost/pdfviewer/pdfviewer?sid=ae027cac-6661-4868-9629-9e764927b980%40sessionmgr111&vid=0&hid=105 (accessed April 21, 2015).

Craik, J. *The Face of Fashion: Cultural Studies in Fashion*. London: Routledge, 1993.

Davis, F. *Fashion, Culture and Identity*. Chicago: University of Chicago Press, 1992.

Dirlik, A. "Chinese History and the Question of Orientalism," *History and Theory* [Electronic], vol. 35, no. 4 (1996): 96–118, Available online at: http://www.jstor.org/discover/10.2307/2505446?uid=3739192&uid=2&uid=4&sid=21103310056621 (accessed 28 January 2014).

Dirlik, S. and U. Yaman. "Ve Tanrı Cemil"i Yarattı!," April 18, 2011. Available online at: http://www.reportare.com/index.php?option=com_content&view=article&id=76:ve-tanr-cemili-yaratt&catid=40:c&Itemid=81 (accessed July 24, 2012).

Eicher, J. B., and B. Sumberg. "World Fashion, Ethnic and National Dress." In *Dress and Ethnicity, Change Across Space and Time,* ed. J. B. Eicher. Oxford: Berg, 1995.

Featherstone, M. *Consumer Culture and Postmodernism*. Los Angeles: Sage, 2007.

Georgeon, F. *Osmanlı–Türk Modernleşmesi*. İstanbul: Yapı Kredi Yayınları, 2006.

Göle, N. *Melez Desenler: İslam ve Modernlik Üzerine*. İstanbul: Metis, 2008.

Hürriyet. "Turkish Fashion Designer Atıl Kutoğlu Salutates Mozart at NY Fashion Show." July 2, 2006. Available online at: http://www.hurriyetdailynews.com/default.aspx?pageid=438&n=turkish-fashion-designer-atil-kutoglu-salutes-mozart-at-ny-fashion-show-2006-02-07 (accessed June 3, 2014).

İnalcık, H. *Türkiye Tekstil Tarihi Üstüne Araştırmalar*. İstanbul: Türkiye İş Bankası Kültür Yayınları, 2008.

Kafadar, C. "Selçuklu ve Osmanlı"da…" In *Anadolu"da Çağlarboyu Kadın*, ed. C. Kafadar. Ankara: Türkiye Kültür Bakanlığı Yayınları, 1993.

Kaiser, S. *Fashion and Cultural Studies*, Oxford: Berg, 2012.

Karaağaç, Ş. "Ottomania New York'ta." September 12 2005. Available online at: http://www.halklailiskiler.com.tr/yazi.php?id=1055 (accessed July 25, 2012).

Kawamura, Y. *The Japanese Revolution in Paris Fashion*. Oxford: Berg, 2004.

Kondo, D. *About Face: Performing Race in Fashion and Theatre*. London: Routledge, 1997.

Koren, L. *New Fashion Japan*. Tokyo: Kondansha International, 1984.

Kozaman Som, S. "İstanbul'da Moda Sektörü: Üretimden Tasarıma." In *Yaratıcı İstanbul: Yaratıcı Sektörler ve Kent*, eds C. Enlil and Y. Evren. İstanbul: İstanbul Bilgi Üniversitesi Yayınları, 2011.

Lenhert, G., and G. Mentges. "Fusion Fashion: Culture beyond Orientalism and Occidentalism." In *Fusion Fashion: Culture beyond Orientalism and Occidentalism*, eds G. Lenhert and G. Mentges. Frankfurt: Peter Lang, 2013.

McLoughlin, P. "Ottoman Opulence," 2012. Available online at: http://www.brownbook.me/ottoman-opulence/ (accessed 24 July 2012).

Mears, P. "Formalism and Revolution: Rei Kawakubo and Yohji Yamamato." In *Japan Fashion Now*, ed. V. Steele. New York: Yale University Press, 2010.

Monden, M. *Japanese Fashion Cultures: Dress and Gender in Contemporary Japan*. London: Bloomsbury, 2015.

Nederveen Pieterse, J. "Globalization as Hybridization," *International Sociology,* vol. 9, no. 2 (1994): 161–84. Available at: Sage Journals, doi: 10.1177/026858094009002003. (accessed 16 June 2014).

Nederveen Pieterse, J. *Globalization & Culture: Global Mélange*. Plymouth: Rowman & Littlefield, 2009.

Özarslan, S. "Designer Kutoğlu: Ottoman Motifs Set my Collections Apart." May 9, 2010. Available online at: http://www.todayszaman.com/newsDetail_openPrintPage.action?newsId=209728, (accessed June 3, 2014).

Özer, İ. *Osmanlı"dan Cumhuriyete Yaşam ve Moda*, İstanbul: Truva Yayınları, 2006.

Polhemus, T. "What to Wear in the Global Village." In *Global Fashion Local Tradition,* eds J. Brand and J. Teunissen. Utrecht: ArtEz Institute of the Arts, 1994.

Reillo, G. and P. McNeil. "Introduction." In *The Fashion History Reader: Global Perspectives*, eds G. Reillo and P. McNeil. London and New York: Routledge, 2010.

Şeftalici Sonay, H. *Terziden Tasarımcıya*. A Thesis Submitted in partial fulfillment of the Requirements of Mimar Sinan Fine Arts University for the Degree of Master of Arts. İstanbul: Mimar Sinan Fine Arts University, 2005

Sezer Arığ, A. *Atatürk Türkiye'sinde Kılık Kıyafette Çağdaşlaşma.* Ankara: Siyasal Kitabevi, 2007.

Skov, L. "Fashion Trends, Japonisme, and Postmodernism." In *Contemporary Japan and Popular Culture*, ed. J. W. Treat. London: Cuzon, 1996.

Taşçıoğlu, M. *Türk Osmanlı Cemiyetinde Kadının Sosyal Durumu ve Kadın Kıyafetleri.* Ankara: Akın Matbaası, 1958.

Teunissen, J. "Global Fashion Local Tradition." In *Global Fashion Local Tradition,* eds J. Brand and J. Teunissen. Utrecht: ArtEz Institute of the Arts, 2005.

Turquality Commission. "Objectives of TURQUALITY" (2007). Available online at: http://www.turquality.com/about-us/objectives-of-turquality (accessed July 25, 2012).

Yan, G. and C. Santos. "'China, Forever': Tourism Discourse and Self-Orientalism." *Annals of Tourism Research,* vol. 36, no. 2 (2005): 295–315. Available: Science Direct/Elseiver, doi:10.1016/j.annals.2009.01.003. (accessed 26 July 2012).

BELDI SELLS: THE COMMODIFICATION OF MOROCCAN FASHION[1]

M. ANGELA JANSEN

Introduction

When my close friend Lina[2] got married in 2006, she asked me to help her with her wedding outfits. The fact that I was writing a PhD on the Moroccan fashion industry automatically made me *the* authority on the latest fashion trends. Although this was far from the case, I accepted her request with alacrity, for it gave me the opportunity to take a closer look at the consumption process of Moroccan fashion. Being from an upper middle-class family, it was out of the question that Lina would order her outfits from a so-called traditional tailor in the *medina*.[3] As she explained it, the tailor would not be up-to-date on the latest fashion trends, there would be no assurance that he would finish the garments on time, and there would be no guarantee of quality. After extensive enquiries among her female family members and friends, studying Moroccan fashion magazines for months, and visiting a large range of Moroccan stylists and designers in Rabat and Casablanca, Lina chose a young designer, a new talent, who had just participated in the renowned yearly fashion event *Caftan*. The showroom of this young designer was located in a stylish apartment building in Agdal, a fancy suburb of Rabat, and we were received in a smart salon where the international channel FashionTV was playing on a wall-mounted flat screen. After the customary greetings and compliments, we were shown the Moroccan fashion magazine *Femmes du Maroc* (also responsible for the event *Caftan*), which featured the designer's latest collection. However, it soon became clear that this was not at all what my friend Lina had in mind; she had actually brought pictures of designs by other designers that she had cut out of fashion magazines to illustrate what she wanted. She had also brought her own fabrics, some of which had been bought by her mother's friend during her pilgrimage to Mecca, and others which had been given to her by her future husband.[4] Over the next three months, we would come back four times for fittings and to supervise the production process. Each time Lina would bring with her another set of female family members, female friends, and future female in-laws who would vivaciously contribute their opinions and suggestions (which did not necessarily benefit the process). It became clear that these women played a crucial role in the negotiation process of the price, which seemed to be an imperative part of the ritual. Lina ended up ordering three outfits: a *beldi-classique* three-pieced white *tekšiṭa* to make her entrance on the *maria*, a *beldi-modern* three-pieced blue *tekšiṭa,* and another *beldi-classique* three-pieced lavender *tekšiṭa.* Although she would wear five outfits in total for her wedding, the characteristic wedding dress from Fes and the final *touche-marocaine* style ivory wedding dress would be rented from the *neggafa* and the fashion designer himself, respectively.[5]

What struck me most about the experience, was that Lina did not actually choose the young designer for his work, but rather because of his reputation, based on the fact that he had participated in the high-profile fashion event *Caftan*, which I shall explain further below. She did not select any of his designs for her own outfits, but rather imposed her own ideas, and even her own fabrics on him. To me this felt like going to Karl Lagerfeld, bringing pictures of Jean-Paul Gaultier's work, and insisting he uses IKEA fabrics. Although Lina favored a designer over a so-called traditional tailor, claiming that he would be better informed on the latest fashion trends, two out of the three garments she ordered were so-called "classic," and only one so-called "modern" (see below for a description of these different categories).

Based on extensive archival, collection, and field research between 2005 and 2012, this chapter deals with some of the complex consumption patterns described above. It aims to illustrate that the introduction of foreign fashion brands on a large scale in Morocco at the turn of the twenty-first century did not threaten Moroccan fashion, but on the contrary, boosted its development through the introduction of new consumption patterns and marketing strategies. It mainly contests a false assumption, following early globalization theory, that globalization leads to cultural homogenization, and rather to the contrary, illustrates how globalization is contributing to a revaluation of Moroccan cultural heritage, as materialized through fashion. Foreign fashion brands have played a decisive role in the revival and commodification of Moroccan fashion, resulting in a shift from anonymous tailors to glamorous fashion designers, from consumption based on demand to consumption based on offer, from a craft to an industry and from imageless workshops to luxurious showrooms and boutiques that suggest services Moroccan consumers have grown accustomed to through their shopping for European fashion.

From the traditional tailor to the fashion designer

No more than a few decades ago, the majority of Moroccan urban garments were produced by anonymous tailors in anonymous workshops in the *medina*. Clients would be loyal to one tailor, who was usually a member of the family.[6] New garments would be ordered once every two to three years, and used for a specific set of occasions, such as weddings and religious celebrations (except for the *jellaba*, a long outer coat with long sleeves and a hood, which is also worn on a daily basis). Changes were slow, and were mainly dictated by what fabric merchants and tailors had on offer. Cuts, colors, and decorations were easy to determine based on age, marital status, and the occasion for which the garments would be worn.

Figure 7.1 A so-called "traditional" tailor in the old Arab city center of Fes, Morocco. Photograph by the author.

While European fashion was first adopted by the Moroccan elite in the mid-1930s, it was only in the years after Independence (1956) that it became truly part of Moroccan identity. European fashion became a symbol of (Euro) modernity following its active promotion by King Mohamed V, who consciously had his children portrayed wearing it, riding horses, swimming, driving a car— living a (Euro)modern life (Daoud 1993: 245). Moroccan fashion, on the other hand, became a symbol of Moroccan nationalism and tradition, especially during the struggle for independence. And, while it was reduced to the context of religious and social celebrations, European fashion became dominant in everyday life. Simultaneously, the elite from Fes, in particular, traded their Arab-style townhouses (*ryads*)[7] in the old city centers for European-style villas in the new French-built city centers of Rabat and Casablanca, which among other things led to a shift from an extended family arrangement to a nuclear family format. They were the first to send their daughters to school, and to adopt a European lifestyle, including European fashion.[8] However, this elite was also strongly nationalistic, and highly valorized Moroccan fashion as a means of distinguishing themselves from the foreign (European) oppressor (Rachik 2003: 91). Due to these rigorous lifestyle changes, however, Moroccan garments were no longer considered suitable for an active and cosmopolitan life, as they consisted of endless layers of heavy and rigid fabrics, wide cuts, as well as wide brocade belts, which seriously restricted women in their movement.[9] Therefore, it is hardly surprising that the first generation of Moroccan fashion designers in the mid-1960s were women of the elite.

Although they had little or no formal training in fashion design, these women were knowledgeable in Moroccan handwork as part of their privileged education,[10] as well as in the latest European fashion trends.[11] These ladies "liberated" Moroccan women from their heavy vestimentary heritage by introducing fluid and light (French) haute couture fabrics, reducing the amount of layers, as well as the widths of cuts, and giving Moroccan fashion a so-called "modern" look.[12] As members of the elite, they were well connected (internationally), which gave them the opportunity to present their work to an international clientele. As this was also the time of the hippie spirit and ethnic chic in both Europe and the United States, they soon acquired international fame and many got to dress influential celebrities, fashion icons, and even royalty. Consequently, their international success unquestionably contributed to their national success, where for the first time, Moroccan women were given the opportunity to express both their sense of fashion and modernity through Moroccan fashion.[13] What this generation of fashion designers probably did not realize, however, is that by proposing their own designs to their clients (as opposed to clients dictating their ideas to tailors), by presenting their collections in glamorous boutiques in luxurious (international) hotels (as opposed to imageless workshops of tailors), which were an important part of their (brand) image, and by signing their collections with their (brand) name, they were the first to challenge the existing consumption patterns of Moroccan fashion. Nevertheless, their collections were limited to an exclusive group, since there was not yet a supporting industry to disperse their designs to a larger audience.

It was not until the late 1990s that fashion was democratized in Morocco. This happened particularly through the success of a national lifestyle press. Under the influence of foreign lifestyle magazines available on the domestic market, Moroccan lifestyle magazines started to develop in the mid-1990s, meeting with remarkable success. As the first editor-in-chief of one of the first Moroccan lifestyle magazines, *Femmes du Maroc*, Aisha Zaim Sakhri explains it, this success largely resulted from the fact that Moroccan readers not only found it difficult to identify with the topics presented in the foreign magazines, but also had limited access to the consumption goods featured in them.[14] Consequently, these national magazines played an important role in giving Moroccan women a new sense of identity (Skalli 2006: 61), their main aim being to promote "a modern Moroccan woman in a modern Moroccan society." As Aisha Zaim Sakhri states:

> [E]specially in the early years of the magazine, the idea persisted that everything that was modern, was coming from Europe. In order to stay true to one's Moroccan identity, women thought they had to stay traditional. We wanted to break with this idea by showing our readers that modernity could come from within.[15]

Such magazines played an important role in the conceptualization of a so-called Moroccan modernity. In order to illustrate their ideas, the magazine focused on the modernization of Moroccan urban dress. According to Aisha Zaim Sakhri:

> Moroccan dress was something that was considered truly Moroccan and purely traditional and it was playing an important role in society. But at the same time, it was also considered to be a heavy load on the shoulders of Moroccan women and therefore we believed that it had to be modernized.[16]

These magazines had limited access to European fashion, since only a few boutiques in Casablanca were selling European fashion at the time. They, therefore, literally had difficulties filling their fashion pages.[17] It was, thus, only logical that they turned to what was available on the local market, i.e. Moroccan fashion, but even that proved to be problematic, since only a few Moroccan designers were actually designing Moroccan fashion collections. The majority were designing European fashion, due to the fact that the few fashion schools that had opened up in Morocco in the mid-1980s, taught European fashion

Figure 7.2 Cover of the Moroccan fashion magazine *Ousra*. Photograph by the author.

design, since they were catering to a Moroccan textile industry that was based on subcontracting to a European market.[18] Moroccan fashion was still a craft that could be mastered by becoming an apprentice to a skilled tailor.

In 1996, *Femmes du Maroc* launched a yearly fashion event called *Caftan*, to stimulate the design of so-called modern Moroccan fashion. As Lina's case testifies, this event grew to become Morocco's most influential fashion event of the year and many consumers await it to be informed on the new fashion trends. Simultaneously, since the job options for Moroccan designers after graduation were limited, and setting up a business in Moroccan fashion was much easier than European fashion, increasing numbers of Moroccan designers switched from European to Moroccan fashion design (or at least to some sort of hybrid style). The problem remained, however, that they did not have the skills to actually produce these garments and were, therefore, still largely dependent on specialized traditional craftsmen.[19] What they did possess, however, were the skills to design European fashion, which they started to apply to Moroccan fashion, introducing close-fitted silhouettes, revealing necklines, pants, skirts, corsets, etc. Due to their formal schooling, they became the first Moroccan fashion professionals with training in fashion management, marketing, and strategy, which had a significant impact on the development of Moroccan fashion.[20]

From a craft to an industry

The introduction of foreign fashion brands on a large scale at the turn of the twenty-first century democratized fashion in Morocco. Due to the liberalization of the Moroccan textile market under European pressure, in particular, and a steadily growing economy, Morocco was inundated by foreign fashion brands in the form of franchises. Ranging from low- and middle-priced (French and Spanish) brands like Zara, Massimo Dutti, Mango, Stradivarius, Bershka, Promod, and Etam to high-end brands, such as Louis Vuitton, Dior, and Yves Saint Laurent, stores opened in the economic capital of Casablanca, the tourist center Marrakech, and the administrative city Rabat, in particular. The *piece-de-resistance* of foreign fashion brands is without a doubt the MoroccoMall (2011). With a total surface of 250,000 m², it is the largest shopping mall in North Africa, offering over 600 brands, including the French *Galeries Lafayette*, Prada, and Gucci, as well as the Hennes & Mauritz and *GAP*.[21]

The introduction and success of these foreign fashion brands in Morocco can be explained through larger processes of globalization, whereby the increasing encounter with foreign lifestyles through media, traveling, and (temporary) migration accustomed Moroccans to foreign commodities. Many of these brands were already familiar, particularly to the middle- and upper-social classes, due to their studies and travels abroad. Progressively these commodities were adjusted and integrated into Moroccan urban life. Although official numbers are lacking, and it can only be estimated that merely 10 percent of the Moroccan population can afford to buy products offered by these foreign fashion brands (Vallée 2006: 33), their introduction has uncontestably had a significant impact on consumerism in Morocco. For example, under the influence of foreign fashion brands, the anonymous workshops of traditional tailors and fabric merchants have become overshadowed by so-called modern

Figure 7.3 The first Zara store on Massira El Khedra in the center of Casablanca, Morocco. Photograph by the author.

fashion boutiques and showrooms of Moroccan stylists and designers. As Lina's case clearly exemplifies, their settings correspond more to an image that has come to inspire client' confidence, suggesting a range of professional services and qualities Moroccan consumers have grown accustomed to through their shopping for European fashion. The irony of the story, however, is that both stylists and designers are still dependent on the skills of Moroccan tailors and craftsmen to produce Moroccan fashion, resulting in large workshops, where the "unstylish" craftsmen are hidden behind a stylish façade.

Furthermore, in the same way that Moroccan customers have grown accustomed to shopping around for European fashion, they have started shopping around for Moroccan fashion and, therefore, are no longer loyal to a particular (family) tailor. And, under the influence of foreign fashion brands, Moroccan fashion has become commoditized, whereby a shift occurred from consumption

Figure 7.4 A boutique selling Moroccan fashion in the shopping mall Twin Centre in Casablanca, Morocco. Photograph by the author.

based on demand to consumption based on offer (Rasing 1999: 239). The offer, in turn, has increased remarkably in the last decade through such factors as the commercial exploitation of specific social and religious events like the fasting month of Ramadan and the wedding season in summer. Since these are traditionally two important occasions when Moroccan fashion is consumed, the industry has become particularly focused on them, whether it is through an array of fashion events promoting the latest fashion trends, fashion magazines featuring special editions, or boutiques offering special promotions.[22]

Niche markets have been created and/or stimulated, like informal Moroccan fashion for a wider range of occasions, and for men and children. For example, two new hybrid-clothing categories that have developed in the last few years are *beldi wear* and *touche marocaine*, which are suitable for informal occasions or day wear. *Beldi wear* is less luxurious and elaborate Moroccan fashion adapted for daily use, while *touche marocaine* is European fashion with characteristic Moroccan iconography, mainly consisting of decoration techniques. Additionally, the market is stimulating Moroccan men to consume by increasing the offer of Moroccan fashion for men, with a particular success for Moroccan male prêt-à-porter. Also, specific occasions in the year like *cšura*[23] are commercially exploited for children to consume Moroccan fashion, and the offer has increased impressively, ranging from haute couture brands like Alrazal to prêt-a-porter offered by Yousra.

An important characteristic of Moroccan fashion, however, is that consumers continue to insist on the uniqueness of their Moroccan garments, as well as the importance of handwork. Thus, it is difficult to industrialize or mass-produce Moroccan fashion, and it demands a network of stylists and traditional tailors with ateliers and craftsmen to translate the latest fashion trends into affordable wear. This particular phenomenon has made it a very complex undertaking to characterize the Moroccan fashion industry, since, on the one hand, "one-of-a-kind" and hand-made are qualities of haute couture, but, on the other, the highly diverse range of qualities of materials and handwork, as well as the level of creativity and innovation have made it impossible to put everyone into one category.

From the local to the global (and back)

Since the 1990s, an increasing number of social scientists have challenged the belief that globalization leads to cultural homogeneity based on a Western format, insisting that receivers of cultural flows are not passive agents but unravel, translate and customize foreign influences (Appadurai 1996; Inda and Rosaldo 2002; Lechner and Boli 2008). As was clearly illustrated above, instead of threatening the local market, foreign lifestyle magazines inspired a wide range of successful Moroccan lifestyle magazines, whose added values of proximity and identity rendered them more popular than foreign magazines (Skalli 2006: 61). In the same way, the introduction of European fashion brands on a large scale did not threaten the continuity of Moroccan fashion, but on the contrary, set the trend for new consumption patterns and marketing strategies applied to Moroccan fashion. As I have argued elsewhere (Jansen 2013: 14), an important reason why these two clothing styles do not threaten each other's existence is because they have different values, fulfill different needs, and, therefore, represent different markets. Where European fashion represents aspirations of change and progress, as well as global participation, Moroccan fashion fulfills needs of continuity, cultural anchorage, and local distinctiveness. As Susan Kaiser (2012: 2) argues, people do not want either/or but and/both. They do not feel the need to choose, since both clothing styles are inextricably connected (Eicher and Sumberg 1995: 303) in the construction of multiple dynamic identities. Thera Rasing (1999: 238–9), in this respect, speaks of interacting identities, explaining that people are dealing with processes that go on simultaneously; on the one hand they adopt "new" ways of living under external influences, and on the other, they hold on to "old" customs and beliefs. This is not contradictory, she says, but shows interacting identities. Moroccans are convinced they can have "the best of both worlds" and as the Moroccan sociologist Fatima Mernissi puts it, drawing on the example of two widespread commodities in Moroccan society:

> Moroccans want to reconcile both realities by constantly traveling back and forth between tradition and (post)modernity. [...] They want, as it were, the mosque and the satellite without sacrificing the one or the other [...] The mosque provides them with cultural anchorage and rootedness, while the satellite seems to offer alternatives to some repressive mechanisms of tradition (in Skalli 2006: 6).

Thera Rasing (1999: 238–9) argues that foreign commodities constitute a significant nexus between the global and the local and that they are dominant in cultural transformations. Fashion, in its turn, is a powerful commodity to negotiate continuity and change, tradition and modernity as well as values of local and global and is simultaneously ambiguous and contradictive. For example, during my extensive interviewing of ninety respondents in Morocco's three major cities (Fes, Marrakech and Casablanca) in 2005–6, many respondents heavily criticized the work of contemporary Moroccan fashion designers, saying that they are "not Moroccan," "too modern," and/or "too European." Nevertheless, the majority agreed that it is due to the "modernization" introduced by fashion designers that Moroccan fashion has become so successful today. Many acknowledged using these collections as sources of inspiration for their own garments. Susan Kaiser (2012: 45) notes in this respect that what contributes to fashion's ambiguity (mixed meanings) is its relation to ambivalence (mixed emotions). She argues that fashion suggests what is to come and it is a process that allows articulating abstract ideas and negotiating ambiguity. Both fashion and culture, she argues, simultaneously undergo continual change and continuity, and these simultaneous processes are complex and even contradictory (2012: 12). For Kaiser:

> fashion can best be understood as *change within continuity*, whereas culture reveals practices that emphasize *continuity within change*. Each concept, in its own way, offers a lens through which to make sense of simultaneity: how different ideas or processes not only coexist but also interact dynamically (2012: 13).

Fred Davis (1992: 18 and 43) argues that fashion articulates and represents collective tensions and moods that it makes visual and material and that it sheds light on potential meanings and opportunities for change. As Jennifer Craik (2009: 234) formulates, fashion is a relentless cycle of anticipating the future yet drawing on resonances of the past. This involves balancing the present with the future and the past, she says. Potential clients may be frightened by trends that are too different from what they wear now, she explains, but reject anything that looks old fashioned or out of fashion, so a careful balancing act is needed to predict a newness that is exciting but still has some familiarity.

It is not (any longer) a simple matter of Moroccan versus European fashion since new hybrid clothing categories have been introduced over time. Fashion in Morocco today roughly fits into five categories, ranging from *beldi-classique* and *beldi-moderne*, to *beldi-wear*, *touche marocaine*, and *mode Européenne*, whereby the first category is considered suitable for formal social and religious occasions, and the second can be worn for less formal occasions, or for formal occasions, but only by "young" (i.e. unmarried) people (Jansen 2014). The third and fourth categories, in their turn, are informal Moroccan fashion due to their (too) high level of European influences, while the last category is considered fully European. These last three categories are suitable for so-called modern occasions ranging from leisure and office activities to formal "foreign" contexts (receptions, inaugurations, galas, etc) although it is hard to generalize and exceptions do occur.

Through the interviews with my respondents, it became clear that the categorization of fashion reflects a constant negotiation process based on the degree of *"localness/traditonalness"* and *"foreignness/modernity"* of a garment with respect to its shape, cut, fabric, colors, and decorations. It is far from an exact science and strongly influenced by personal opinion. What is considered *beldi-classique* by one respondent, can be easily categorized as *beldi-modern* by another. Again, what is really being negotiated, is continuity and change, tradition and modernity, whereby the first is associated with the local, and the second with the global, and especially with euromodernity. For example, Moroccan society is, to a large extent, influenced by Arab culture through film, music, and Muslim fashion, but this is never associated with modernity. The way Jonathan Inda and Renato Rosaldo (2002: 3) explain this, ideologies related to modernity are in the majority made up of elements of the Enlightenment worldview such as freedom, welfare, human rights, democracy, and sovereignty. Many developing nations, they claim, adhere to policies which at least ostensibly aim to "modernize" their politics, infrastructures, and economies, but often their own prevailing ideologies do not correspond with those proposed from "outside." In this respect, a "Moroccan modernity," as first promoted by Moroccan fashion magazines, and later by King Mohamed VI, has become a desirable alternative for euromodernity, and is believed to be more in harmony with prevailing local ideologies and values.

Beldi as a brand

People in a consumer culture no longer consume for merely functional satisfaction, but in order to give meaning to their lives (Richard Elliott & Andrea

Davies 2006). The consumption of commodities is an important aspect in the construction of identities, or as Wendy Gordon and Virginia Valentine (2000: 12) put it:

> [T]he 21st century consumer shifts identities and uses a vast wardrobe of brands to create herself into whoever she wants to be. Others construct their own stories about her by decoding her brand attire at that moment within a particular context.

They argue that people want to belong to something bigger than themselves, and that they make sense of the world around them by creating stories and clues (Gordon and Valentine 2000: 6, 10, 12). These clues, they say, are communicated consciously and unconsciously, not only in the course of social interaction, but also through overt brand communication and covert brand body language. They explain that it is not the company that owns a brand, but rather the consumers by giving meaning to a brand, "by owning it." They argue that customers create brands, while companies create brand identities. Also, the relationship a consumer has with a brand is continually changing and, therefore, the meaning of a brand can only be understood in the context of the discourse in which the brand is being consumed.

A brand, as Benoit Heilbrunn (2006) formulates it in his article "Culture Branding between Utopia and A-topia," is no longer just a sign added to a product to differentiate it from another product, but a semiotic engine whose function is to constantly produce meanings and values. Brands create value not just by the products or services they represent, but by the meanings they generate (McCracken 2005). In the words of Clifford Geertz (1973), people are creatures of meaning, and questions of meaning and identity are being primarily answered by the culture in which they grow up. Cultures provide the symbolic tools needed to create a sense of identity. The idea forwarded by ID Branding (2010: 7–8) suggests that brands work in exactly this way, namely, in order to be relevant to consumers and sustainable over time, brands must operate much like culture, they argue. Consumers will embrace a particular brand as part of their own identity, they say. Consumers thus, in essence, join the brand's culture and participate in that culture as a way of expressing to the rest of the world (and to themselves) who they are and what they believe in.

The other way around, cultures are becoming more and more like brands. Moroccan culture materialized through Moroccan fashion has become a brand under the name *beldi*. As I explain in my book *Moroccan Fashion* (Jansen 2014), the term *beldi*—meaning "traditional/local/authentic" in Moroccan Arabic, as opposed to *rumi* meaning "new/foreign/industrial"—has come to represent everything that ·is "good" about Morocco, from grandmother's homemade cooking, to Moroccan handcrafts. *Beldi* allows people to dream of the unique skilful crafts from Fes, which is considered the capital of Moroccan civilization, where Moroccan handwork originated and was raised to perfection in the course of centuries. Where *beldi* only a few years ago was still associated with the countryside, backwardness, and old-fashionedness, today, in a rapidly developing urban society, *beldi* allows people to escape for a moment and dream about Morocco's glorious past. This search for authenticity, as Marilyn Halter (2000: 17) observes, is very much related to nostalgia for an idealized and fixed point in time when folk culture was supposedly untouched by the corruption that is automatically associated with commercial development. Hence, she says, the more artificiality, anonymity and uncertainty apparent in a postmodern world, the more driven are the quests for authentic experiences and the more people long to feel connected to localized traditions seeking out the timeless and true. Moroccan fashion sells a fantasy materialized by Moroccan fashion designers through the skills of Moroccan artisans. According to Loubna Skalli (2006: 56), an ideological "retraditionalization" refers to a politicization of tradition to combat, in a self-conscious defense, traditional norms that are threatened by others. While Moroccan fashion is considered uncomfortable, expensive, and time-consuming to purchase by a large majority of the respondents, both men and women, it is equally valued as "important," as "part of Moroccan tradition" and as indispensable for formal social and religious occasions.

Conclusion

This chapter has tried to illustrate how a series of phenomena in post-colonial urban Moroccan society have not threatened Moroccan fashion, but on the contrary, boosted its development through the introduction of new consumption patterns and marketing strategies. It aimed to illustrate how globalization has contributed to a revaluation of Moroccan cultural heritage, materialized through fashion. A first generation of Moroccan fashion designers, in the 1960s, revolutionized the consumption of Moroccan fashion by proposing their own designs in their own glamorous boutiques under their own (brand) name. By doing so, they were the first to create and sell a brand rather than an imageless craft. A second generation, in the late 1990s, through their professional training in (European) fashion design, marketing, and strategy, pushed this development even further. Supported by the success of a national fashion press and their strongly mediatized fashion events, they were widely featured in glamorous fashion spreads and broadcasted on national television, which not only enabled them to reach a large audience, but also to position themselves as national celebrities. This resulted in the popularity of the glamorous fashion designer over the imageless tailor, who became associated with informality, low quality and low social status, while fashion designers and stylists became associated with luxury, glamor, and, most of all, professionalism. The Moroccan fashion press, in its turn, also contributed to an important image change of Moroccan fashion by taking it out of its "traditional" context of social and religious gatherings, and putting it in a "modern" context of fashion magazines and shows; they turned it into a desirable commodity.

The aim of this chapter was to show that the introduction of foreign fashion brands on a large scale at the turn of the twenty-first century did not threaten the continuity of Moroccan fashion. The anonymous workshops of tailors and fabric merchants in the old city centers became overshadowed by fashionable boutiques and showrooms of designers in the new city centers. Thus, under the influence of foreign fashion brands, Moroccan consumers are no longer loyal to one (family) tailor, but rather shop around for Moroccan fashion in the same way they do for European fashion. In addition, under the influence of European prêt-à-porter, Moroccan consumers no longer have the patience and/or knowledge to order Moroccan fashion custom-made, having to purchase the fabrics and garments separately, as well as knowing about materials, qualities, and techniques. Today, stylists and designers are offering their clients "all-in-one," by proposing their own fabrics, designs, and decoration techniques. Moreover, under the influence of foreign fashion brands, Moroccan fashion is no longer consumed based on need, but rather on what is being offered, and the amount on offer has increased dramatically in the last decade. Particular annual events have become commercially exploited, with Ramadan and the wedding season in summer as the absolute highlights. The majority of the fashion events are organized prior to these two events, and a large range of boutiques and shops, including supermarkets, feature Moroccan fashion around these periods.

However, Moroccan fashion is limited to specific social and religious occasions and contexts, which limits its consumption considerably. Therefore, the industry has particularly focused on the market for so-called informal Moroccan fashion for expansion in recent years, as well as Moroccan fashion for men and children. Nevertheless, Moroccan consumers continue to insist on two important characteristics when it comes to Moroccan fashion, and that is handwork and exclusivity. So, under the influence of European fashion brands, "modern" values like image and service have come to play important roles in the consumption of Moroccan fashion, but without affecting so-called traditional values of craftsmanship and exclusivity.

Finally, the growing impact of foreign (European) cultural influences, as a result of globalization, did not in any way threaten local culture, but on the contrary, resulted in a reevaluation of local cultural heritage as a means of local distinctiveness. Moroccan fashion has never been this popular, and it is exploited to a maximum, from advertising to entertainment on television. A wide variety of companies, from telephone providers to tile producers, are using modern Moroccan fashion in their advertisements to sell their products. In short, it has become a brand under the name *beldi*, a symbol *par excellence* of a "Moroccan modernity," delicately balancing between tradition and modernity, between continuity and change, and between the local and the global. Moroccan fashion plays on people's nostalgic longings for "nationalism," "tradition," and "authenticity," while simultaneously representing promises of change, progress, and participation in global discourse.

As illustrated by Lina's case, on the one hand, consumers are both attracted and reassured by the modern fashion designer, as opposed to the traditional tailor, who they believe will be able to advise them as a professional, and offer them modern services relating to the timeframe and quality of the work, even though the actual work is still, in fact, executed by a "traditional" tailor. Most importantly, the designer provides prestige among family and friends. On the other hand, Moroccan consumers are not willing to give up their "traditional" privileges to impose their own fabrics, their own models, and, most of all, to negotiate the price, as is done with a traditional tailor.

Figure 7.5 Modern Moroccan fashion used in a billboard advertisement of a telephone provider. Photograph by the author.

Notes

1. This chapter was presented as a conference paper for the 16th IFFTI Annual Conference held on January 27–31, 2014 at Bunka Gakuen University, Tokyo, Japan.

2. The names of respondents in this article were altered for privacy reasons.

3. This is the old Arab city center, as opposed to the new French city center.

4. This is a new interpretation of an old custom. Although it is not clear when this change occurred, in the early twentieth century brides would receive fabrics from their husbands as part of their wedding gift on the day of their wedding. Now, since contemporary brides want to use these fabrics for their actual wedding outfits, they often get them before the actual wedding.

5. The *tekšiṭa* is an outfit that consists of two long T-shaped garments, usually with long sleeves, and held together with a belt. It is worn by women for formal social gatherings. The *maria* is a heavily decorated platform that is used to carry in the bride. This is also a new interpretation of an old custom, for the bride used to be carried from her father's house to her future husband's house through the streets, hidden from view by curtains. Now it is just a way to offer the bride a "grand entrance." The *neggafa* is the Moroccan version of the wedding planner. *Beldi-classique*, *beldi-modern*, and *touche-marocaine* are newly introduced categories of Moroccan fashion, as is discussed in more detail in the later paragraphs.

6. Mainly for practical reasons because the contact between men and women who were not related was problematic.

7. This is a multi-level townhouse, based around a central courtyard, and usually inhabited by an extended family.

8. Zhor Sebti (Moroccan fashion designer from the first generation), interview with the author, Casablanca, November 17, 2006; notes on file with author.

9. Tamy Tazi (Moroccan fashion designer from the first generation), interview with the author, Casablanca, July 9, 2004; notes on file with author.

10. Moroccan girls of the elite learned how to sew and embroider at a young age as part of their respectful young girl's upbringing.

11. Tamy Tazi (Moroccan fashion designer from the first generation), interview with the author, Casablanca, July 9, 2004; notes on file with author.

12. Ibid.

13. Zhor Sebti (Moroccan fashion designer from the first generation), interview with the author, Casablanca, Nov. 17, 2006; notes on file with author.

14. Aisha Zaim Sakhri (first editor-in-chief of the Moroccan lifestyle magazine *Femmes du Maroc*), interview with the author, Casablanca, December 15, 2006; notes on file with author.

15. Ibid.

16. Aisha Zaim Sakhri (first editor-in-chief of the Moroccan lifestyle magazine *Femmes du Maroc*), interview with the author, Casablanca, December 15, 2006; notes on file with author.

17. Ilham Benzakour (editor-in-chief of the first Moroccan lifestyle magazine *Citadine*), interview with the author, Casablanca, December 27, 2006; notes on file with author.

18 Zineb Joundy (Moroccan fashion designer of the first generation), interview with the author, Casablanca, November 21, 2006; notes on file with author.

19 Albert Oiknine (Moroccan fashion designer of the second generation), interview with the author, Casablanca, July 9, 2004; notes on file with author.

20 For a third generation of Moroccan designers, emerging at the turn of the twenty-first century, please see Jansen (2014).

21 www.moroccomall.net (accessed 27 January 2014).

22 Meryam Al Alami (director of the fashion department of College Lasalle), interview with the author, July 13, 2006; notes on file with author.

23 This is a religious celebration that has been on the verge of disappearing for which children are given sweets, toys and new clothes.

References

Appadurai, Arjun. *Modernity at Large*. Minneapolis: University of Minnesota Press, 1996.

Craik, Jennifer. *Fashion: The Key Concepts*, Oxford, New York: Berg, 2009.

Daoud, Zakya. *Féminisme et politique du Maghreb: Soixante ans de lutte*. Casablanca: Editions Eddif, 1993.

Davis, Fred. *Fashion, Culture and Identity*, Chicago, London: The University of Chicago Press, 1992.

Eicher, Joanne, and Barbara Sumberg. "World Fashion, Ethnic and National Dress." In *Dress and Ethnicity: Change Across Space and Time*, ed. Joanne Eicher, 295–306. London: Berg, 1995.

Geertz, Clifford. *The Interpretation of Cultures*. New York: Basic Books, 1973.

Gordon, Wendy, and Virginia Valentine. *The 21st Century Consumer—A New Model of Thinking*. MRS Conference, Acacia Avenue, 2000.

Halter, Marilyn. *Shopping for Identity: The Marketing of Ethnicity*, New York: Schocken Books, 2000.

Heilbrunn, Benoit. "Culture Branding Between Utopia and A-topia." In *Brand Culture*, eds Jonathan E. Schroeder and Miriam Salzer-Mörling, New York: Routledge, 2006.

ID Branding (2010). *Give Them Something to Believe In: The Value of Brand Culture*. Available online at: http://www.brandchannel.com/images/papers/405_BrandCulture_final.pdf (accessed 27 January 2014).

Inda, Jonathan X., and Renato Rosaldo. *The Anthropology of Globalization: A Reader*. Oxford: Blackwell Publishers, 2002.

Jansen, M. Angela. "Three Generations of Moroccan Fashion Designers: Negotiating Local and Global Identity." In *Fashioning Identities: Cultures of Exchange*, ed. Sarah Heaton, 161–80. Oxford: Inter-Disciplinary Press, 2013.

Jansen, M. Angela. *Moroccan Fashion: Design, Tradition and Modernity*. London: Bloomsbury, 2014.

Kaiser, Susan. *Fashion and Cultural Studies*, Oxford, New York: Berg, 2012.

Lechner, Frank J. and John Boli. *The Globalization Reader*. Oxford: Blackwell Publishing, 2008.

McCracken, Grant. *Culture and Consumption II: Markets, Meaning, and Brand Management*. Bloomington: Indiana University Press, 2005.

Rachik, H. *Symbolizer la nation: Essai sur l'usage des identities collectives au Maroc*. Casablanca: Editions Le Fennec, 2003.

Rasing, Thera. "Globalization and the Making of Consumers: Zambian Kitchen Parties." In *Modernity on a Shoestring: Dimensions of Globalization, Consumption and Development in Africa and Beyond*, eds Richard Fardon, Wim van Binsbergen, and Rijk van Dijk, 227–46. Leiden, London: EIDOS, 199.

Skalli, Loubna H. *Through a Local Prism: Gender, Globalization and Identity in Moroccan Women's Magazines*. New York: Lexington Books, 2006.

Vallée, Samuel. "Les Confectionneurs marocains mettent le pied dans la distribution." *Le Journal du Textile* (Avril 2006): 33.

PART IV

LOCAL CONSTRUCTS OF THE GLOBAL

8

HISTORY, ART, AND PLASTIC BAGS: VIEWING SOUTH AFRICA THROUGH FASHION

VICTORIA L. ROVINE

It can be that the simplest objects used by people throughout society acquire, through their widespread use, the power to profoundly reflect on the lives of the various members of that society. –Strangelove
(GIBSON AND PATER 2007).[1]

Introduction

Commodities, as Kopytoff and others have demonstrated, may have biographies as eventful as those of the people who use them (Kopytoff 1986). Even the most prosaic goods may acquire dramatic biographies, as vividly illustrated by the modest containers at the center of this exploration. Through the work of two fashion designers, I explore the South African lives of the plastic containers, often called "China bags," though they have other names as well. The life stories of these bags illustrate how fashion can be used to investigate local constructions of modernity that emerge out of global markets and media, as these humble containers defy their rootlessness to become deeply local.

My investigation also illuminates aspects of South Africa's fashion scene, which is exceptional in Africa. Like its fine art markets (which, as I will describe, intersect with the fashion design industry), fashion's education, production, and marketing infrastructure resemble European and North American systems. Although designers struggle to build careers there as elsewhere, the nation's fashion shows, journalism, and range of markets does provide opportunities for unconventional work to find audiences, such as that of the two South African designers at the center of my meditation on commodities and identities.

My exploration of China bags is inspired by the work of two South African artists: Carlo Gibson and Ziemek Pater, fashion designers who worked collaboratively under the name Strangelove from 2001–9. Using clothing as their medium, Gibson and Pater animated China bags, enabling the objects to enact their own life stories. They harnessed the bags' potential to serve as containers not for goods, but for identities, histories, and aspirations. Transforming China bags into fashion, an art form that is inseparable from the bodies for which it is created, Strangelove literalizes the roles of commodities and global networks in the shaping of contemporary South African identities.

South Africa's recent political, social, economic, and legal transformations are reflected in virtually all of the nation's creative industries, including fashion. These transformations have included the final violent throes and the demise of the Apartheid system, the implementation of the world's most inclusive national constitution, the dramatic growth of formal and informal urban populations, a steep rise in crime, and the scourge of HIV/AIDS. While the work of many of the country's visual artists reflects the tensions between liberation and hardship, continuity and transformation, national pride and xenophobia, Strangelove's use of fashion to interrogate historical and contemporary inequities sets them apart.

To pursue the biographies of China bag fashions, my analysis draws on several influential works from a growing anthropological subfield focused on consumption and commodities as windows onto social structures. Strangelove's work vividly enacts and extends Gell's analysis of the absorption of commodities across cultures, exemplifying the production of new meanings through consumption (Gell 1986). Gell explores the functions of commodities in global networks, tracing objects' shifting significance, as they are adapted to diverse cultural and individual identities. My analysis of the cultural weight of China bags in South Africa is also informed by Jean Comaroff's analysis of historical South African dress practices at the intersection of cultures (Comaroff 1996). Through an exploration of Tswana dress in the mid- to late-nineteenth century, she provides rich insights into the contemporary worlds of China bags. Commodities were key to the negotiation of power between European missionaries and Tswana communities.

Comaroff's analysis of Tswana dress in historical perspective reminds us that Strangelove—and all of Africa's contemporary fashion designers—represents the latest incarnations of long histories of innovative transformations of attire. While attaining historical depth beyond the late nineteenth century is difficult, evidence of African consumers' interest in the new styles and creative adaptations is evident in the Benin bronzes of the sixteenth century, and Kongo ivories of the same era, which depict the incorporation of European forms into local styles of dress. In South Africa, the brilliantly colored beadwork that has become a hallmark of traditional dress in many Nguni cultures (Zulu, Xhosa, Ndebele, and others) is the product of fashion systems; much to the chagrin of eighteenth- and nineteenth-century European traders, consumers' preferences for bead colors and sizes changed from year to year. Sandra Klopper cites a vivid passage from an 1854 letter by a British visitor to southern Africa: "the Natives […] are as capricious in their taste for beads, as any English lady in the choice of her bonnet" (Klopper 2000: 31). These past innovations may rightly be considered fashion, the result of the desire for innovation and novelty; a reminder that South Africa, like the rest of the continent, has long participated in global fashion systems.

Finally, Strangelove's work with China bags evokes the paradoxical experience of modernity in contemporary Africa, where the modern is for many an absence and an aspiration, visible yet just out of reach. The China bag poignantly evokes that absent or, as I will propose, failed modernity. Ferguson's critique of the model of "multiple" or "alternative modernities" provides the framework for this analysis (Ferguson 2006). Rather than accounting for the vast disparities between Africans' and Westerners' access to prosperity and material comforts as "alternative" versions of modernity, Ferguson calls for a reassessment of the meanings of modernity. He considers it as an embodied experience rather than a temporal or a theoretical status; Strangelove's work literalizes this embodiment of modernity.

Strangelove's fashion theater

From 2001–9, Ziemek Pater and Carlo Gibson worked together as the conceptual design team Strangelove.[2] Since 2009, the brand has continued to create fashion and fine art under Gibson's direction. From their earliest fashion shows, Strangelove pushed the boundaries of fashion design, moving clothing into fine arts contexts, as for the quality of their clothing design and production. A 2006 review described the brand's reputation for theatricality: "Their shows are characteristically, perhaps infamously, unconventional, and they have married their penchant for beautiful clothes with a love for art and theatre." (Buys 2006) Strangelove's performances are more than promotions of their fashion design. Through their unorthodox approach to clothing design and presentation, Gibson and Pater use the medium as a platform for explorations of culture and history in South Africa, and, more specifically, in the distinctive urban milieu of their home, Johannesburg. According to Pater, clothing is a means to an end, one medium among many used to create a narrative: "We've discovered that the most profound thing you can do with clothing is storytelling. Structurally, clothing cutting is interesting but it has a limit" (Pater 2005). Gibson and Pater collaborated with dancers, visual artists, musicians, choreographers, and actors, creating works of art that explore multiple aspects of South Africa's cultures and histories.

Figure 8.1 Strangelove (Carlo Gibson, Ziemek Pater), in collaboration with Nelisiwe Xaba, *They Look at Me and That's All They Think*, 2007–8. Courtesy of Carlo Gibson.

A performance entitled *They Look at Me and That's All They Think* (2007–8), created in collaboration with choreographer/dancer Neliswe Xaba, featured a dramatic costume made of white parachute fabric. Tailored above the waist, the dress expanded to create a tent-like form with an enormous bustle extending from the rear. This bustle makes reference to Saartjie Baartman's physiognomy, or, more accurately, the European fascination with her physiognomy. Baartman was an indigenous KhoiKhoi woman who was taken to Europe, in 1810, to be displayed as the "Hottentot Venus." The garment is central to the work, for it not only embodies Baartman; at some points in the performance it becomes an element of the set, behind which Xaba dances in silhouette. Clothing, in this collaboration of choreographer and designers, enables the body to narrate histories and identities in multiple dimensions. The story told through image and movement is richly symbolic of South Africa's long history of racialized oppression, restoring agency and dignity to its protagonists.

Along with their performance work, Strangelove is known for their ready-to-wear garments, manufactured and sold from the company's Johannesburg boutique, located in the Parktown neighborhood. The China bag projects, which are the focus of this exploration of Strangelove's oeuvre, were manifested in both realms of their production, prominently featured in several performance pieces and subtly reflected in their ready-to-wear lines.

Taxi Rank: animated commodities

Pater and Gibson have employed China bags as both artistic media and characters in dramatic narratives. Cheap plastic bags, ostensibly valued only for the goods they contain, draw in associations and emotions, as they circulate in global and local markets. China bags are foreign, even as they represent the local; they signify prosperity in the context of poverty; they are omnipresent, yet nearly invisible. Strangelove use the bags' contradictory associations to comment on the paradoxes that characterize their city and their country. One performance that literally embodies these contradictions took place far from the fashion runways and exclusive neighborhoods, where most fashion designers promote and sell their work.

On an inner city loading dock in June 2003, a crowd gathered for a performance created by Gibson and Pater. The event, entitled *Another Day at the Strangelove Taxi Rank*, was planned to coincide with South African Fashion Week, a major event that attracts the country's large fashion community. Instead of gathering at Sandton, the upscale suburban shopping and convention center, at which nearly all of the fashion week events were taking place, Strangelove brought its audience to a loading dock in the Carfax neighborhood, an industrial area in downtown Johannesburg, where their studio was then located.[3] In the middle of the loading dock sat several large, striped bags, made of white, red, and blue plastic fibers. Audience members moved around and between the bags as they found places on the cement floor that would become the stage. While they waited, cardboard shadow puppets performed on a makeshift screen, portraying taxi vans, street signs, and people waiting for rides, all accompanied by the sounds of honking cars, chugging engines, and travelers hailing drivers.[4]

As audience members found places to stand, the bags began to move. Arms and legs emerged and the bags began to interact. First, two of the bags got to their feet, revealing tall rubber boots. The bags then began to dance, performing in the style known as gumboot dancing, a distinctively South African form of entertainment (Erlmann 1989: 262; Gillespie 2008: 84).[5] Although it has become a tourist attraction today, gumboot dancing emerged out of the painful history of migrant labor, in which the horizons of workers were limited by their race in the Apartheid system. It was an outlet for creativity and means of covertly preserving the dances that were one aspect of the migrants' cultural heritage. On the loading dock in Johannesburg, the rubber boots worn by the bags could not help but evoke these associations.

As the two bags danced, a third began to move. This bag wore no boots and, it soon became clear, was a female character. One bare leg emerged from the bag, toe pointed elegantly. Slowly, deliberately, two hands appeared and began carefully unrolling a long stocking, beginning with the toes, pulled over the curving ankle, stretched along the smooth calf, suggestively lingering. The crowd hooted as the hands stroked the stocking-sheathed leg, a clear allusion to the use of a condom. In South Africa, where HIV/AIDS has thoroughly infiltrated public consciousness, references to condoms are intensely meaningful as part of widespread public discourses on safe sex.[6]

A birthing scene followed, in which the female bag lay on the ground, legs spread uncomfortably wide. The birth produced a group of small bags tied to a string of bag handles—a plastic umbilical cord. In the final element of the performance, the female bag slowly climbed to the top of a set of stairs, awkwardly moving on all fours. The audience and the gumboot-wearing bags cheered her on, as she pulled herself to the top where she stood, exhausted and triumphant. In this pantomimed drama, China bags were transformed into characters that struggled and triumphed, reproduced and entertained, all without escaping the restrictions of their lives by unzipping their bag bodies. Through these humble plastic bags, the designers created narratives and personalities as well as subtle social commentary on globalization by evoking the country's history of migrant labor, economic inequity, and the struggle to survive against immense odds.

The plastic bags that were their medium for *Taxi Rank* appear elsewhere in Strangelove's work. They used China bags as props in a series of photographs called *Johannesburg Walkabout*, created in collaboration with photographer Hannilie Coetzee. These were fashion photographs of a kind, because the

Figure 8.2 Strangelove (Carlo Gibson, Ziemek Pater), in collaboration with Hannelie Coetzee, from the series Soweto Walkabout, 2005–6. Courtesy of Carlo Gibson.

models wore Strangelove clothing, yet the city was as much the focus of the images as the fashions. Each image is set in unusual urban landscapes, in empty fields and beside highways. The models are engaged in ordinary activities—buying fruit from a stand, eating fast food from a paper bag, even urinating on a highway embankment. A China bag appears in each image; in some scenes the humble containers appear prominently, in others they are nearly absorbed by the barren urban landscapes. But their constant presence, once noted, lends them significance.

Strangelove also used China bags to show and to create fashion, sending models holding China bags down the runway at a 2005 fashion show. At the same event, they presented clothing made of the bags. These garments made use of the bags as textiles, disassembling the containers to tailor the plastic fibers into dresses, shorts, and other forms. In late 2008, the designers won a fashion competition in which they used a China bag to create a wedding dress.[7] The clothing made of China bags was never sold, largely because the work of disassembling and reworking the bags was labor intensive, but the garments dramatically enacted the bags' reach deep into people's daily lives.

Gibson and Pater's use of the bags depends upon the form's familiarity for diverse audiences. Initially, Gibson had worked with China bags as a student at the Johannesburg Technikon, where he and Pater met. Like many designers, he regularly used them as containers to transport his fabrics and other materials. Though they are made elsewhere, Gibson found that the bags "gave him the feeling of being African." He wondered how he could animate the bags, "to make them full of the life they carry" (Gibson 2009). The containers draw their local meanings from their presence in markets, where merchants and consumers use them to transport food, clothing, and other products. China bags also provide insights into circuits of labor migration, where they carry personal belongings rather than products for sale. And they link the intensely personal economy of an individuals' struggle to survive with networks of industrial mass-production and global merchandizing, dominated in recent decades by China, the country that lends the bags their name.

Strangelove's description of the bags' significance is founded in the containers' central yet unheralded role in countless lives, as illustrated by excerpts from a 2007 conference presentation by the designers (Gibson and Pater 2007):

These bags are used by hawkers and street vendors to transport goods daily, products ranging from fruit and vegetables to cheap Chinese imported clothes and shoes. These bags also carry home the acquisitions of migrant workers from Zimbabwe, Malawi, and other countries when they pay return visits home after their stints of working in the City of Gold [Johannesburg].

Looking more deeply into the bags' contents, Gibson and Pater have found that the containers evoke profound sentiments:

this seemingly basic item begins to represent emotional content [...] the association of the return of a father from a long working stay in the big city; the pride a parent feels having returned home from working in a faraway place bearing vital consumable items: mielie meal, sugar and, if all has gone well, perhaps a few items of luxury.

In addition to their emotional significance, China bags can stand in for the ironies of local consumption practices within a global economy:

Thanks to its low price the China bag has, in its own way, colonized most continents of the globe. Ironically, thousands of subsistence traders in Africa carry the very goods in those bags that indirectly undermine any possibility of the growth of a stable manufacturing sector in this continent's economies.

Fashioning modernity in South Africa

Strangelove's animations of China bags, in their many manifestations, both illustrate and extend theorizations of the traffic in commodities and identities across cultures. Appadurai's analysis of the cultures of globalization addresses the diffusion of commodities and cultural practices, noting that these potential agents of homogenization may paradoxically enhance cultural differentiation: "globalization itself is a deeply historical, uneven, and even *localizing* process" (Appadurai 1996: 17).[8] He describes clothing as one such localizing commodity. Indeed, clothing is exceptionally nuanced, mobile, and accessible—amenable to the subtleties of shifting identities. Far from homogenizing, Strangelove's intervention into the circulation of an emblematically global commodity draws out distinctively local meanings.

Jean Comaroff's assessment of dress as a tool for conversion, colonization, and resistance in nineteenth-century South Africa offers a historical instance of this localizing process, as non-local clothing forms were transformed into markers of local identities. Using the example of a British missionary society among Southern Tswana communities, Comaroff's analysis exposes the ironies and innovations of consumption. She describes the unintended outcomes of missionary efforts to deploy clothing as a means of reforming the "heathen" Tswana. The re-imagined meanings of global commodities produced new manifestations of "traditional" culture. Comaroff explores how imported garment styles, instead of bringing the Tswana closer to European culture, were combined with indigenous elements to create "rural folk dress" that marked Tswana women's identities. Ironically, she notes, "significant features of this style would endure for decades—or rather, be actively reproduced as "tradition""￼ (Comaroff 1996: 37). Fashion, fueled by the introduction of new forms, was an ideal tool for the Tswana to reinforce a sense of ethnic identity that had been destabilized by missionary pressures, for fashion "epitomizes the power of the commodity to encompass the self" (Comaroff 1996: 21).

The textile known as *shweshwe* or *isishweshwe* offers another South African example of this declaration of local identities through imported forms, implicitly pushing back against homogenization. This cloth has become an icon of South African identity despite its history as an imported form (Leeb du Toit 2005). *Isishweshwe* is characterized by small, neatly ordered geometric patterns, and a limited color palette of blue, brown, occasionally red, maroon, or brown. The cloth was originally made using indigo dye, but since the late nineteenth century, it has been made using a synthetic form of indigo developed in Germany. In South Africa, its status as imported (arriving with German settlers in the nineteenth century) long precluded its inclusion in conventional conceptions of "authentic" South African attire.

Since the late 1990s, however, *isishweshwe* has become a symbol of national identity. South African manufacturer Da Gama Textiles is the only producer globally still using the nineteenth-century process associated with "authentic" *isishweshwe*: copper rollers etched with patterns that are used to apply an acid solution to blue dyed cotton percale, bleaching out white patterns. Numerous South African fashion designers have made use of the textile, including Amanda Laird Cherry, Bongiwe Walaza, David West, and Ephymol. In the words of one young design student, "shweshwe is the celebration of a cultural heritage that embraces the new" (Counihan 2005: 63). Or, as cultural critic Adam Levin notes, the cloth has been transformed from the attire of matrons who have little access to fashion into the garb of choice for trend-setters: "*Shwe-shwe* fabric—once the domain of overweight aunties—is now a favorite of young black and white women" (Levin 2005: 173).

Like the Tswana dress analyzed by Comaroff, and the *isishweshwe* that has been adapted to youth markets, Strangelove's use of China bags vividly enacts Gell's analysis of consumption across cultures. Gell documents how the Muria of India create cultural meanings for objects, transforming them from uninflected goods into symbolic forms that articulate their own identities: "What distinguishes consumption from exchange is not that consumption has a psychological dimension that exchange lacks, but that consumption involves the incorporation of the consumed item into the personal and social identity of the consumer" (Gell 1986: 112). Those forms that are consumed become elements of "personalia," the complex of attributes by which people are located within social networks (Gell 1986: 113).

That some commodities are imbued with meanings as part of their consumption, signifying relationships and histories, is not the most provocative aspect of Gell's analysis. The commodities in question, which are central to Muria personalia, have non-local origins. The Muria employ non-local commodities, including most notably clothing and jewelry, as markers of local identity. Further, Gell notes that "the Muria have imposed their own set of social evaluations on them [non-Muria prestige goods], which are quite distinct from the ones operative among the groups with whom these goods originated" (Gell 1986: 121).

This conception of commodities as elements of personal identities, absorbed from outside one's self as well as outside one's culture, is dramatized and expanded by Strangelove's China bags. The translation of bags into clothing, shown on runways or worn for performances, makes them into personalia—elements of personal identity—and further into personalities themselves. In the *Taxi Rank* performance, Strangelove draws the China bag deeper still into social and individual identities by animating the forms, literally making commodities into social actors.

China bags: local everywhere, global at home

The container at the center of these explorations of identities and consumption, the China bag, is made of polypropylene fibers, woven into a fabric that is both light and strong, as well as inexpensive. While the bags appear in many colors and patterns, the most common style is red, blue, and white plaid. The bags may also be adorned with woven or printed images and patterns. My recent observations in a random assortment of locations—Mali, Peru, South Africa, France, Niger, and the United States—indicates that the most common China bag motifs include names of cities and countries, along with iconic images from those locations (Eiffel Tower, London Bridge), cartoon characters, and animals.

The bags are made in a variety of sizes, but always in the same rectangular shape, with no interior pockets or dividers, two simple, strap-like handles, and a zipper closure. Their lack of structure makes the bags extremely versatile—they conform to the shape of whatever they contain, and when partially full they can be wedged into corners in the backs or on the tops of taxis and buses (Klopper 2010). When not in use, they can be neatly folded flat, the size of a newspaper.

Figure 8.3 China Bags and other products for sale, Bamako, Mali, 2008. Photograph by the author.

Their origins are obscure—their omnipresence makes tracing their moment of inception exceptionally difficult. What matters most is that they are everywhere, and that they are useful in every context.

Eminently practical, these containers seem to leave little room for symbolic or emotional baggage, for irony or humor. In markets, bus stations, and airports the world over—indeed, nearly anywhere people and goods converge—China bags can be found, filled with recent purchases, goods for sale, all sorts of possessions on the move. The China bag's global circulation and its role in contemporary South Africa make it a window onto the ways in which commodities and globalization have been theorized as elements of modernity in Africa. Because it is defined by change from what has come before, fashion is inextricably connected to chronology. Even when clothing trends reach into the past for sources of inspiration, their focus on innovation gives the past "the scent of the modern" (Benjamin 1999: 252). A constant drive to leave the present behind binds fashion to a constantly changing modernity. Strangelove's China bags play with this expectation of modernity, implicitly challenging its assumptions.

Strangelove's work is elucidated by Ferguson's critique of models of "alternative," or "multiple" modernities, used (primarily in academic circles) to describe contemporary non-Western cultures. He asserts "the alternative-modernity formulation misses what may be most important about the current mutation in the meaning of 'modernity' for Africans" (Ferguson 2006: 185). Theoretically, modernity replaces tradition; it is marked by cultural practices that share more with other "modern" societies than with long-standing local practices. But this is not the lived expectation of modernity in much of Africa. Instead, "modernity" means economic and personal security, access to funds, goods, and services that ensure a good life. Ferguson describes the irony of underdevelopment in many African communities that are increasingly marginalized by global markets. For people whose standard of living is declining, who are denied access to the trappings of modernity, aware of yet experiencing only vicariously its comforts and privileges, the modern may be a remembered past rather than a promised future. Ferguson describes the attitudes of Zambian mineworkers: "We used to be modern—or, at least, well on our way—but now we've been denied that opportunity" (Ferguson 2006: 186). Jean and John Comaroff encountered a similar perception in South Africa, where a Tswana farmer described modernity as a status that is nearly but never quite achieved: "things modern […] seem always to be in the next village" (Comaroff and Comaroff 1993: xii).

The China bag is a distinctively modern product, yet it emerges out of a modernity that might also be past, or just out of reach. It is perfectly designed for this failed modernity. Its production and its use emblematize the alienation of industrialization, one marker of modernity. The name of the bag signals this distant manufacture, and it calls to mind the changing meanings of China in Africa today. China is neither the remote, exotic "Other" nor the Communist behemoth that used to represent a strategic alternative to South Africa's alliance with the Soviet Union (Taylor 2000). Instead, China is now a dominant player in the same global capitalist arenas as other market economies. According to a recent analysis of South Africa's clothing economy by the Trade Law Centre for Southern Africa, "The overwhelming features of clothing imports [...] into South Africa since 1996 has been the dramatic increase in these imports and the dominance of China in these imports" (Sandrey and Fundira 2008). The tensions surrounding China's threat to domestic textile and fashion markets is apparent even to the casual observer. During a visit to Durban, in the upscale Gateway Mall, I visited a Young Designers Emporium, a chain of stores that feature garments by young South African designers. In the window, a large and brightly colored sign proclaimed: "Cheaper than China [...] 100% South African." In her presentation at a business seminar, during the 2005 South African Fashion Week, fashion consultant Rhona Carter decried China's dominance, calling it a "monster" that would undersell and out-compete national manufacturers (Carter 2005). The China bag represents this dominance.

The bags' modernity is further dramatized by their medium: they are made of a substance that is entirely disconnected from the natural world, made of "polymers" rather than any recognizable raw materials. Yet, despite its global reach and synthetic materials, in many ways the bag is remarkably low tech. The polypropylene of which it is made can be transformed into any shape, any texture. In most of its uses, polypropylene is molded or extruded; the weaving technique used to create China bags seems positively quaint, an anachronistic reference to the limitations imposed by conventional textile production. The design of the bags is also dramatically low tech—little more than a box with handles, all right angles with no additional pockets or stylistic embellishments.

As noted earlier, China bags are most commonly striped or plaid, in red, white, and blue, or other primary colors. These unremarkable abstract motifs offer little fodder for interpretation. The bags adorned with place names, such as Paris and New York, in contrast, may bear symbolic weight in the many of the economies where China bags circulate. They seem to underscore the failure of the modern in the places where many Africans live. Their romantic representations of these world cities and sites contrast dramatically with their environments, in crowded markets, strapped to the tops of buses and informal taxis. Strangelove's use of these humble, utilitarian containers in the rarified field of fashion design creates a similar frisson, drawing attention to the cultural associations borne by this inconspicuous object.

Fashion: identity and industry in South Africa

"Every 1 million rands of sale in the clothing sector creates 11 jobs compared with five jobs in gold mining for the same amount of sales."
—Etienne Vick, organizer of the 2008 SA Clothing and Textile Workers' Union.[9]

The medium that lies at the heart of Strangelove's production—fashion—is a particularly rich field of creativity in South Africa, and one with broad implications in light of the country's history. Labor organizer Etienne Vick's comparison of job production in the gold mining and the clothing industries, asserting that clothing is a more effective engine for employment, brings together two realms in which the differential treatment of races was vividly enacted under Apartheid. Both also represent sites of control over indigenous bodies. The need for a readily controllable labor force for the gold mines around which Johannesburg was founded in the late nineteenth century drove many of the early manifestations of Apartheid. Mbembe describes this system of embodied racism: "In relation to blacks, both the techniques of power and profit were, ever since the founding of Johannesburg, centered on the body: the individual body of the migrant worker and the racial body of the populace" (Mbembe 2008: 52). While mining controlled bodies in order to extract value from the land, dress offered a means of shaping identities to enforce or resist social control.[10] Personal identity—primarily racial but also ethnic and regional identity—was the central determining factor in the system that developed out of this drive to control the lives and labor of South Africans before and during the Apartheid period (1948–1994).

In a reflection of this history, bodies and the clothing that adorn bodies have been central preoccupations for South African creative expression in the years since the end of Apartheid. In her discussion of the prominence of the body as subject matter in contemporary South African studio art, van der Watt notes: "For it is on the body more often than not that identity seems to converge [...] often the visible part of identity, such as race, is taken to stand in for the whole..." (Van der Watt 2004: 49). Klopper's analysis of clothing and politics in the post-Apartheid era demonstrates that the clothed body has been a key site for the negotiation of complex new identities: "New and reviewed visions of fashionableness have played a central role in these recent attempts to develop a post-Apartheid identity, in part because dress provides unlimited possibilities for the renegotiation and performance of notions of self" (Klopper 2000: 216). That bodies and the clothing that adorns them have become key elements of the cultural symbolism in South Africa should not be surprising, given the country's recent legacy of oppression. In light of this history, Strangelove's use of clothing as their medium of expression adds another layer to their engagement with the legacy of South Africa's past.

May 2008: another connotation of China bags

In the summer of 2008, Strangelove's adoption of China bags as an icon of South Africa's cultures of migration, globalization, and the struggle to get by collided with another, tragic aspect of the bags' significance. The bags' association with migration took an ominous turn that summer, as economic disintegration in South Africa's northern neighbor Zimbabwe sent desperate refugees fleeing from poverty and near-starvation across the border into South Africa. The association of plastic bags with migration and dislocation is evoked in the names by which they are known for some South Africans: *Mashangani*[11] and *khonza ekhaya*. *Khonza Ekhaya*, a Zulu term for the bags, literally means "goodbye at home," a reference to the expectation that people who leave home with a packed bag are leaving forever (Klopper 2010).

Mashangani refers to the Shangani or Shangaan people, from Tsonga-speaking communities in the northeast of South Africa, as well as in Mozambique and Zimbabwe. The term also signifies non-local identity, used in reference to people of Zimbabwean and Mozambican origins, often carrying negative conno-tations (Ashforth 1998).[12] The bag is associated with their migration into South Africa from homes across the border in search of employment and goods. In the fraught environment of contemporary South African identity politics, immigrants—specifically immigrants from other African countries—are blamed for "stealing" jobs from South Africans.[13] A range of other social ills are attributed to those identified as foreigners, as Simone notes in his discussion of Johannesburg: "a large measure of xenophobia prevails, where foreign Africans are blamed for an overcrowded informal trading sector, the growth of the narcotics trade, and the general deterioration of the inner city" (Simone 2000: 434). In the summer of 2008, as Zimbabwe continued its tragic descent into chaos, the influx of Zimbabwean migrants became the central element in an explosion of xenophobic violence across South Africa. According to a May 2008 article on the events in the *Mail and Guardian*, more than sixty people were killed and thousands displaced; government sources estimated the number of people displaced by the violence at 30,000, while some NGOs placed the number at 100,000.[14]

The news was filled with stories of brutal beatings, burning of houses, and random interrogations of Zimbabweans, Mozambicans, and others who had lived in South Africa for decades but whose names indicated roots elsewhere. News photographs of refugees fleeing the country vividly illustrate the desperate conditions these people faced. China bags appeared repeatedly in the scenes at border crossings and in the churches and other locations where Zimbabweans sought refuge, underscoring the omnipresence of these plastic bags, which were pressed into service as beds for some. I was in South Africa at the time, and my discussions about fashion were tinged with the bewilderment and repulsion so many South Africans felt at the sight of this ethnic violence, a horrible echo of the Apartheid era. For Strangelove, two white South African artists whose own biographies include immigration from Poland and Italy, the violence spawned doubt about the future of the country, and thoughts of departure. For them, the China bag has, unfortunately, still more layers of meaning now, as a symbol of violence, fear, and the failure of global markets.

Coda: China bags in Chinatown

This analysis of an ostensibly unremarkable commodity's rich symbolic potential ends with a brief introduction to further twists in the China bag's biography, absorbing new meanings in markets that are worlds away from the struggles of South Africa's migrants and immigrants. In 2006 and 2007, Jack Spade (the men's line of the well-known bag designer Kate Spade) and Louis Vuitton each created high fashion versions of the China bag. For Jack Spade, the bag and associated accessories were marketed as "The Chinatown Collection," a reference not to the bags' country of origin, but to Chinatown in New York. This was an ironic spin on the phenomenon of counterfeit designer bags, associated with the shops in Chinatown that skirt the law to sell Gucci, Louis Vuitton, Kate Spade, and other brands' knock-offs. A year after the Jack Spade bags, Louis Vuitton produced a "street bag" that appears to be indistinguishable from cheap China bags—the same size, shape, standard red, white, and blue-plaid pattern. These bags, however, are made of leather rather than plastic, and they are embossed with a large Louis Vuitton logo. The China bag reproduction phenomenon inspired one observer of fashion and counterfeit designer bags to summarize the absurdity of this strange fashion loop:

> Any day now, if it hasn"t happened already, I expect copies of the Louis Vuitton Street bag to turn up in Manila's [or New York's] bazaars, transported in the same plastic shopping bags it stylishly parodies. The luxury house rips off the counterfeiters, who then rip off the luxury rip-off. At which point we wander into the realm of meta-fashion. (Zafra 2007).

Strangelove's China bag garments might be viewed as ironic meta-fashions, toying with the lowbrow associations of their material. But in South Africa today, the China bag is inextricably knitted into the struggle to get by—they are the luggage used by migrants who seek a livelihood yet risk becoming targets of others' frustration; the containers for goods whose acquisition marks the success of a returning family member; the products of distant manufacturers whose cheap goods put South Africans out of work. These bags are neutral sounding boards, sensitive to the reverberations of the lives around them, a powerful medium for art, fashion, and social commentary.

Notes

1 Many thanks to Carlo Gibson and Ziemek Pater for their time, good humor, and wonderful work. I thoroughly enjoyed all of our conversations, in South Africa and the United States.

2 Carlo Gibson continues to direct the Strangelove brand, producing clothing and collaborating on a range of art-related projects. Ziemek Pater is working in other aspects of the fashion industry.

3 The event was conceptualized in response to an invitation from the French Institute of South Africa, the French embassy's cultural agency, to participate in events surrounding Bastille Day. Ziemek Pater, interview by the author via email, July 27, 2009.

4 The screen was made of sheets of pattern-making paper, the puppets of cardboard, and lights were inexpensive lanterns mounted onto long, handheld poles. Carlo Gibson and Ziemek Pater, interview by the author, Johannesburg, July 29, 2005.

5 Erlmann speculates that gumboot dancing originated among stevedores on the docks of Durban; Gillespie locates the origins of the practices in the mining camps of the Johannesburg region.

6 The deficiencies in South Africa's past national HIV/AIDS policies, including most notably former president Thabo Mbeki's denial of a causative link between HIV and AIDS, have been much discussed and deservedly condemned. Safe sex was, however, endorsed and promoted by governmental policies during the Mbeki era, and increased condom distribution has been assessed as one positive element of HIV/AIDS policies of the period. See, for instance, Mbali 2003: 315.

7 The event, called a Style War, was sponsored by the Tropika fruit juice company.

8 Of clothing, Appadurai notes: "The globalization of culture is not the same as its homogenization, but globalization involves the use of a variety of instruments of homogenization (armaments, advertising techniques, language hegemonies, and clothing styles) that are absorbed into local political and cultural economies." (42)

9 "Fashion Unions Take to the Street," *Design Indaba* 3rd Quarter (2008), 5.

10 Nelson Mandela's strategic use of clothing exemplifies the power of dress as a means of resistance. In his autobiography, Mandela described his choice of attire for his first court appearance in the trial that sent him to Robben Island: "I entered the court that Monday wearing a traditional Xhosa leopard-skin *kaross* [cloak] instead of a suit and tie [...] I had chosen traditional dress to emphasize the symbolism that I was a black African walking into a white man's court. I was literally carrying on my back the history, culture and heritage of my people" (Mandela 1995: 384–5).

11 Gibson and Pater had heard this name used for the bag, and I have also found in use on some South African blogs. I have located no published documentation of the term.

12 In his investigation of spiritual belief and social anxiety in Soweto, Ashforth elucidates an informant's reference to Mashangani, noting that the term refers to "the most despised ethnic group in South Africa concentrated on the border with Mozambique and consisting of large numbers of immigrants to South Africa from that country" (Ashforth 1998: 50).

13 Neocosmos convincingly argues that while poverty and high unemployment may partially explain this xenophobic tendency, one must also look to South Africa's public policy on immigration, to discourses on national identity, and to media coverage of immigration-related issues as sources of prejudice and violence. (Neocosmos 2008: 586–94).

14 "Toll from xenophobic attacks rises," *Mail and Guardian* (May 31, 2008). http://www.mg.co.za/article/2008-05-31-toll-from-xenophobic-attacks-rises (accessed 20 December 2010).

References

Appadurai, Arjun. *Modernity at Large: Cultural Dimensions of Globalization*. Minneapolis: University of Minnesota Press, 1996.

Ashforth, Adam. "Reflections on Spiritual Insecurity in a Modern African City (Soweto)." *African Studies Review* 41 (3) (1998): 39–67.

Benjamin, Walter. "Theses on the Philosophy of History." In *Illuminations*, ed. H. Arendt, trans. Harry Zohn. London: Pimlico, 1999 [1968].

Buys, Annie. "Happening on the Fringe of Fashion." *Mail and Guardian* (July 21, 2006): np.

Comaroff, Jean. "The Empire's Old Clothes: Fashioning the Colonial Subject." In *Cross-Cultural Consumption: Global Markets, Local Realities*, ed. D. Howes, 19–38. New York: Routledge, 1996.19-38.

Comaroff, Jean, and John Comaroff. *Modernity and Its Malcontents: Ritual and Power in Postcolonial Africa*. Chicago: University of Chicago Press, 1993.

Counihan, H. "Shweshwe: The Long History of the Latest Trend." *Urban Fabrics* (July 2005): 62–3.

Erlmann, Veit. "'Horses in the Race Course': The Domestication of Ingoma Dancing in South Africa." *Popular Music* 8 (3) (1989): 259–73.

Ferguson, James. *Global Shadows: Africa in the Neoliberal World Order*. Durham: Duke University Press, 2006.

Gell, Alfred. "Newcomers to the World of Goods: Consumption among Muria Gonds." In *The Social Life of Things: Commodities in Social Perspective*, ed. A. Appadurai. New York: Cambridge University Press.

Gibson, Carlo. Interview by the author via telephone, July 23, 2009.

Gibson, Carlo, and Ziemek Pater. "Objects, Agents, and Spaces of Circulation" (paper presented at African Visual Cultures: Crossing Disciplines, Crossing Regions, Carter Lectures on Africa, University of Florida, March 28–April 1, 2007).

Gillespie, Kelly. "Moralizing Security: Corrections and the Post-Apartheid Prison." *Race/Ethnicity* 2 (1) (2008): 69–87.

Klopper, Sandra. "Re-dressing the Past: the Africanization of Sartorial Style in Contemporary South Africa." In *Hybridity and Its Discontents: Politics, Science, Culture*, eds A. Brah and A. Coombes, 216-32. New York: Routledge, 2000a.

Klopper, Sandra. "From Adornment to Artefact to Art: Historical Perspectives on South-East African Beadwork." in *South East African Beadwork*, eds M. Stevenson and M. Graham-Stewart, 9–43. Vlaeberg, South Africa: Fernwood Press, 2000b.

Klopper, Sandra. Personal communication via email, January 22, 2010.

Kopytoff, Igor. "The Cultural Biography of Things: Commoditization as Process." In *The Social Life of Things: Commodities in Social Perspective*, ed. A. Appadurai. New York: Cambridge University Press, 1986.

Leeb du Toit, Juliette. "Sourcing Amajamani/isiswhweshwe and its Indigenization in South Africa." Unpublished paper, 2005.

Levin, Adam. *The Art of African Shopping*. Cape Town: Struik Publishers, 2005.

Mandela, Nelson. *Long Walk to Freedom: The Autobiography of Nelson Mandela*. London: Abacus, 1995.

Mbali, Mandisa. "HIV/AIDS policy-making in post-apartheid South Africa." In *State of the Nation: South Africa 2003-2004*, ed. J. Daniel, A. Habib, and R. Southall. Cape Town: HSRC Press, 2003.

Mbembe, Achille. "Aesthetics of Superfluidity." In *Johannesburg: The Elusive Metropolis*, eds S. Nuttall and A. Mbembe. Durham: Duke University Press, 2008.

na. "Toll from xenophobic attacks rises," *Mail and Guardian* (May 31, 2008a). http://www.mg.co.za/article/2008-05-31-toll-from-xenophobic-attacks-rises (accessed 20 December 2010).

na. "Fashion Unions Take to the Street." *Design Indaba,* 3rd Quarter (2008b): 5.

Neocosmos, Michael. "The Politics of Fear and the Fear of Politics: Reflections on Xenophobic Violence in South Africa." *Journal of Asian and African Studies* 43 (6) (2008): 586–94.

Pater, Ziemak. Interview by the author, Johannesburg, July 29, 2005.

Sandrey, Ron, and Taku Fundira. *Quota Imports of Chinese Clothing into South Africa: the First Year Analysis* (Stellenbosch, South Africa: Tralac Trade Brief 4, 2008). Available online: www.tralac.org.

Simone, Abdoumaliq. "Going South: African Immigrants in Johannesburg." In *Senses of Culture: South African Culture Studie*s, eds S. Nutall and C. Michaels. Oxford: Oxford University Press, 2001.

Taylor, Ian. "The Ambiguous Commitment: The People's Republic of China and the Anti-Apartheid Struggle in South Africa." *Journal of Contemporary African Studies* 18 (1) (2000): 91–106.

Van der Watt, Liese. "Towards an 'Adversarial Aesthetics': A Personal Response to Personal Affects." In *Personal Affects: Power and Poetics in Contemporary South African Art*, ed. D. Brodie. New York: Museum for African Art, 2004.

Zafra, Jessica. "Emotional Baggage." *The Standard, China's Business Newspaper* (May 19, 2007). Available online at: http://www.thestandard.com.hk/news_print.asp?art_id=44747&sid=13547179 (accessed 1 December 2011).

9

CONSTRUCTING FASHIONABLE DRESS AND IDENTITY IN BHUTAN[1]

EMMA DICK

Introduction

While working as Head of Fashion in LASALLE College of the Arts in Singapore (2007–10), I was approached by Singapore International Foundation (SIF) to act as a Specialist Volunteer Overseas to co-develop a tailoring curriculum for the Ministry of Labour and Human Resources in Bhutan, in an international development project funded by the United Nations Development Programme (UNDP) in 2008–9. In this chapter, I present a critical reflection on our curriculum and broadly situate the role of international development projects focused on textiles and dress within discourses of globalization. I examine how the interaction with non-governmental and inter-governmental agencies may combine with ideas about dress and identity within the recipient country. I wish to personify the processes through which these "hybrid" identities are constructed, both physically and metaphorically, through ideas about fashionable dress present in garments and online discussions about them to challenge simplistic essentialist thinking about the ways in which "fashion" is adopted by a "non-Western" culture.

As a small developing nation, Bhutan may seem an unlikely location to situate a discussion of fashionable dress and identity. There exists a popular consensus that fashion is a modern cultural practice that evolved through the emergence of capitalism and consumer culture and exists in modern cities in the "developed" world. Scholarship offers a variety of opinions. Craik (2009: 19–20) suggests that:

There is a powerful perception and myth that non-Western cultures have stable and unchanging clothing codes, perhaps driven by the synchronic approach to ethnographic case studies and an apparent desire to cleave discernable differences in taxonomy between artificial binary categories of "us" and "them."

Such binary categories are made even more emphatic in the case of "developing" countries, variously orientalized as "exotic," "ethnic," or "wild" backdrops for photo shoots, and as open sources of "authentic" inspiration for designers in the international fashion press. References to Bhutan in American *Vogue* assert a mythical association with Shangri-La, an imagined utopia presented by James Hilton's 1933 novel *Lost Horizon*, which describes a pristine medieval Buddhist culture, somewhere in the high Himalayas. The *Vogue* discourse about Bhutan is evident from the 1960s onward, as the country was beginning to engage actively in international socio-political networks. Bhutan is described as "one of the magic words [...] organized around castle-strongholds (like mediaeval Scotland)" (*Vogue*, June 1963), ruled by "a charming family from a small, imperilled kingdom in the Himalayas" [whose name translates as] "Fearless Thunderbolt, Master of Cosmic Power" (*Vogue*, July 1967). The narrative continues, practically unchanged, to the present. In 2005, U.S. designer Jane Mayle described Bhutan as a "mythical, magical land almost untouched by the modern world" (*Vogue*, June 2005). Condé Nast Traveller magazine, in October 2008, lavished an eight-page editorial on Bhutan entitled, "*Flying Tiger, Thundering Dragon*," featuring images of Asian supermodel Ling Tan, juxtaposed beside masked Buddhist dancers, a prayer wheel, an archer, and Buddhist monks. These fashion editorials echo exactly the phenomena Niessen, Jones, and Leskowich (2003: 18) suggest:

> Contemporary ways of knowing and representing the Oriental Other as timeless, exotic, untouched, dangerous, passive, inscrutable, or oppressed are the legacies of earlier Orientalist frameworks developed to understand and subjugate Asia.

The enduring Condé Nast discourse on Bhutan acts as a driving force to impel the fashionistas of the world to make pilgrimage and transform the Shangri-La myth into reality. Designer Derek Lam holidayed in Bhutan in 2011. Polymath businessman Sir David Tang, founder of Shanghai Tang, reportedly celebrated his fiftieth birthday there in 2004. Christina Ong, founder of worldwide fashion distributor Club 21 owns a luxury hotel there. For Autumn/Winter 2012, Proenza Schouler captured the "magical beauty of Bhutan," along with a self-confessed pastiche of "everything Asian" (*i-D* online, 2012). Diane von Furstenberg and Christian Louboutin traveled to Bhutan in May 2012 to stock up on items, including an embroidered vest for Louboutin to wear to the Met Ball. *Diane's Diary* conveys a well-meaning, yet rather patronizing rhetoric of the "Other," as she describes meeting the Bhutanese Royal Family:

> It is like being in a fairy tale. They look and behave like a fairy tale King and Queen. They are so incredibly nice, simple and caring about their lovely Kingdom (von Furstenberg, 2012).

Due to the country's physical inaccessibility in the high Himalayas, accessed by only the national airline, Drukair, and a deliberate low-impact, high-yield tourism policy, which sets a minimum daily cost for tourists of US $200, Bhutan manages to embody the Shangri-La myth, and attains a level of cultural distinction by association with the rich and successful who can afford to holiday there.

However, this imagined Shangri-La land is in sharp contrast to the economic daily reality of Bhutan, termed one of the world's smallest and least developed economies by OECD, eligible for official development assistance, and tabulated by The World Bank to have an average annual gross national income per capita of US $2,370 (World Bank, 2014). Bartering for basic foodstuffs is practiced, and the average life expectancy is calculated within the lowest 30 percent of the world. Money played virtually no role in Bhutan until the 1960s, when tax

Figure 9.1 Mount Everest's summit seen from above the clouds through the window of a Drukair flight to Bhutan, June 2009. Photograph by the author.

could still be paid in the form of textiles (Pommaret, 1994: 174). Little private enterprise exists, and employment opportunities are precarious, especially for the burgeoning young population. The median age of the country is twenty-five years (CIA, 2012). Public concern is expressed in the national press about the dangers of drug abuse and the violence simmering among a disaffected youth, who have limited future prospects locally, but are now connected to images of the material wealth and opportunity of the "outside" world, since television was introduced to the country in 1999, to broadcast the fourth King's silver jubilee.

It is against this backdrop of economic uncertainty that our tailoring curriculum was developed, to provide a possible career path and creative opportunities for future generations. Developing nations such as Bhutan may adopt certain elements of the "historically and geographically specific system of dress" (i.e. "Western") that Entwistle (2000) identifies, during encounters with international development agencies and individuals. This is how the hybrid identities, theorized by Appadurai (1990), begin to emerge in the discussion of globalization. Current Anglophone-centric scholarship offers a range of definitions for theorizing "fashion," which broadly agree on its ephemerality; its fundamental need for continual changing of styles; and its geographical, historical, and cultural locus of power in the post-industrial cities of Paris, London, New York, and their descendants in the second- and third-tier global network of cities now staging "Fashion Weeks" as a powerful indicator of national economic, cultural, and creative success.

I do not believe that it is particularly meaningful to try to enforce one universal definition of "fashion," and, from the evidence presented by Bhutan, I would suggest that multiple world fashion "systems" exist in chaotic and variously changing relationships to one another (see, for example, Craik, 1993; Riello and McNeil, 2010; Kaiser, 2011). By looking at the production of garments in Bhutan, through the example of our curriculum, and the production of ideas about what constitutes fashionable identity by a local Facebook group called Bhutan Street Fashion, I offer, here, a preliminary suggestion of how people within Bhutan actively engage with, and construct, their own ideas about fashionable dress and identity.

Driglam namzha: a national dress code

The historical and cultural context of dress in Bhutan is framed by the existence of a Buddhist monastic dress code, following models established in the seventeenth century, which since 1989 has been fairly rigorously applied as mandatory in civil society. *Driglam namzha* is an important example to emphasize that what constitutes "traditional" dress is hardly traditional, authentic, or static, but in this case has been adopted for very particular political and social impact. Bhutan was never colonized, thus, the internal socio-political, cultural, and economic structures evolved without undue external influence. The insistence on strict codes of public behavior and dress forms part of a conscious agenda of nation building by the Royal Government of Bhutan, to avoid any threat of internal political fragmentation into different factions based along ethnic lines, which, it was feared, could cause Bhutan to become subsumed into its neighboring Hindu states, as had happened to Sikkim, in 1975. The official dress code is based on the traditional dress of the *Ngalop* ethnic group, the dominant social and religious group within Bhutan, said to descend from the earliest bearers of Tibetan Buddhism into the country in the ninth century CE. The national dress code, rigorously applied since 1989, tightly regulates public attire at all official sites, but does not apply to Hindu priests or foreigners, an exception which, in itself, promotes potentially problematic ideas about national and ethnic identity within an otherwise relatively non-hierarchical society (Pommaret, 1994: 173). Shortly after the institution of the strict dress code in 1989, an estimated 80,000 Hindu *Lhotshampas* of Nepali origin from the south of Bhutan fled as refugees from Bhutan, not wishing to be assimilated into the dominant ethnic-political group.

The national dress for men, *gho,* is the same garment as worn by most Tibetan males, but is hitched up to the knees to give greater freedom of movement. The word *gho* literally means "garment," while the Tibetan equivalent item of dress is called *chuba*. The *togo* is a shirt with long white cuffs worn underneath the *gho*, the term borrowed from an item of monastic dress. In addition to the *gho*, the national dress code requires men on official business to wear a *kabney,* a large scarf of a specified color, according to their rank in civil or religious society. This is wrapped around the body from the left shoulder to the right hip. A red *kabney* indicates male members of the royal family or higher-ranked officials in the civil service. White is the color worn by ordinary citizens, and saffron yellow may be worn only by the King and the chief abbot, or *Je Khenpo*. As Bhutan is one of the world's youngest multi-party democracies, modern color codes have been created for *kabneys* worn by members of the new National Assembly and National Council, and established by the constitution in 2008 (*Bhutan Observer*, 2011). The wearing of *kabney* is said to have begun in the time of Gautama Buddha, and the exchanging of scarves with all official communication was observed by the few Europeans who visited Bhutan in the eighteenth century on diplomatic and trade missions, such as George Bogle, who visited Bhutan on behalf of the East India Company, in 1774, and Captain Samuel Turner, in 1783 (Turner, 1800; Stewart, 2009; Teltscher, 2003).

For women, national dress consists of a *kira*, a rectangle of cloth, usually about three meters in length of hand-woven textile, which is wrapped around the body, folded into a wide pleat in the front, fastened at the shoulders with brooches, called *tinkhup,* or *koma*, and secured with a tight narrow cloth, or *kera*, wrapped around the waist. The *kira* is worn on top of a loose long-sleeved Tibetan-style blouse, or *wangu,* and the look is completed with a short wide-sleeved jacket, or *tego*. The jacket sleeves are aligned with the blouse sleeves and folded back with them into cuffs worn a little above the wrist. A shoulder cloth, or *rachu,* is worn draped across the left shoulder (Myers and Bean, 1994).

In private, Bhutanese people often wear "Western-style" clothing, of "pants" and "shirts," but anyone engaged in public life must abide by *driglam namzha*. This means all civil servants, students, people engaged in the tourism industry, or those who represent Bhutan officially, in any context, must follow these rules and regulations, even though they are perhaps inevitably at odds with the everyday dress practices of some Bhutanese, some of whom prefer Western dress:

> I like wearing my tracksuit or my jeans. But I know I will get stopped by the police [...] then I just say that I am on my way to play football. They can't fine me since they can't prove I am not (Whitecross, 2009: 67).

Fines enforced for breaking the *drighlam namzha* amount to approximately three days' wages for the average Bhutanese, so the incentive to dress within the law is quite strong. The young Bhutanese people whom I interviewed seem to have no problem in following *drighlam namzha,* where required, and dressing in "pants and shirts" when off-duty. The imposition of conformity through dress and appearance, propagated through the newly codified *Dzongka* national language section of *Kuensel*, the state newspaper, also diminishes the potential applicability of dominant "Western" theories about fashion to accurately describe the current practices of everyday dress in Bhutan. The two contexts of "official" and "off-duty" allowed the Bhutanese to hold both sets of values in their mind simultaneously, to exhibit a dual-consciousness of dress.

A definition often quoted for the term "fashion" is from Joanne Entwistle (2000), who determines it as, "a system of dress found in societies where social mobility is possible." This concept does not correlate with Bhutanese ideas of state sovereignty, which are fundamentally different to those presented by European history. Furthermore, fashion is overwhelmingly construed as a materialistic and superficial field of practice, which seems difficult to reconcile with the non-materialistic philosophy of Buddhist culture. Changes in style may happen more subtly and at a slower rate in Bhutan than in a highly developed economy, but an alternative system of social identification through dress and appearance, governed by its own logic of temporality and location is visible in the traditional dress practices of people throughout Bhutan and exists alongside a range of influences from encounters with the development agencies, celebrities, tourists, and media influences present in the capital city, Thimpu, and other urban centers throughout the country.

The national press regulates and mediates local concerns about how to interpret *driglam namzha* correctly (see, for example, Yeshi, 2008) alongside an emergent discourse of nostalgia for the loss of authentic national dress practices as older styles of garments become superseded by modern hybrid garments with stitched elements to emulate the appearance of wrapped and folded cloth, and modern closures and fastenings adopted for reasons of practical wearability:

> Today, it is very rare to see Bhutanese women wearing the complete National Dress. With the hook, half-*kira* and the jacket-*tego*, *kera* and *wangu* may soon also be heading for the museum like the *thinkhab* (BBS, 2007).

Parallel to this narrative of nostalgia and cultural loss, reports appear in the same newspapers encouraging readers to wear stiletto gladiator sandals with their *kira*, adopt Korean style spectacles, and tweed jackets that emulate characters in the *Twilight* movie franchise, and how to style cardigans, imported from Bangladesh. The seeming contradictions of change and continuity, tradition, and modernity are encapsulated by the dual consciousness of dress.

Alongside the Royal Family, who are almost universally admired within Bhutan as equitable forward-thinking bearers of modernity, one of the most revered and recognisable figures actively shaping Bhutan's contemporary culture on the domestic and international scene is the incarnate lama and movie producer Khyentse Norbu, also known as Dzongsar Jamyang Khyentse Rimpoche, who offers a view that supports Entwistle's belief that social mobility and fashion are in some way connected. He clearly understands the politics of fashionable dress and the need to equate ideas of modernity with those of "traditional" culture, to give it currency among the youthful population of Bhutan. He advises that Bhutanese people should be looking to practice elements of the ancient culture in ways that are relevant, vibrant, alive, dynamic, inspiring, modern, and even "fashionable" to combat increasing problems arising during the transition through elements of development, modernity, and increased urbanization. One specific example which he offers is to "eliminate clothing items that embody class distinctions, such as scarves and robes showing rank" (Walcott, 2011: 257). One of the most respected Buddhist masters in the world is also encouraging a paradigm shift in the way that Bhutanese culture and society is visibly embodied through the dress code. He understands and believes that the right to enjoy a culture is not "frozen" at some point in times past, when culture was supposedly "pure," or "traditional."

Multiple parallel examples exist worldwide which illustrate similar tensions in the process of economic and social development in the pursuit of modernity, a result of anachronistic notions of the "authenticity" of the culture (see, for example, Gilbert, 2010: 38). Choosing which aspects of traditional culture to keep, which to discard, and which to update in what ways, is an extremely problematic area for governmental authorities and inter-governmental agencies to decide. Such evolution is by nature an ongoing, fluid, contradictive, and never-ending process. Time-limited policy-driven grant-funded development programs based on deliverables might interfere with cultural evolution that would otherwise take years to emerge.

Such anachronistic notions of "authenticity" are significant in the analysis of the *driglam namzha* and the discourse of cultural loss expressed by the national press. This is where I begin to situate my own contribution to the construction of ideas about fashionable dress and identity in Bhutan, through my participation in the co-development of a tailoring curriculum for Chumey Vocational Training Institute in Bumthang, Central Bhutan.

The construction of hybrid dress styles: tailoring curriculum for Chumey Vocational Training Institute, Bumthang, Bhutan

The demand for a curriculum directly addressing the perceived skills gap in tailoring in Bhutan had emerged through a series of events implied in the process of nation-building through dress code and appearance. A national design competition coordinated by UNDP Bhutan to design and manufacture uniforms for the Drukair female cabin crew (UNDP, 2007: 16) had highlighted the difficulties of manufacturing standardized garments in Bhutan. The wish to supply uniforms for the military and police out of local manufacture, rather than outsourcing production to India, and the growing demand for quality items of national dress to clothe the civil service, contributed to the formulation of a development project to request capacity building training in garment design and manufacture through UNDP in Bhutan. Singapore International Foundation responded to the call for proposals and identified LASALLE College of the Arts Singapore as the appropriate academic partner to provide expertise in curriculum development and technical skills training in tailoring. Regional geographies of development may be influenced by a number of personal and professional networks, with Bangkok and Singapore viewed as particularly powerful hubs of global aka "Western" expertise and technological innovation within the South East Asia region.

The scope and framework of the curriculum was established by the Dean of Design in a preliminary needs assessment exercise in 2008. In that year and 2009, my colleague, Peck Leng Tan, and myself made a series of missions to Bhutan to develop content, and deliver a structured vocational curriculum and a training program for those who would go on to become the trainers in the final iteration of the Tailoring Program at Chumey Vocational Training Institute.

The mode of delivery was based on the "Training of Trainers" facilitation model, designed to produce a sustainable cascade of knowledge, learned through active participation, which can be passed onto the next cohort of trainees. This approach is used widely throughout the development sector, and it is thought that skills learned through such methods survive long after the initial trainer has delivered the first iteration of the course, and moved on.

Through a series of discussions with a range of stakeholders from Chumey Vocational Training Institute, private tailors already established in Bhutan, the Ministry of Labour and Human Resources, UNDP Bhutan, Singapore International Foundation, and many other agents of development whom we encountered in Thimpu during that period, we agreed to develop a curriculum that would enable the tailors and new trainees to produce high-quality garments for the internal market, and also create innovative garments from traditional textiles using Western-style tailoring methods and quality standards.

These "hybrid" garments were perceived to be in demand among the wealthy tourists who visit Bhutan, and are seen as a good opportunity for developing enterprise, entrepreneurial skills, and personal creative outlets for the aspiring fashion designers whom we met among, and alongside, the cohort of trainees. The gradual evolution of traditional dress codes to include items targeted at wealthy tourists existed prior to the development of our curriculum, which may

Figure 9.2 Emma Dick and Peck Leng Tan with Staff and Trainees on Tailoring Curriculum at Chumey Vocational Training Institute, Bhutan, September 2009. Photograph by Peck Hoon Tam.

now have in some small part contributed to the technical innovations and further moves away from any anachronistic notions of "traditional" dress, frozen at a fixed point in time somewhere in the imagined seventeenth century.

The final curriculum consisted of six modules, distributed over two years of full-time study. In line with the vocational training framework that was being developed for Bhutan at the same time, the practical to theory ratio was established as 80:20, although these figures may have evolved since the first iteration of the program was established.[2] The six modules were as follows:

Module 1: Production Methods and Introduction to Flat Pattern-Making
Module 2: Understanding Fabric
Module 3: Understanding Garment Construction: Womenswear and
         Menswear
Module 4: Design Detailing and Garment Construction
Module 5: Production of Small Products
Module 6: Introduction to Production Chain Management

With the introduction of Helen Armstrong's comprehensive manual *Patternmaking for Fashion Design* as one of our core texts, our curriculum aimed to introduce trainees to the fundamentals of hand and machine sewing and the basics of constructing garment blocks by hand to understand and develop the fundamental aspects of "Western" techniques of garment design and production from the very start of Module 1. Pre-existing knowledge and skill was variable among our first cohort of trainees. Some had little experience but demonstrated tremendous commitment to learning when applying to join the project by competitive entry. Others had been practicing as tailors for many years, using a combination of techniques evolved and created locally through encounters with experienced tailors from neighboring India, or picked up from previous training courses variously organized by different disparate development initiatives. There had been no systematic structured delivery, development or assessment of tailoring knowledge and skills within Bhutan prior to our curriculum, and formalizing the current state of knowledge and practical skill would be one of the key indicators of our success.

We encouraged trainees to experiment with locally available textiles, closures, and fastenings to enhance the functionality and wearability of garments designed for working in. As already mentioned above, such simple innovations in production had already caused the lamenting of cultural loss in the national press, a fundamental agent in mediating, constructing, and maintaining a sense of national identity (Crane, 2008: 364). The hook fastening is gradually replacing the *kera* belt in some garments in Bhutan. The half-*kira* is a stitched form of the lower half of a *kira*, sewn to emulate the correct folds and pleats of a "traditional" wrapped *kira*. This garment closely resembles "Western" notions of a "skirt." The jacket-*tego* is a hybrid garment with contrasting collar and cuffs stitched directly inside the openings of a "traditional" style *tego*, to emulate the full appearance of wearing a *wangu* underneath, but without the need for the additional garment.

Further embedded in the hybrid language of UK-centric curriculum design and standards codified by Bhutan Department of Trade, two of the learning outcomes the trainee should demonstrate on successful completion of Module 4 of the curriculum are listed thus:

Identify and select details that are traditional and non-traditional. Apply these details in traditional and non-traditional context (Curriculum, 2010: 35).

This binary categorization between the traditional and non-traditional is present also in Module 5, which links quality control to "appropriate commercial standards e.g. *Bhutan National Seal*" (Curriculum, 2010: 39). The Bhutan National Seal is aimed at:

Establishing national quality benchmark standards for Bhutanese handicraft products and encouraging the producers/ artisans to be more innovative and creative in their designs, while preserving the age-old traditional craft skills and knowledge (Bhutan Department of Trade).

The judging criteria for the Bhutan National Seal are divided into the same two words referenced in our curriculum. Products classified as "traditional" will be judged on their "authenticity, design and finishing skills, technique, material and marketing," and for items deemed as "non-traditional," the first judging criterion is changed to "innovation," while all the rest remain the same. The criteria of "innovation" and "authenticity" may be read as well-intentioned anachronisms, further preserving the mythical authenticity of Bhutanese dress, while also legitimating designed products wholly derived from the same semi-mythic traditions as *driglam namzha*.

Technical innovation that enhances creative possibilities available to aspiring designers creates a further blending of the distinctions between the "traditional" and the "non-traditional." Synthetic and processed yarns have become prevalent in Bhutan, through trading links with India, Bangladesh, and Thailand. A frame loom introduced from Tibet has "augmented the existing technology of back-tension looms and sparked the creative development of brocaded wool twill weaves" (Myers and Bean, 1994: 18). Article 27 of the International Covenant on Civil and Political Rights highlights the difficulties of trying to codify legal frameworks to protect indigenous cultures, while at the same time trying to anticipate to what extent modern technology could form part of such traditional activities and how these could be defined and protected legally as a part of "traditional" culture (Gilbert, 2010: 37). Joseph Lo, chief technical adviser for the

Culture Based Creative Industries project for UNDP Bhutan 2004–9 confirmed similar difficulties in the Bhutan context, in trying to define markers of authenticity within cultural production, how to innovate within those boundaries, and how to measure indicators of success:

> It is really problematic trying to codify skills and abilities which are really tacit knowledge and trying to get them to fit into a structured framework (Lo, 2012).

Lees (2011) suggests that some inter-governmental organization-authored projects become limited by definitions, caught up in documenting the "authentic" to the detriment of supporting new ideas and innovations. One school of thought would suggest that ordinary individuals are disempowered, rather than empowered, by the intervention and activities of international inter-governmental agency-driven development projects:

> Global NGOs come in from the outside very often armed with their own ideas of what is wrong and what should be done to remedy the situation. At precisely this point the issue of representativeness arises to bedevil thinking on civil society (Chandhoke, 2002: 46 cited in Crane, 2008: 374).

This logic should perhaps be applied to issues of representation in its broadest sense, and in our case to the political, aesthetic, and cultural sovereignty governing self-representation through fashionable dress and identity construction. The context of our curriculum project should be framed within these broad concerns about cultural autonomy and representation, although the active role, which the Royal Civil Service of Bhutan takes in ensuring self-negotiated ideas of traditional culture, is significant, and our curriculum was developed through a process of genuine stakeholder engagement and collaboration.

These examples from our curriculum may be implicated within the construction of hybrid dress practices and notions of fashionable dress and identity now evident in the national press in Bhutan. The impossibility of unadulterated cultural neutrality on the part of development agents, including myself, may connote diffuse transnational cultural imperialism on the part of global development agencies. These inter-agency encounters underscore the anachronistic logic presented in a false dichotomy between categories of "traditional" and "non-traditional." Such binary logic presents an approach markedly different from the holistic ideas expressed by incarnate lama and movie producer Rimpoche, who aims to reconcile tradition and modernity, as one universally understood language. Few ordinary people, however, possess the transcultural omniscience represented and suggested by Rimpoche. He presents the same universal philosophy beautifully in his film *Travellers and Magicians*

(2003). The central character, Dondup, performed by non-actor and prominent BBS journalist Tshewang Dondup, dreams of escaping to America, smokes cigarettes, listens to rock music, and wears a denim *gho*. Dondup represents the frustration of the present-yet-absent hybrid modernity of contemporary rural Bhutan, existing at a further area of remove from the hub of development agents and cultural intermediaries congregating round inter-governmental agencies based in Thimpu, the capital city.

The production of garments through our curriculum presents a narrative of institutionally measurable modernity in dress emerging through structured encounters between agents of inter-governmental development in vocational education. A complementary and related example is unfolding online via the pages of the Facebook group called Bhutan Street Fashion (BSF). BSF has emerged as an active trend discussion forum, and was established by Karma Wangchuk, whom I worked alongside in 2009, while I was developing the Tailoring curriculum, and he was working for UNIDO in Bhutan. It is interesting to compare a different set of ideas about fashionable dress and identity in Bhutan, quite distinct from the ideas of cultural nostalgia for the loss of traditional heritage reported in some of the mainstream print media in Bhutan. BSF offers an opportunity both to view the construction of ideas about fashionable identity by documenting and discussing what is worn by people on the streets, and to understand the range of people within and outside Bhutan who are driving, and contributing to, this active and energetic discussion in virtual space.

Bhutan Street Fashion (BSF)

The STREETS is where the inspiration is. Masses r the new CLASSES. showing the fashion on the street …we show you like it is…no pretensions and no wannabe Mother Teresa promises, no HIDDEN agenda, no moral policing… Everyday life FASHION on the street (Bhutan Street Fashion, 2010).

Bhutan Street Fashion (BSF) was established on Facebook on June 19, 2010, and, at the last count, had 41,095 followers (March 7, 2016). Founder Karma Wangchuk studied Fashion Design in India, and lives in Thimpu. He describes himself as a:

Design student and Fashion Illustrator at the start of my journey […] I am an accidental photographer with no formal training. I am more a visual person and therefore my blog has more images n sketches and less writing but I promise to write more (Wangchuck, 2012).

Figure 9.3 Bhutan Street Fashion Facebook group example page from July 2010. Image with permission from BSF.

BSF began as a location for candid street-style photography shots of people "spotted" in their daily lives in Bhutan.[3] As Rocamora observes in her discussion of fashion blogs, such images overwhelmingly attract positive comments by the online community of followers (Rocamora, 2011). Encouraged through the "like" function, group members engage in communal online discussions usually expressing support and admiration for the subjects' sartorial choices and to Karma for his innovation in starting up the group.

Miaka Wangmo Go Bhutan street fashion.. :) CLICK CLICK CLICK ♥ :) i offer ma services :) LOL
21 July 2010 at 12:16 · Like · 1

[…] actually its always been there people just didnt notice it i guess =)
28 July 2010 at 07:26 · Like · 2

Jiwan Gurung indeed it is true...glad dat v r catchin up wid d world..BSF..u all r doin a gr8 job...kudo's 2 u all...
29 July 2010 at 05:16 · Like

[…] i should have put both the pics tiogether n made the fans choose the look .. tuff dude Vs Chic dude
20 August 2010 at 13:21 · Like

[…] actually both these pics are the same kid […] its amazing what clothes n a haircut can do […] pretty boy to macho =)
20 August 2010 at 13:32 · Like

Karma Kaso Sonam great collection…luv d pics..guess our country is rele developin si…
21 September 2010 at 12:01 · Like

The fluent use of informal "text speak" abbreviations throughout the participants' conversations highlights the widespread ease of expression in English—and not Dzongkha—as the language of dedicated followers of street fashion in Bhutan. This makes the group widely accessible on the global Facebook network, which does not yet offer a version in Dzongkha. It also highlights the gap between official language policy and everyday language usage in, and about, Bhutan. Throughout the photo comments for the album "Street Trend in Bhutan 2010" emerges a collective sense of what "Bhutan Street Style" means to the participants in the discussion. Gentle jokes are made about each other's style preferences, but Karma is usually present in the discussion, marshalling potentially offensive comments with direct remarks such as,

[…] ʃ@KYT .. agree .. Stereotyping is equivalent to racism …
14 October 2010 at 05:58 · Like · 1

Taking on the role of "moderator," Karma manages an extremely fluent dialogue about the consensus of meanings and derivations of the various ensembles represented in his and other members' photographs. Information is passed on about popular fashion ideas from Korea, Taiwan, and Singapore, and about how places like Mongar, the fastest growing region in Eastern Bhutan, compare to these East Asian countries. Shopping tips are shared about where to get the best fake Converse-style shoes in Bangkok, and how to make your own T-shirts, clothes, and accessories, using simple DIY techniques. At one stage, Karma enters into a definition of fashion terminologies to correct what he views as misunderstandings about the meanings imparted by the words "Chanel," "Marc Jacobs," and "vintage," related to an image of a girl with a handbag he has taken:

belle époque era mens beautiful era . …VINTAGE is a terminology used noadays for second hand clothes n BTW the clothing from the 1920s to 1980s is considered vintage so there u go …
11 October 2010 at 08:31 · Like · 2

Over the six years since the group was founded, the regularity of the postings and volume of commentary has increased and the range diversified. Karma and his collaborators have gained in confidence and are in demand as photographers, stylists and people to be talked about in fashion related projects across emerging print magazines, including *Yeewong*, launched in September 2009 and *Bhutan Time Out*, launched in April 2012. BSF has amassed followers from all over the world, and regularly posts photographs of readers in front of a range of global mythic locations, such as New York Fashion Week, the Houses of Parliament, in London, and the Merlion in Singapore, carrying a hand made sign of allegiance to BSF. References made in international media about BSF, such as Cartner-Morley's (2011) article about the royal wedding of the fifth King, and *Marie Claire* writer Fabrizio interviewing favorite TV personality Namgay Zam, are also posted on the page. This demonstrates a self-awareness of the positioning BSF commands in reference to the global fashion media, attracted in some measure by the exotic Otherness of Bhutan, established by the Shangri-La myth, and echoed in the pages of mainstream fashion media, such as *Vogue.* The page has become a dynamic discussion forum for a virtual global community of more than 41,000 people interested in Bhutan Street Fashion, and also contributing to its future ontology.

BSF has been successful in captivating the minds of a virtual worldwide community beginning to actively construct the rhetoric of fashionable dress and identity in Bhutan from observation, documentation, and representation of the people on the streets, and how this relates to global online social media visual culture. Images of people "Style Spotted" on the streets of Thimpu show them wearing a multi-colored array of *gho*, *kira,* pants, and shirts, stylishly accessorized with "geeky" glasses, "Aviator" sunglasses, and small purses crafted out of hand-woven *kira* fabric, for example. The King and Queen are frequently cited as style icons, both in their national dress and in pictures of them traveling overseas in "Western" dress. The written comments show a wide variety of opinions and perspectives on fashionable dress and identity, but the overwhelming attitude of users of the site is positive toward *drighlam namzha*, even though the visuals demonstrate a sophisticated awareness and practice of a whole world of clothing styles that exist outside the official dress code. Where users celebrate Western clothing styles through imagery, they are often quick to balance this with a positive comment about national dress:

Aernest Tree mind you the gho loks allways the best haha
14 August 2010 at 16:27 · Like · 3

Aernest Tree gho dang kira for ever
14 August 2010 at 16:28 · Like · 4

> [...] we know that showing a lil appreciation for our Western cousins the fact
> is we wear them too
> 15 August 2010 at 14:00 · Like · 2

The dual consciousness present in everyday people's attitude toward *drighlam namzha* is present in the pages, images, and commentary evolving through the online community. Rimpoche stands as the ideal candidate to legitimize a similar process from within the official structures of the Buddhism-based constitutional monarchy. As incarnate lama and movie producer he embodies an extremely powerful balance between the same realms of "authenticity" and "innovation" signified in the Bhutan National Seal judging criteria. His dual role has captivated journalists worldwide, but has also attracted some disbelief that one person can actually perform two such differently perceived functions in realms usually presented as mutually exclusive. He counters these suspicions thus:

> It indicates to me that from certain standpoints working in film is viewed as almost sacrilegious, like I am breaking some kind of holy rule [...] Film is a medium and Buddhism is a science. You can be a scientist and at the same time you can be a filmmaker [...] Buddhism is not against idolatry—it uses statues as representations [...] Film could be seen as a modern day *Thangka* (traditional Buddhist painting or cloth banner) (Prayer Flag Pictures, 2002: 13).

If film is viewed by some as a sacrilegious medium, fashion would almost certainly be seen by the same people as profane. There is so far very little written about the relationship between fashion and inter-governmental development initiatives. Such a body of work may begin to emerge, given the growth of the ethical fashion sector and the range of organizations promoting equitable trade alliances, in preference to unilateral or bilateral aid, and enabling market linkages between producers and consumers. Figures like Rimpoche act as a cultural catalyst in this process. The popularity of online groups such as BSF allows almost unrestricted non-hierarchical and intercultural dialogue between multiple stakeholders to take place. Such forums will inevitably begin to generate even more complex multi-layered forms of hybrid fashionable identity to emerge in Bhutan and elsewhere in cyberspace. Future iterations of development projects such as our Tailoring curriculum could easily draw upon the rich market insight, sub-cultural capital and trans-national awareness that BSF possesses. All of these qualities are significant in the process of constructing fashionable dress and identity in Bhutan, and should serve to clearly challenge simplistic binary thinking about how the West and the non-West engage in discourses about dress.

Conclusion

The geographical inaccessibility and the psychological "Otherness" of Bhutan, formed through the myth of Shangri-La, derive in part from the semi-mythical foundation stories of the unification of the country and reassertion of *driglam namzha* to the present day. A discourse about fashionable dress and identity formed in Bhutan exists in the international fashion press that retains these metaphors of inaccessibility and authenticity. Within Bhutan, this nebulous discourse has become reified through real hybrid garments, constructed through arenas such as our curriculum, and also generated a discussion of fashionable dress and identity in the pages of Bhutan Street Fashion. Translation between these different ways of systematizing knowledge creates a clash of structural logic in the way that these ideas about Bhutan are conceptualized and held together in the competing languages of fashion journalism, international development and Facebook.

The belief in systematizing knowledge is deeply linked to ideas forged by the European Enlightenment, "the 'modern' subject manages to control ideas, classify objects, produce knowledge about identities, and, thus, secure meaning about them" (Constantinou, 1998: 29–30). It is not meaningful to impose such values on a culture that independently developed its own entirely different logic of enlightenment. In Buddhist terms, to be "enlightened" means to have woken up and to understand the world, so that the mind and the body are not separated, but are in perfect harmony with one another. Thus, binary systems that exist to impose "rational" order on the world are deeply unenlightened from this perspective. Rimpoche echoes beautifully the complexity with which we should frame the study of non-Western dress, when he says:

> I believe that all these systems [of global governance] are well-intended but I don't believe that one particular system can work for everyone. In fact I don't believe that every human being on Earth has to learn one particular system […] Buddhism is a wonderful philosophy. It's a wonderful system. But Buddhism is different from Buddhists. Within Buddhist institutions we see downfalls, corruptions. No system has worked thoroughly in this world (Prayer Flag Pictures, 2002: 19).

Roland Barthes (1992 [1967]: 300) said that fashion is an order made into disorder, the conversion of reality into myth, blurring the memory of past fashions to make the current "euphoric." There are multiple fashion systems operating under different logics and notions of temporality, all of which are perpetually being reconsidered and constructed in complex hybrid encounters with each other through globalization. The construction of fashionable dress and identity in Bhutan is just one such encounter that demonstrates the complexity and richness of the many fashion discourses present in the non-West.

Notes

1 The author would like to thank the following individuals and organizations who made this research possible: Joseph Lo (PhD candidate at Heriot Watt University, and formerly of UNDP Bhutan), Karma Wangchuk (Bhutan Street Fashion), Pernille Askerud, Karma Lhazom (MOLHR), Peck Hoon Tam (formerly of SIF), Tan Peck Leng, Nur Hidayah and Emily Wills (LASALLE College of the Arts Singapore), Phuntso Norbu (The Institute of Zorig Chosum, Thimpu), Sangay Dorji, Kinley Wangdi, and all the private tailors and students who took part in our Tailoring Curriculum at Chumey Vocational Training Institute, Bumthang, Bhutan.

2 It has not been possible to establish the ongoing status of the tailoring program as this chapter goes to press and as a precarious environment, it is possible that the delivery of the course has evolved further since the last mission Peck Leng made with another colleague, Emily Wills, in 2010. This is one of the challenges of funding for development. When the funding finishes, it is sometimes difficult to ensure the future sustainability of the project.

3 See the photo album, "STREET TREND IN BHUTAN 2010," available online at: https://www.facebook.com/media/set/?set=a.140021779348778.20328.132246 446792978&type=3 (accessed June 30, 2014). Please note that comments from BSF have been recorded and reproduced exactly as they were posted online. These quotes have been used on the basis of fair dealing/use for the purposes of criticism and review only.

References

Appadurai, Arjun. "Disjuncture and Difference in the Global Cultural Economy." *Theory Culture & Society*, vol. 7 (1990): 295–310.

Barthes, Roland *The Fashion System*. Berkeley: University of California Press, 1992 [1967].

BBS (2007) http://www.bbs.com.bt/There%20it%20goes,%20to%20the%20museums. html (accessed July 14, 2012).

Bhutan Observer (2011) http://bhutanobserver.bt/4668-bo-news-about-kabney_colour_ mania.aspx (accessed May 3, 2015).

Bhutan Street Fashion https://www.facebook.com/BhutanStreetFashion/?fret=ts (accessed March 7, 2016).

CIA (2012) https://www.cia.gov/library/publications/the-world-factbook/geos/bt.html (accessed May 3, 2015).

Constantinou, Costas M. "Before the Summit: Representations of Sovereignty on the Himalayas." *Millennium: Journal of International Studies*, vol. 27, no. 1 (1998): 23–53.

Craik, Jennifer. *The Face of Fashion: Cultural Studies in Fashion.* London: Routledge, 1993.

Craik, Jennifer. *Fashion: The Key Concepts.* Oxford: Berg, 2009.

Crane, Diana. "Globalization and Cultural Flows/Networks." In *The SAGE Handbook of Cultural Analysis*, eds Tony Bennett and John Frow, 359–81. London: Sage, 2008

Curriculum SIF, LASALLE, and Chumey VTI, *Tailoring Curriculum*. Unpublished handbook, 2010.

Eicher, Joanne B. ed. *Dress and Ethnicity: Change Across Space and Time*. Oxford: Berg, 1995.

Eicher, Joanne B. "Introduction: The Fashion of Dress." In *Fashion* ed. Cathy Newman, 17–23. Washington DC: National Geographic, 2001.

Entwistle, Joanne. *The Fashioned Body: Fashion, Dress and Modern Social Theory.* Cambridge: Polity Press, 2000.

Gilbert, Jeremie. "Custodians of the Land." In *Cultural Diversity, Heritage and Human Rights*, eds Michele Langfield, William Logan, and Mairead NicCraith, 31–44. London and New York: Routledge, 2010.

Hilton, James. *Lost Horizon*. Chichester: Summersdale Publications, (2005 [1933]).

i-D online (2012) http://i-donline.com/2012/05/on-top-of-it/ (accessed June 14, 2012)

Kaiser, Susan B. *Fashion and Cultural Studies.* Oxford: Berg, 2011.

Lees, Emma. "Intangible Cultural Heritage in a Modernizing Bhutan: The Question of Remaining Viable and Dynamic," *International Journal of Cultural Property*, Vol. 18 (2011): 179–200.

Lo, Joseph. Personal interview conducted by the author during June 2012.

Martin, Richard, and Harold Koda. *Orientalism: Visions of the East in Western Dress.* New York: Metropolitan Museum of Art, 1994.

Maynard, Margaret. *Dress and Globalization*. Manchester: Manchester University Press, 2004.

Mendes, Valerie. "Introduction: The Fashion of Fashion," In *Fashion*, ed. Cathy Newman, 29–35. Washington DC: National Geographic, 2001.

Myers, Diana K., and Susan S. Bean. *From the Land of the Thunder Dragon: Textile Arts of Bhutan.* London: Serindia and Peabody Essex Museum, 1994.

Newman, Cathy, ed. *Fashion.* Washington D.C.: National Geographic, 2001.

Norbu, Khyentse. *Travellers and Magicians.* Film. Prayer Flag Pictures, 2003.

Pem, Tandim. "What is in vogue this summer?" *The Bhutan Observer.* August 9, 2010. Available online at: http://bhutanobserver.bt/3096-bo-news-about-what_is_in_vogue_this_summer.aspx (accessed May 3, 2015).

Pommaret, Françoise (1994), "Textiles in Bhutan I: Way of Life and Identity Symbols." In *Bhutan: Aspects of Culture and* Development, eds Michael Aris and Michael Hutt. Kiscadale Asia Research Series No. 5, 173–90. Gartmore: Kiscadale Ltd., 1994.

Prayer Flag Pictures. *Talking with Khyentse Norbu.* Interview by Noa Jones, 2002. UK Media Information Kit: Prayer Flag Pictures / Hanway Films.

Riello, Giorgio, and Peter McNeil. *The Fashion History Reader: Global Perspectives.* London: Routledge, 2010.

Rocamora, Agnes (2011) "Personal Fashion Blogs: Screens and Mirrors in Digital Self Portraits." *Fashion Theory*, vol. 15, no. 4 (2011): 407–24.

Said, Edward. *Orientalism.* London: Penguin, 2003.

Savada, Andrea Matles, ed. *Bhutan: A Country Study.* Washington, DC: GPO for the Library of Congress, 1991.

Skov, Lise. "Dreams of Small Nations in a Polycentric Fashion World." *Fashion Theory*, vol. 15, 2 (2011): 137–56.

Stewart, Gordon T. *Journeys to Empire.* Cambridge: Cambridge University Press, 2009.

Teltscher, Kate. "The Lama and the Scotsman: George Bogle in Bhutan and Tibet, 1774–1775." in *The Global Eighteenth Century*, ed. Felicity A. Nussbaum, 151–64. Baltimore and London: The John Hopkins University Press, 2003.

Tshering Uden Penjor. "Bhutan." In *Berg Encyclopedia of World Dress and Fashion,* vol. 4, South Asia and South East Asia, ed. Jasleen Dhamija, 102–8. Oxford: Berg, 2010.

Turner, Samuel. *Bhutan and Tibet: An Account of an Embassy to the Court of the Teshoo Lama in Tibet Containing a Narrative of a Journey through Bootan.* Varanasi: Pilgrims Publishing, 1800.

UNDP (2007) http://www.bt.undp.org/assets/files/publication/a_report06.pdf (accessed September 14, 2012).

Vogue. "Features/Articles/People: 'I Went to the Wedding at Sikkim.'" June 1963.

Vogue. "Fashion: H.M. the Queen of Bhutan, and Her Children." July 1967.

Vogue. "Fashion: Point Of View: Finding Shangri-La: The Doors To The Remote Himalayan Kingdom Of Bhutan Have Slowly Opened To Western Visitors. Designer Jane Mayle Found A Mythical, Magical Land Almost Untouched By The Modern World." June 2005.

von Furstenburg, Diane (2012) http://www.dvf.com/on/demandware.store/Sites-DvF_US-Site/default/Blog-Post?cid=blog-post-363 (accessed May 3, 2015).

Wangchuck (2012) http://lharikhamba.blogspot.co.uk/ (accessed May 3, 2015).

Whitecross, Richard W. (2009) "Migrants, Settlers and Refugees: Law and the Contestation of 'Citizenship.' in Bhutan." In *Spatializing Law: An Anthropological Geography of Law in Society*, eds Franz von Benda Beckmann, Keebet von Benda Beckmann, and Anne Griffiths, 57–74. Farnham, Surrey: Ashgate, 2009.

Wilson, Elizabeth. *Adorned in Dreams: Fashion and Modernity*, revised and updated edition. London: I.B. Tauris, 2010.

World Bank (2014) http://data.worldbank.org/country/bhutan (accessed March 7, 2016).

Yeshi, Samten (2008) http://www.kuenselonline.com/2011/?p=10494 (accessed June 14, 2012).

PART V

CONCLUSION

10

AFTERWORD: FASHION'S FALLACY

SANDRA NIESSEN

A cohort of scholars has decided to meet regularly to address the Western bias in fashion studies. This volume is one of the results of that decision; the authors have pooled their efforts to write revisionist fashion. Much work is needed to rectify terminologies and perceptions that have been constructed on a false socio-politically constructed West/Rest dichotomy. Nevertheless, the fact that these meetings are necessary gives pause. Has it not already all been said? Fashion studies are Eurocentric, evolutionary, Orientalist, and in urgent need of review and revision. But the cry has not been sufficiently taken up. To be sure, revisionist fashion studies have made headway in the dominant fashion discourse, but not enough. Where recently endorsed, this is often because of current attention to so-called fashion globalization, which is being held up as proof of fashion's universality. However, this perception constitutes a confusion that is symptomatic precisely of the persistence of the West/Rest dichotomy in the study of fashion.

In the middle of the last century, Simmel (1957) pointed out that fashion was found in the West and not in non-Western contexts. Scholars continue to reiterate his claim whether directly or indirectly. Surely what his writing did was to issue an invitation to scholars to test his claim cross-culturally and not to sit cozy with it as a safe mantra. Had empirical testing indeed followed, the study of clothing/fashion in a global context would have taken a different course because the dichotomized thinking would have been put to rest. On the other hand, in Simmel's day and even before (and certainly since), there were generally known examples of intercultural interactions in the development of Western fashion that flew in the face of his dichotomous characterizations: tales of the silk road and derring-do related to the spread of natural color materials and recipes from India and South America, the development and spread of Chinoiserie and chintz, the importation of beaver pelts for European top hats, and the European fascination with the Cashmere shawl, to cite but a few, all of which showed the international participation in the development of Western fashion. However, even such commonly known examples have not dislodged the conception of fashion as an originally and exclusively Western phenomenon. Simmel's fashion theory was —and remains—an expression of an entrenched bandwagon fallacy predicated on a Western understanding of the Other (Niessen 2010).

Toby Slade's chapter in this volume especially adds to the arsenal of proof that the global interplay in the clothing domain is complex, age-old, and flies in the face of a West/Rest discourse. Will his contribution make a difference? Will the scales drop from the eyes of fashion conservatives who will then stand back and say, "My goodness, we clearly have to rethink fashion and cross-cultural clothing systems!"? It is enticing to conceptualize a world in which that would be the case, but currently that is only ridiculously naïve. The fashion world turns on a different axis. It is not looking for truth and analyses to find it. Instead it plays with myth and appearance in its commitment to obtaining profits and is thus incontrovertibly vested in its Western ideological stronghold. It is clear that the weight of additional historical evidence of global linkages will not transform the fashion world. Not only for this reason, there needs to be a strict(er) separation between analytical writing on fashion and the fashion process (including the textual component). The two have different goals and priorities.

The central tenet of Simmel's characterization of fashion is rate of style change, fashion purportedly changing relatively quickly and non-fashion, by definition, depending on stability. Fashion continues to be characterized in this way even in the latest fashion textbooks. This is highly problematic if only because it perpetuates the "rate of change" myth for a new cohort of students. At the very least it needs to be logically discredited as a delimiting characterization. It implies a cross-cultural framework but this claim has not been specifically tested using comparative data. Since Simmel's day there has been time to do systematic cross-cultural survey work, but it has not been a priority. On the grounds of scientific method alone, as a delimiting characterization it fails.

Furthermore, when rate of change is invoked in fashion textbooks (one senses a grasping at straws to try to come-up with something that will support the position that fashion is found only in the West), this is simultaneously problematic because the characterization does not delimit and it is untrue. Today's increasingly fast-changing world has emptied it of any definitional value that it might have had. Given this, in addition to the absence of comparative data to substantiate the claim, the only function that allegiance to this "distinguishing property" can serve is to perpetuate the illusion of a West/Rest dichotomy. As such, it is a cog in the wheel of the bandwagon West/Rest fallacy.

Another frequently used textbook definition of fashion is "non-localized changing styles." This definition is safely neutral and implies no West/Rest dichotomy. It is interesting, therefore, to note the inconsistencies with which it cohabits. I am referring here to the depictions of fashion history as a parade of Western dress styles, starting with Greek and Roman times, and, following the example of the conservative "old" art history, working up to the present. A recent addition to the fashion history literature, entitled *Fashion, the Whole Story* (Fogg 2013), incorporates a selection of dress forms from a handful of cultures in the American Southwest, Africa, and Asia, by way of enlightened acknowledgment that fashion has been found elsewhere in the world and not just in the West. The illustrations from these other cultures are situated in the book at the beginning of the historical parade of Western fashion. The fashion history was not adapted to accommodate a broader, multicultural definition of fashion; rather the Other was admitted in a cursory way without any clear criteria of selection and no cross-cultural analysis. First giving lip service to the idea that fashion may not be exclusively Western, the layout of the book then situates these exceptions within a Western evolutionary/historical framework. This treatment of fashion history only serves to reveal, yet again, the underlying West/Rest dichotomy. The token additions make it painfully evident that the critique of fashion has not been integrated thoroughly and that the dominant framework of fashion history persists unrevised. Fashion history is presented as Western history *a priori*. This is a co-opted conventional understanding of fashion posing as fashion analysis.

It may seem unduly pedantic to spend on such definitions when an exciting and burgeoning fashion literature, including the chapters in this volume, apprise the reader of a dynamic global fashion development against which these definitions seem only to call up yesteryear. Nevertheless, this problem is so prevalent in fashion textbooks that it is necessary to continue to address them. Moreover, as I point out at the outset, unless we understand why this fallacy is so persistent, it will continue to inform present and future fashion studies. This can be demonstrated with respect to fashion globalization.

Until now, fashion studies have been co-opted, at least partially, by the ideologies of fashion and the entrenchment of the West/Rest dichotomy in the study of fashion serves as proof. As critical academics whose job it is to probe and see through fallacies, many of us also bear the burden of preparing students to work in the fashion industry. This can lead to conflict of interest. Moreover, trying to escape the ideologies of fashion is a tall order when it is the fate of all of us, academics or not, to wear clothes and in our everyday lives, to sartorially negotiate the social markers of status and power. In this sense, "seeing through clothes" is like trying to kick a food addiction, while still needing to eat to survive. Regardless of the great strides that have been made in fashion research, these circumstances may at least partially explain why the distinction between fashion analysis and the fashion process is still insufficiently clear. It also explains why so few have chosen to examine the global power relations embodied in clothing systems.

These failings are perhaps our strongest evidence of the need for solid and systematic enquiry into why the well-formulated and exceptionally serious criticisms of the bandwagon West/Rest fallacy in fashion studies have had insufficient impact. This same fallacy has been exposed in the studies of history, art history and anthropology, but they remain inextricably entrenched in fashion studies. Unless the perniciousness and the extent of the dichotomous West/Rest bias are thoroughly understood and the criticisms generally acknowledged *and* integrated, the dichotomized notion of dress (fashion/non-fashion) will persist as a skewed foundation for fashion studies. Every analytical structure that we build atop it will reflect, to a greater or lesser extent, the original fallacious imbalance. A veritable fashion syndrome has grown up around the dichotomy.

An example of this is the problematic term "world fashion." The term was coined to designate the "dress of ordinary people," including apparel items, such as jeans, sweatshirts, T-shirts, trousers, skirts, blouses, shirts, blazers, business suits, and the like" rooted in Euro-American heritage, but now found "across the globe" (Eicher 1995: 4; Eicher and Sumberg 1995: 300). The term emphasizes the similarity in appearance of items of clothing, but does not take account of the meanings associated with the clothing. We know that these outfits have a different meaning in different cultures (see for example, Hansen 2000). The spread of "world dress," if we apply sociologist Georg Simmel's observation that people dress according to their aspirations, speaks volumes about where the dominant centers of global power are located. The standardization of appearance thus simultaneously reveals and masks political relations, an ambiguity that the term "world fashion" does not convey because it designates only sameness in appearance, and obfuscates inhering power differences.

The contributors to this volume have taken it upon themselves to operate within a new fashion paradigm, a very tall order. They must perforce make do not only with concepts but also with terminologies that are already enmired in conventional conceptions.

A disruptive (non-dichotomous) fashion discourse begins with the recognition that the systems of dress anchored in all cultures around the world (body decoration is a human universal) have their own distinctive features and dynamics (though they may be inter-related to a greater or lesser extent) and that this diversity has been obscured by the dichotomous study of dress in which the Western dress system (Western fashion: a system rooted in Western capital dynamics) has been given a privileged position while "the rest" have been lumped together, more or less undifferentiated, as a consequence of ideological, untested and unverified assumptions and characterizations. The fashion/non-fashion dichotomy suggests a difference in clothing kind and process ignoring and denying the dense historical connections in production and trade between the different parts of the world to which the terms are ascribed, and fails to ascertain what is universal, and what distinct in the various systems spawned by human creativity throughout the world. The goal of a renewed and disruptive discourse is to critique the fallacies in this ideologically based study of universal dress, revise skewed understandings and accepted wisdom about fashion and thereby rewrite fashion in its broadest cross-cultural, not-exclusively Western sense.

Fashion's fallacy on the global stage

The emergence of so-called "fashion globalization" adds a particularly complex and confusing layer to the West/Rest issue. This is exacerbated because we have not yet completed the project of explaining the fallaciousness of the West/Rest dichotomy in fashion studies. It is (too) easy to point to the mushrooming of Fashion Weeks, as many do, as proof that the West/Rest dichotomy is receding into the past. The traditional centers of fashion hegemony appear to be eroding as multicultural design themes proliferate. This evokes the triumphant response: "See!", "'They' do have fashion! The proof is available all over the world!" The implication is that fashion is no longer Western and its study no longer ethnocentric. The term "fashion globalization" is misleading, however, in the same way as the term "world dress" is misleading; it also veils the same power relations. "Fashion globalization" is an expansive step in the socio-economic development of Western fashion. To hail "fashion globalization" as proof that the "rest" also has fashion, is to dwell in appearances and, ironically, to continue to privilege the Western clothing system, in fact side lining other fashion/clothing systems, while purporting to finally recognize them. Although there is overlap; there is especially difference between documenting the process of "fashion globalization" (the emergence of/(the appearance of) the local indigenous on the fashion stage), and rewriting the study of fashion to do away with the false West/Rest dichotomy by acknowledging the unique dynamics in local clothing/fashion systems found throughout the world throughout time.

It is difficult to even discuss this issue because of terminological entrenchment. For example, to refer to the dynamics in local, indigenous clothing systems throughout the world as "fashion" subversively de-privileges the conventional, exclusive Western "right" to the term but also serves to confuse the reader who does not know which "fashion" is being referred to: the Western kind that is proliferating on a global stage, or the localized, indigenous forms that are disappearing as rapidly as the first is expanding. To refer to the former as fashion and the latter as non-Western fashion settles us back into precisely the dichotomy that we are trying to escape. The matter is all the more pernicious and confusing because the global economy reifies Western fashion dominance in real and not just ideological terms.

In this volume, Şakir Özüdoğru wrestles with the problem of ascertaining what is really going on when Turkish designers take a position in the global fashion parade. He cites Polhemus' prediction that "Western dominance in the fashion system" will disappear but he, nevertheless, also has doubts arising from his observation that "the dominant fashion capitals of the West have maintained their positions" (pp. 84–87) despite the entry of non-Western newcomers on the globalized fashion stage. Where lies the truth? Why this ambiguity?

We live in baffling times. The global economic system, a social construct, has grown not only out of control, but also beyond our ken. Economist Joseph Stiglitz (2012) crunched the numbers to ascertain that in 2012, 1 percent of the population of the United States held 40 percent of the wealth while 80 percent of the population holds only 7 percent, a trend that has continued apace. When physicist, James Glattfelder (2011), tried his hand at developing mathematical models to determine who controls the world, his answer was: shockingly and increasingly few. When we know that the United States holds 20 percent of the wealth of the entire world, and we juxtapose that fact with how wealth is distributed in that country, the global ramifications of this distribution are mind-boggling. And the tide has not yet changed.

There is no reason to assume that fashion economics are exempt from this trend. Despite fashion globalization, there are indications that the West has never held the reins of fashion economics more tightly. A group of holding companies are disproportionately large players in the field. It is no longer the styles that reveal the social ladder. If fashion once trickled down that ladder to reveal the social pecking order, the game is now about manipulating the system to suck capital upward. The most powerful wealth is no longer manifest through opulent display, it is behind the scenes manipulating the production and marketing of opulence. In all of its manifestations, opulence is a marionette. The game is about the essentially invisible power pulling its strings.

Many scholars have noted that fashion is economics. What would a fashion system that reflects these extreme global power and economic relations look like? The answer would inevitably be—if it is true that fashion is a mirror of the times: what we know as fashion globalization, the system in all of its facets and not a particular "look" or "looks." Not fashion houses, as they no longer vie independently for the top; they are owned by holding companies. Not the work of particular fashion designers as they are hired and fired at will. Not fashions as these are plucked from London, Milan, Deli, Jakarta, Marrakech, Sydney, and just as easily dropped (a recent, purportedly analytical, fashion publication characterized Western styles as the result of free and unencumbered creativity in contradistinction to clothing systems limited by tradition and social meaning. Meanwhile, another variation on the West/Rest theme underscoring the need to explore the political economy of global fashion influences, style creation, and marketing). Fashion globalization is the distribution of the steps of fashion's ladder all around the globe engaging the participants in variations on the same marketing game and the same upward capital flow.

If we claim that fashion globalization is eroding the original Western centers of fashion it behoves us to support this conclusion using empirical data, but the finances of fashion are currently also beyond our ken. What percentage of fashion's wealth is held by whom? What role does fashion globalization play within these fashion economics? How do the dynamics of fashion globalization intersect with the structures that channel power and wealth? What latitude do designers throughout the world have within this global system? Do we need to add the prediction of the erosion of Western fashion to the heap of fallacious, untested fashion wisdom based on appearances and ideologies? Unapprised of the economic data, we remain mystified and in the realm of what Sakir Özüdoğru, citing Yan and Santos, called "images and narratives" (2009: 86), co-opted by fashion's own story and lacking an analytical framework to document fashion dynamics and expose the fallacies in global fashion analysis.

There is evidence to suggest that if fashion globalization is *not* eroding the original Western centers of fashion, the emergence of a global fashion phenomenon *does* correspond to the decline of local cultural/clothing systems. In 2003, I described what I referred to as a "trajectory of fashion" among the Batak people of North Sumatra, Indonesia. The historical progression began more than a century ago when the Batak lived in relative isolation. During the early stages, they selectively incorporated exogenous novelties, "Batakizing" them, while building their unique, local aesthetic. External pressures expanded during the colonial era, reducing their latitude for selective incorporation of external elements. The unique features of Batak clothing and textiles went into decline, as weavers were pressed to imitate external fashion trends in order to compete for a segment of the market pie and wearers were pressed to demonstrate their participation in their expanded social environment. Today, the Batak textiles most desirable and thus viable on the national market display the now fully fledged national fashion aesthetic. To make them, the unique features of the Batak aesthetic were pushed aside or into the background. More recently, local designers have started to use archival images of the Batak in their villages as a marketing tool to give their individualized fashion creations the aura of cultural authenticity. The self-Orientalized, folklorized, mythologized, and objectified result is successful on the fashion stage. In the meantime, the once-dynamic indigenous clothing tradition of the Batak people is on the brink of extinction (the few remaining elderly weavers have few successors), leaving only the "appearance" of Batak in the form of fashion creations manipulating images and myths for marketing purposes. The work of the indigenous fashion designers is far from a symptom of revival or even maintenance of a local tradition even though it is often perceived and promoted as such.

Fashion dynamics are universal, but the emergence of globalized fashion around the world is not *sui generis*. Far from rendering the West/Rest dichotomy a historical artefact, understanding globalized fashion requires dissection of the global relations built into Western dress and the implications of the global economy for clothing traditions everywhere.

The disappearance of indigenous culture is one of the most pressing and simultaneously most neglected (also by fashion studies) issues of our time. The global economy grants little room for the survival of alternative cultural and economic systems and globalized fashion, because of its focus on profits, can do little for the well-being of indigenous fashion systems. Şakir Özüdoğru's conclusion that "globalization is not leading to cultural homogenization but, on the contrary, stimulates cultural heterogenization through the (re)invention of and emphasis on local cultural heritage" does not constitute an answer to his question about whether fashion globalization engenders cultural loss. It only constitutes an acknowledgment of complex plurality in the process of fashionalization.

The interface between the dominant Western fashion system and indigenous fashion systems is where the negotiations about identity and power take place, and where meaning is constructed and lost. It cannot be surprising, therefore, that most of the contributions to this volume focus on that dynamic nexus. A balanced approach to fashion writing would do justice not only to the process of entry into the global system but also to the departure from local, indigenous (disappearing) fashions/culture. A degree of co-optation is implied when the story of global fashionalization is focused on the entry, particularly when framed in terms of success, and when a struggle for the maintenance of an indigenous system is deemed anachronistic. It is also a symptom of the West/Rest dichotomy when only half of the story is told. The other half has never been fully attended to in conventional fashion analysis. Lumped as "the rest," it is largely unknown and not understood. Indeed, in this sense, fashion theory parallels the process of fashionalization illustrated In this volume by the chapters by Jennifer Craik and Janaki Turaga. Visual elements from their culture of origin, where they have deep, mystical meanings unknown except to those steeped in the culture, are extracted from those dense meaning systems and then paraded as commodities down fashion street cloaked in new mythologies and exogenous narratives.

Longitudinal, two-sided studies of wide scope are needed to show the impact of fashionalization on the longer term. Only then can the answers to the questions "What is being lost?" and "what is being gained?" and "By whom?" be answered. Without critical frameworks to situate what is happening at the macro level in the fashion globalization process, we run the risk of being seduced by its delicious visuals on the runway level, co-opted like fashion consumers.

To conclude, embarking on a corrective, disruptive, non-co-opted history of fashion is a long-term project. It must include a self-reflexive critical evaluation of the development of the concept of fashion to explain the current vestedness in fashion's conventional definition. Only this will provide a firm foundation for rewriting fashion history so that it rests on a non-dichotomous understanding of global dynamics rather than privileging the dynamics of the fashion process in the West. Fashion globalization will be unmasked as a Western phenomenon with deep historical roots, and a capacity to transform fashion systems throughout the world.

References

Eicher, Joanne B., ed. *Dress and Ethnicity*. Oxford: Berg, 1995.

Eicher, Joanne B., and Barbara Sumberg. "World Fashion, Ethnic, and National Dress." in *Dress and Ethnicity*, ed. Joanne B. Eicher. Oxford: Berg, 1995.

Fogg, Marnie. *Fashion: The Whole Story.* London: Thames and Hudson, 1013.

Hansen, Karen Tranberg. *Salaula: The World of Secondhand Clothing and Zambia.* Chicago: University of Chicago Press, 2000.

Niessen, Sandra. "Afterword." In *Re-Orienting Fashion: the Globalization of Asian Dress* by S. Niessen, A. Leshkowich, and C. Jones. Oxford: Berg, 2003.

Niessen, Sandra. "Interpreting 'Civilization' through Dress." In *Encyclopedia of World Dress and Fashion, Vol 8: West Europe, Part I: Overview of Dress and Fashion in West Europe*, 39–43. Oxford: Berg Publishers, 2010.

Simmel, Georg. "Fashion." *The American Journal of Sociology* 62 (6) (1957): 541–58.

Stiglitz, Joseph. *The Price of Inequality: How Today's Divided Society Endangers Our Future*. W.W. Norton & Co., 2012.

INDEX